Era of the Passenger Liner

Nicholas T. Cairis

PEGASUS BOOKS LTD.

London ◆ Boston

© Nicholas T. Cairis 1992

Published by PEGASUS BOOKS LTD.
London, England
Manufactured in the United States of America

Library of Congress Cataloging-in-Publication Data
Cairis, Nicholas T.
    Era of the passenger liner/by Nicholas T. Cairis.
        p.   cm.
    Includes bibliographical references and index.
    ISBN 0-929624-03-3
    1. Ocean liners–History–20th century. 2. Passenger ships–
History–20th century. 3. Steamboat lines–History–20th century.
I. Title.
VM381.C27   1992   92-8575
387.2'432'0904–dc20   CIP

CONTENTS

"Though we travel the world over to
find the beautiful, 'we must carry
it with us' or we find it not"
                              Ralph Waldo Emerson

Preface

The invention of the steam engine and the screw propeller well over a century ago added a new page in the history of passenger shipping. The evolution from packet ship and clipper ship to paddle wheelers came about within a small time period. The industrial revolution contributed to marine technology with iron hulls replacing wooden-built ships, steam replaced sail. By the turn of the century the steel-built ship made her debut and great leviathans came off the shipways measuring several thousand tons.

Contributing to this immense growth in the shipping industry were the waves of immigrants who sought a new life. The lure of the New World created the impetus to build bigger and bigger ocean liners. Many lines built ships specifically for this trade with steerage accommodations for over one thousand and as much as two thousand persons. The quarters were dormitory style and the amenities spartan like.

Ellis Island, which lies in the outer reaches of New York harbour, was the keyhole through which millions would pass for processing. Opened in the 1890s, the white and red brick edifice with its huge halls has since been converted to a museum as a monument to the diverse peoples who passed through. Ellis Island is actually a window into many an American's genealogy since mostly all had a relative who was screened here. They came from the United Kingdom, Ireland, Scandinavia, Germany, the Low Countries, France, Italy, Hungary, Russia and the Balkans. In 1907, a peak year, over one million came to America's shores each with his or her own particular dream. They all came in ships and were the backbone of the shipping lines. This lucrative cargo of human freight caused the lines to vie with one another to attract customers. Speed was a major factor and companies like Cunard concentrated on building fast greyhounds like the sisters *Mauretania* and *Lusitania* with speeds exceeding 27 knots. Their swiftness also earned them government sanction by earning the privilege of carrying the mails and financial subsidy.

Cunard's major competitor, the White Star Line, built slower but more luxurious liners for its first and second class clientele while still catering to the third class element. The same could be said for the Hamburg-American Line, which also built floating palaces while its foremost contender, the North German Lloyd, concentrated on speed.

Enter the American financier J.P. Morgan, who attempted to amalgamate all of North Atlantic shipping under one household. Under the banner of the International Mercantile Marine, Morgan purchased the White Star Line, Red Star Line, American Line, Dominion Line, Leyland Line, Atlantic Transport, and a substantial amount of stock in the Holland-America Line. Cunard Line stockholders, exhorted by royal will, held out. The American monopoly eventually dismembered its holdings and free competition prevailed.

The writing on the wall caused governments to pay closer attention to passenger shipping. The United States had created the U.S. Shipping Board to help subsidize its merchant shipping with building and operating subsidies. The French had made a practice of it for years. Their ships some of the most luxurious.

When the United States enacted more stringent immigration quotas the steamship lines began to offer more amenities to the public. This resulted in a proliferation of majestic liners in the years preceding the First World War. Ships like the Hamburg-American Lines trio, *Bismark*, *Imperator*, and *Vaterland*; Cunard's *Aquitania*; White Star Line's *Olympic* and the ill-fated *Titanic*; French Line's *France*; and Holland-America Line's *Rotterdam*.

The post-war period witnessed changes in class accommodations. The saloon type category known as steerage would later become third class. First class would always remain at the top and second class would later emerge as cabin class. There were variations on these such as tourist third later on. The third class designation would eventually be deleted, leaving the term tourist. In the early twenties many ships were converted from coal burners to oil-firing and simultaneously a number of ships became cabin class ships with space for cabin and tourist only. During one of the earlier transitions there existed a third cabin category

when the lowest category, steerage, began to be phased out with cabins for four and six people in place of the dormitory type accommodations.

Above decks on the promenade and boat decks were situated the first class cabins, mostly outside. Inside cabins without a view were less expensive as were those staterooms below the main deck. Many of these were dispersed between either first or second class depending on their situation. Today's ships offer only first class accommodations, but in reality the consideration paid determines the cabin in which one will voyage. In the heyday of the liner there were three separate dining rooms for each of the classes and three lounges with restriction areas for one's classification.

The social convention of life ashore was brought to sea aboard these floating cities that ferried across the Atlantic. Whilst the elite travelled in the utmost luxurious conditions, some with their own private deck space and a retinue of maids and valets, the middle class were accommodated in comfortable quarters, a hotel style bill of fare, and lively soirées. Below decks, and in some cases below the waterline, third class held on to the richness of their dreams and sustained themselves on such intangibles as hope and promise amidst hostelry-like conditions.

Sailing day was a day of excitement for all who sailed. An army of porters would be on hand to help load the hundreds of steamer trunks. Exuberant chatter filled the air and drowned out the clank of the trunks. Bouquets of flowers were brought to passengers' cabins by white-jacketed stewards. There was the first salt smell of the sea and the sound of escaping steam. Then the chilling sound of the ship's horn was heard and tooting tugs nudge the floating leviathan from her quay, turning her to the direction of the open sea.

Ships are, as man has dubbed them since time immemorial, ladies. Regal ones at that. Several have borne the names of reigning queens. These same queens sent them down the ways when they were christened, as have numerous princesses and duchesses as well.

The floating mass of steel held together with millions of rivets bedecked with miles of teak and brass fittings surely possessed a soul. The majestic Grecian columns in the dining room with painted ceiling and murals, the inlaid interiors of walnut and satinwood veneers, mahogany furniture handmade in every period style from Rococo and Chinese Chippendale to art deco; indoor Roman baths and French cafés, chintz, leather, bone china, silver and crystal added the finishing touches. Each liner had its own distinctive character and was manned by a contingent of disciplined and professional officers, stewards, engineers, chefs and seamen. The ship was a symbol of goodwill which embodied the best in technological know-how and culture of the country whose flag it flew. A nation's calling card if you will.

The race for supremacy of the seas was rewarded by the Blue Riband in the form of a large silver gilt cup to the steamship line which had the fastest liner to cross the Atlantic. The coveted distinction changed hands several times, mostly between the British and German lines. As the years rolled on the liner became bigger and faster. Superliners, they would eventually reach over one thousand feet in length and measure upwards of 80,000 gross tons.

At the outset the Germans led the way with the North German Lloyd sisterships *Bremen* and *Europa* both in the 50,000 ton category and with speeds exceeding 28 knots. They in turn wrestled the Blue Riband from Cunard's now aging *Mauretania* in 1929. The Grand Old Lady, as she was fondly known, had held the title for over two decades.

The year 1929 was a turning point in economic growth worldwide. With the coming of the Great Depression many lines were forced to merge or go bust. Several Italian lines consolidated their fleets to form the Italian Line which brought out the *Rex* and *Conte di Savoia* in 1932, both in the 50,000 ton range. The *Rex* enjoyed a brief glory when she snatched the Blue Riband from the *Europa* in 1933 with a speed of 28.92 knots. The race for prestige was on. Despite the grave economic situation between the years 1929–1936 the largest liners were laid down. When the French Line's *Normandie* made her debut in 1935, the world looked in awe at the 83,000 ton liner. And when she won the Blue Riband in turn the owners of Cunard took an appraising eye. In the spring of 1936 the *Queen Mary* entered service for Cunard Line. That summer she outpaced the *Normandie* at a mean speed of 30.14 knots. The rivalry between the two giants continued back and forth when the *Normandie* won back the title a year later. In 1938 the *Mary* made a crossing at a speed of 30.99 knots and continued to hold the regal honour of being the fastest ship afloat until U.S. Lines' United States in 1952 with her phenomenal speed of 34.51 knots. She crossed the North Atlantic in 3 days, 12 hours and 12 minutes from Bishop Rock to Ambrose Lighthouse, 9 hours and 36 minutes sooner than the *Queen Mary*.

There is no argument that marine technology had reached its zenith in the years preceding the Second World War. The interior opulence of the ships was unmatched and when the war came to a close the world and the North Atlantic ferry would be a very different place. Gone were the young debutantes with their black-tie escorts attending the captain's ball off to catch the latest fashions in Paris. The changing passenger list was now made up of cigar-wielding garment business men to copy the latest fashions for mass production.

Looking back in retrospect it appears that the fifties witnessed the beginning of the end of an era. Those travelling across the ocean were a mixed group, a new generation from different walks of life. A chapter in maritime history had come to a close.

The sixties were lackluster for the shipping industry as the air lines became more popular attracting a new breed of traveler. And for a time it seemed as though the outmoded passenger liner would sail into oblivion. The oil embargo of the following decade sealed the fate for a number of operators. The casualty list of household names grew longer and longer. Greek Line, Swedish-American Line, the Italian Line and French Line to mention a few. United States Lines as well as other American-flag operators fell victim to government policy with the termination of operating-differential subsidies which had allowed them to compete with foreign lines.

The everyday pace of life gained momentum in the fast moving seventies and the old maxim of "getting there is half the fun" fell out of context for the time being.

A century old mode of travel and style had been eclipsed. The race which had begun for economic supremacy over the sealanes had brought the merchant marines of England, America and the Continent to a halt. The subsidies had ended; the mail contracts were now awarded to the air lines who gnawed further at shipping revenues. Unable to compete on a technological plane despite added amenities to draw customers, superliners like Cunard's *Queen Mary* and *Queen Elizabeth* were put up for sale. The French Line's grandiose *France* got an early retirement when the French government terminated its subsidy.

Even the record-breaking *United States* with her phenomenal speed of over 35 knots and crossing time of three and a half days did little to attract customers. She too, was withdrawn from service by 1969. Countless other intermediate liners were laid up as well. The cruising aspect of shipping had yet to develop and Cunard sold its lovely 34,000-ton *Caronia*, built expressly for cruising.

The Greeks and the Norwegians, who for some reason appear to have an insight into the world of shipping, began to develop other markets. As early as 1965 the Greek-owned Home Lines brought into service the *Oceanic*, built exclusively for cruising. The company had abandoned the business of liner service in the sixties and concentrated on this steadily growing market. Of course it was difficult to convert liners which had been engaged in the trade from England to Canada or other northern ports to fully outfitted cruise ships with outdoor pool and large lido areas for sunbathing. Most of this tonnage was either laid up or sold.

The Italian Sitmar Line had purchased Cunard's *Carinthia* and *Sylvania* and converted them to cruise ships successfully, as did the Norwegian Cruise Lines when it purchased the *France* and renamed her *Norway*. There are several instances of these success stories of converting liners and even ferries into cruise ships.

One of the first of those to see the writing on the wall were the Scandinavians. And though the Swedish-American Line had been devoting much of its services to cruising in the years of the liner's demise, they got out of the business at the turning point. On the other hand, the Norwegian-America Line, with its yacht-like *Sagafjord* and *Vistafjord*, were and still are great successes in this new arena.

By the late seventies, travel on the North Atlantic had reached a nadir with only the Polish Ocean Lines' *Stefan Batory* and Cunard's *Queen Elizabeth 2* maintaining service. The latter only when she was not cruising.

In a vain attempt to stay afloat, several of the lines before closing down had been selling 'cruises to nowhere' for those who just wanted to party off shore. Ships would pull out of New York and sail around in circles for a few days. The new course seemed to illustrate the liners' predicament, but there was a beacon on the horizon.

Ship conversions began to increase as liners were rebuilt into cruise ships. Destination the Caribbean and surrounding waters. Liners to the sun. Within a short time new orders were being placed for this new breed of ship. Gone were the stately ships. The majestic Cunarders, the sleek North German Lloyd greyhounds, the elegant floating hotels of the French Line. A gay and gilded era had come to an end but in its wake the cruise ship had emerged.

The grey clouds hung over the industry for nearly a decade but by the 1980s the tide had surely turned for a period of astounding growth within the industry.

Social change from the turn of the century to the present has undergone dramatic transition. The three-tiered cabin classification aboard ships would be faded out in the cruise ship market. It was a gradual process which began to erode these now archaic standards back in the mid-seventies. Financial pressures on the population soon eliminated the 'cabin class' category altogether by the mid-seventies. There would always be a segment of the populace to fill the first class cabins, but this too was a dwindling number. The Edwardian concept of classification itself became a misnomer within a society of professed equality and the class categories were merged into a 'single first class' capacity. Or so it is called. However, the location and amenities of one's cabin still designates price.

The technological aspect of the industry had also witnessed dramatic change over the decades. Whereas Britain was building ships for the whole world rivalled only by Germany in the years before the First World War, orders were few and many shipyards had closed down for good.

In the late sixties Finnish designers drawing schematics for such banal craft as ferryboats began to add flair to the outward appearance to these otherwise utilitarian vessels. The industry took notice and the Finnish shipyards began to fill orders for the major cruise lines. The industry began making giant strides and a number of operators were compelled to send their ships back to the shipyards to be jumboized by the insertion of a mid-body section extending the ship's length with additional cabin fittings and public rooms.

The eighties witnessed extraordinary growth for the cruise ship industry with nearly one hundred seventy cruise ships in operation world-wide. The 1990s have ushered in a period of still greater growth and still bigger ships. Once again we have ships measuring in the 70,000-gross ton class. *The Sovereign of the Seas* has a passenger capacity for 2,276 people. Given her architectural construction and shallow draft of 25 feet, she was designed like many of her peers for the calmer waters of the Caribbean and inland rivers like the Amazon. Crossing the North Atlantic in January would demonstrate that such vessels are a different breed from their predecessors. Social reform has also brought a different element of vacationer into the market. A veteran steward from Cunard, White Star Line or the French Line would most probably look with disdain on the voyager of today. All progress is not always progressive. It would be difficult to recreate the synergy and gaiety of the past of yesterday on today's ships. The world is a very different place. People likewise. And those things once taken for granted, like the oceans and seas, have even undergone change. . . .

There are many factors which contribute to the makeup of a liner and to explore this facet of the industry would entail another volume in itself. Other maritime authors have contributed books to this segment of the industry whereas I make no attempt to elaborate in this area with the exception of an occasional sentence or two attributed to social circumstances etc... And though my interest in the subject is all encompassing, I have confined my books to chronicling the events in the individual services of these ships. My affinity is limited to passenger liners whose magnetic draw, I feel, interests a growing number of people. Some of the facts will evoke memories for many readers as they do for me, personally. Still others will be enlightened to this splendid fashion of travel created by man.

When the single-screw passenger liner *Stefan Batory* was taken out of service a couple of years ago, she left a legacy of her own. Her owners, Polish Ocean Lines, also abandoned the North Atlantic ferry. Despite the fact she represented an eastern bloc country she was a lovely ship. Her history was a bit odd since she had been laid down as a cargo ship and finished off by the Holland-America Line in 1952 as a passenger liner when traffic on the transatlantic run began to perk up a bit. The Polish Ocean Lines operated her in the traditional fashion of a bygone era. Her absence left Cunard's *QE2* to carry on the tradition. And although there are a number of ships sailing today with the prefix of Royal..., Sovereign..., and countless absolutes with titles from Countess to Princess, there is only one Queen....One of her forerunners, the *Queen Mary*, lies permanently docked in Long Beach, California as a witness to a generation of stately ships much like the drydocked *Cutty Sark* at Greenwich, England stands as testimony to the era of the clipper ship.

The forthcoming pages attempt to give the reader an overview of travel on the North Atlantic as well as the South Atlantic and other routes serviced by the represented lines within the text. The companies chosen are household names whose vessels were prominent on both sides of the Atlantic. Some may be disappointed not to see a particular company's ships and I must apologize but, in order to keep the book within reasonable bounds, I had to select the better-known steamship line for each nation represented, i.e. when it came to England, Cunard was selected over White Star, North German Lloyd over the Hamburg-American Line etc. Of course not all the ships of those lines represented will have found their way into this volume due to size once again. Included are only ships measuring over 10,000 gross tons. In all there are eighteen companies. Five more than the first and second editions and over seventy more liners. When the first edition came out in

England twenty years ago I was but a student running down to Lloyds whenever I could to open the enormous leather bound books in the statistics department and library. Since I have gathered new information and revised and corrected to the best of my knowledge nearly every entry, which includes, I trust, everyone's favourite liner.

Although a White Star Liner, I included a special entry for the *Titanic* due to the ship's profound impact on ship lore. How ironic. The research for this edition directed me to Harvard University's Widener Library, built and dedicated to Harry Elkins Widener by his mother. The young Widener was a student at Harvard when he perished on the maiden crossing of the *Titanic*. A bronze plaque bears this into account upon entering the great edifice with its towering Greek columns. As one climbs the main staircase to the upper level, there lies Harry Elkins Widener's own private collection of fine hand-tooled leather and gold gilt bindings. Above the fireplace in the private-like chambers hangs a painting of the young man sitting in a contemplative mood; his head tilted; upheld by his right hand, legs crossed; his eyes viewing every visitor. Upon leaving I sometimes looked back and he seemed to approve of my doings....

The events of that fateful evening of April 14, 1912 had shaken the maritime community and people on both sides of the Atlantic. The tragedy was, however, setting new standards for safety at sea. Social change aboard ships was much slower in improving the conditions for the lower classes. In time sanitation, safety, and accommodations became better. Technology played its part in making travel by sea more enticing until sailing was for the most part a luxury no matter in which class one voyaged. Of course research and development are not restricted to the maritime industry alone. The science of aeronautics would soon eclipse the strides made in marine engineering. The liner had gone the route of the packet ship, and the clipper ship, the paddle-wheeler and the steamship. The age of the motor cruise ship is here. No longer is speed a priority. A lethargic cruise to sunny horizons is the new pace for the ship of today. Fuel consumption is down with the ships travelling below normal speed and a newly coined phrase "cruising speed" has entered the mariner's dictionary and kept fuel cost at a minimum and ship owners in the black. The ships of today, though different in so many aspects, attempt to, in their own way, keep alive this lovely world of splendor afloat. At the time of writing, new orders are up. . . .

Explanatory Notes

All facts have been entered in this book to the best of my knowledge as being accurately documented. The information contained stems from various sound resources listed in the bibliography. In stating the specifications and data of each ship there is listed in order the name of the ship followed by the name of the builder, completion date, gross tonnage, dimensions, type of engines, number of propellers, watertight bulkheads, decks, normal speed, passenger accommodations, officers and crew, country of registry, and maiden voyage. A roman numeral preceding the ship's name indicates the sequential ship to carry the name. Following the ships' historical background will be listed a sister ship or ships if any existed in the service of the company.

Passenger accommodations may vary if a ship was in service for a long time period since classes changed over the years and the immigration laws of the early twenties enacted by the United States Government limited the number of people entering the country thereby eliminating the designated 'saloon' and 'steerage' categories. These eventually evolved into an improved 'third class' capacity. In some cases the liners' original complement of passengers listed in parenthetics will be given along with the last known figures. The same rule applies to officers and crew. Since the conversion from coal-firing to oil-firing and other aspects of modern technological improvements limited the number of crew members, the figures listed are the last in the ship's

career. This change-over of the early twenties eliminated the "black gangs" of stokers, trimmers and firemen. The position of pages were eliminated in time as well as the deck steward.

The classification of decks is difficult due to either their actual construction, or designation by architectural inference. Some may consider a certain section of a vessel to be classified as a deck, whereas others may not. The extension of the specified deck area being the problem depending on its length and location in the ship's design. I have formulated my own method by including decks as those which extend the greater part of two-thirds of a ship's waterline length. In the case of others extending only half a vessel's length I have combined the two such areas to equal one deck. These partial deck areas collectively are added to the actual decks to give a general number.

Clarification of some of the technical terms should be defined in order to better understand maritime jargon, i.e. "screw" is used for propeller. The most common misconception is "gross tonnage" to the layperson unfamiliar with shipping. Gross tonnage is a measured unit made up of one hundred cubic feet of enclosed space, and is not, as many believe, a weight measure such as a ship's deadweight tonnage (a ship's load including the total weight of cargo, fuel, stores, crew, and passengers). The date of build is the date of launching if only a launching date is known. In order to distinguish the launching and actual completion there must exist a time difference between the month stated in the completion date and the approximate time of the maiden voyage. One may determine the completion date, if there exists a time difference between the launching date given and completion by actual fitting-out, if the completed date is closer to the date of the maiden crossing. The length given is the overall length which is the extreme length of the ship. In the case of the ship having a bulbous bow the overall length includes any protrusion of that bow. Breadth is the moulded breadth which is the greatest width at amidships from the heel of frame to heel of frame. Depth is the moulded depth determined by the perpendicular depth taken from the top of the upper deck beam at side amidships down to the top of the keel. The draft given is the mean draft calculated by the level of water from bottom of keel to center of the load line disc printed on the ship's hull. The speed stated is the normal speed which the ship is capable of maintaining at sea in normal weather conditions and at normal service draft. Continuing with the biographical text the ship's history is chronicled from the time of ownership of the designated line until its final demise but excluding data under other ownership. In cases where no information is stated in the statistics section, i.e. draft, none was available (example French Line *Chicago*); bulkheads – either none existed or information unavailable (example the Holland-America Line *III Noordam*); the maiden voyage is that made under the ownership of the Line represented in the book. Since the previous two editions, much invaluable information has surfaced and incorporated into the individual entries. Revisions have resulted and errors corrected to the best of my ability. The result, I trust, a more thorough and accurate historical account for reference.

Should any readers have any reason to question the information contained herein, they may take the initiative to write me through the publisher. In due course I shall be most happy to divulge the source of provenance and degree of authenticity with regards to factual data.

My gratitude would be incomplete if I should close without thanking the following people for supplying information and/or photographs. They are: Mr. R. Smol of Bureau Veritas, David Littejohn, Sandra Scott of Lloyd's Register of Shipping in London, Mr. Claros and Mr. Ballet of the Spanish Line, Mr. Vreugdenhil of Holland-America Line, Mr. Bouvard of the French Line, Mr. Rickmann of the North German Lloyd, Mr. Rogers and Eric Flounder of Cunard Line, Mr. Bet of the Italian Line, Tom Brady and Mr. Martin of United States Lines, Mr. Amundsen of the Norwegian-America Line, Mr. and Mrs. Henriksson of the Swedish-American Line, Mr. Sigalas of the Greek Line, Mr. Coutinho of the Portuguese Line, Mr. Tillet and Mr. Sutherland of Home Lines, Mr. Janczarski of Polish Ocean Lines, Mr. Kidsen and Connie Lindval of Scandinavian Seaways, Mr. Armstrong of the Trans-Atlantic Steamship Conference, Mr. Michael Lennon of Waterlooville, Hants, England for several Russian photos, Mr. Ove Nielsen of the Copenhagen Port Authority for photos, The Upper Clyde Shipbuilders of Glasgow, Scotland, The Maritime Museum of Barcelona, The Peabody Museum of Salem, Massachusetts, The Mariner's Museum of Newport News, Virginia and the Southampton City Museum in England. And last but not least, those individuals who through correspondence over the previous two editions have advised me of errors and omissions in various instances, as well as other minutia. I also wish to thank those who have shared their personal anecdotes aboard a number of the liners.

Cambridge, Massachusetts
March 1992

Bibliography

Annual Reports of the Trans-Atlantic Passenger Movement, New York, 1908-1976; *Morton Allen Directory of European Passenger Steamship Arrivals*, Baltimore, 1931 Genealogical Publishing Company 1898–1930; *Trans-Atlantic Passenger Ships Past & Present*, Smith, Eugene W., George H. Dean Co., Boston, MA, 1947, 1963; *Passenger Liners of the Five Oceans*, Gibbs, Vernon C.R., Putnam Co., London, 1963; *Passenger Liners of the Western Ocean*, Gibbs, Vernon C.R., Staples Press, London, 1952, 1957. *Passenger Liners*, Dunn, Laurence, Adlard Coles Ltd., Southampton, 1961 and 1965; *Histoire Compagnie Generale Transatlantique*, Marthe Barbance, Paris, 1853–1955 (French Line); *Det Forenede Dampskibs Selskab DFDS* 1866–1906 (Scandinavian-American Line); *DFDS–1866-1991 Ship Development through 125 Years from Paddle Steamer to Ro/Ro Ship*, DFDS A/S 1991, Copenhagen, Soren Thorsoe, Peter Simonsen, Soren Krogh-Andersen, Frederik Frederichsen Henrik Vaupel. *Nordeutscher Lloyd*, Berlin, Ecksteins Biographescher, 1857–1957 (North German Lloyd); *Den Norske-Amerika Linien 1910–1960*, Erik Vea, Johan Schreiner, and Johan Salond, Grondahl & Son, Oslo, 1960 (Norwegian-America Line); *North Atlantic Passenger Liners*, Cairis, Nicholas T., Ian Allan Ltd., London, 1972; *Passenger Liners of the World Since 1893*, Ciaris, Nicholas T., Crown, New York, 1979; *Cruise Ships of the World*, Cairis, Nicholas T,. Pegasus, Boston, 1989; *Lloyd's Register of Shipping*, London, 1893–1991; The American Bureau of Shipping, *North Atlantic Seaway*, N.R.P. Bonsor, T. Stephenson & Sons Ltd., Prescot, Lancashire, England 1955-61 supplement/Volumes 1 David & Charles, Devon; Volumes 2-5, 1980 Brookside Publications, Jersey, Channel Islands, England. The Record, 1921–1969; The Shipbuilder & Marine Engine Builder, 1907–1942, London; Sea Breezes, Liverpool; Fairplay Magazine, London; Lloyd's List, various years; Cruise & Ferry Catalogue; Steamboat Bill, Company Press Releases; brochures various years; travel guide timetables; various newspaper articles and dates. Original abstracts of ships' times, departures, arrivals and speeds from Cunard Line records of various ships both British & Foreign leaving and arriving in the United Kingdom.

TITANIC

Builder: Harland & Wolff Ltd., Belfast, Northern Ireland
Completed: 1911
Gross tonnage: 46,329
Dimensions: 852' x 92' Depth 59'
Engines: Two 4-cylinder triple-expansion engines and one low pressure
  turbine
Screws: Triple
Watertight bulkheads: Fifteen
Decks: Seven
Normal speed: 21 knots
Passenger accommodations: 2,000 in three classes (1st, 2nd & 3rd)
Officers and crew: 688
Registry: United Kingdom
Maiden voyage: April 10, 1912 Southampton-Cobh (New York)

Built exclusively for the White Star Line and christened *Titanic*. Built at a cost of $7,500,000. Ironically some years before her construction a short story had been written about a ship named *Titan* which had struck an iceberg and sunk. Her measurements were larger than those of the Titanic, but the eerie account later stood as a premonition of the tragic event. The *Titanic*, designed by Thomas Andrews who travelled with the ship on her maiden voyage, had sacrificed prudence for luxury by not extending the forward bulkheads up to the uppermost decks in order to afford passengers more space. The *Titanic* set sail from Southampton on April 10th headed for the open sea. At twenty minutes before midnight on April 14th she struck an iceberg while steaming at 18 knots off the Grand Banks of Newfoundland. The collision ripped a 300-foot gash in the

Titanic's bottomside. The forward compartments began to fill. The ship could remain afloat with her first four compartments filled but, due to the bulkheads not extending high enough above E deck, her fifth compartment began to fill. The ship began to take an increasingly vertical position. At 2:20 a.m. on April 15th she sank to the depths. The *Titanic's* lifeboats with a capacity for 1,178 were lowered holding only 652. Survivors picked out of the water brought the total number of saved to 705 persons, out of a total of 815 passengers and 688 crew members. Her captain, John Smith, went down with his ship. The remaining survivors were picked up by the Cunard Liner *Carpathia* when she arrived on the scene at around 4:00 a.m., in the area of latitude 41 degrees 46'-50 degrees-14' longitude, where the *Titanic* went down. The passengers and crew were taken to New York. The mystique of the *Titanic's* sinking spawned countless written accounts and a few feature films. In 1985, nearly three-quarters of a century after the event, the *Titanic* wreck was located by a joint French-American team. Dramatic photographs were sent to the surface mothership by the remote control 26' submarine *Nautile*. In September 1986 I was personally invited to attend the salvage operations for the White Star Liner *Republic*, which sank outside Nantucket, Massachusetts in January 1909—three years prior to the *Titanic*. The artifacts which were brought up from this time capsule were furnished by the same suppliers that had furnished the other ships of the Line including the *Titanic*. Viewing these artifacts were of particular fascination since those of the *Titanic's* have been left in their resting place and rightfully so.

Sister ships: *Britannic, Olympic.*

Note: The wreck was actually first located on August 15, 1980.

Austro-Americana Line

CANADA

Builder: Blohm & Voss, Hamburg, Germany
Completed: 1898
Gross tonnage: 11,440
Dimensions: 501′ x 62′ Depth: 43′
Engines: Two sets of 8-cylinder, quadruple expansion engines
Screws: Twin
Decks: Three
Normal speed: 12 knots
Passenger accommodations: 2,100 in second and third class
Registry: Austria
Maiden voyage: Trieste-Patras-Naples-Ponta Delgada-Quebec-Montreal,
   arriving on May 15, 1913

Built for the German-owned Hamburg-American Line and christened *Bulgaria*. Sold to the Austro-Americana Line in 1913 and renamed *Canada*. Employed on the Mediterranean route carrying mostly immigrants leaving their homes in Italy, Greece, the Balkans and Portugal for the new world. Made her last voyage for the line on August 28, 1913, when she departed Montreal for the last time. Resold to the Hamburg-American Line in December 1913 and reverted to her original name. Interned at New York on July 27, 1914 and seized by the United States in April 1917 upon U.S. entry into World War I. Converted to a cargo ship under the name *Hercules*. Later renamed *Philippines* in 1919, the ship was returned to the United States Shipping Board in October 1919 and sold for scrap in January 1924. Note: She made only two round trip voyages for the Austro-Americana Line and she may have only been chartered. Information is sketchy.

Sister ship: *Polonia*.

KAISER FRANZ JOSEF

Builder: Cantiere Navale, Triestino, Monfalcone, Italy
Completed: May 1912
Gross tonnage: 12,567
Dimensions: 477' x 62' Depth: 45' Draft: 29'
Engines: Two sets of 8-cylinder quadruple expansion engines
Screws: Twin
Watertight bulkheads: Nine
Decks: Four
Normal speed: 17 knots
Passenger accommodations: 236 first, 802 second and 108 third class
  (figures Lloyd Triestino)
Registry: Austria
Maiden voyage: Trieste-Buenos Aires in February 1912

Built expressly for the Austro-Americana Line and christened *Kaiser Franz Josef*. Employed mostly in the Mediterranean service out of Trieste Patras-Naples-Ponta Delgada-New York service from May 1912, arriving a New York for the first time on June 8. She made her last voyage for the line on July 4, 1914, New York-Ponta Delgada-Naples-Patras-Trieste Passed on to Cosulich Line ownership in 1919 after the transition from the Austrian flag to the Italian due to the new geographical boundarie brought about by the end of the First World War. Renamed *President Wilson*. Sold to the Lloyd Triestino in 1930 and renamed *Gange*. Resold to the Adriatica Line in late 1936 and renamed *Marco Polo*. Burned out by bombing at Tobruk on January 23, 1941.

POLONIA

Builder: Blohm & Voss, Hamburg, Germany
Completed: 1899
Gross tonnage: 11,464
Dimensions: 501' x 62' Depth: 43'
Engines: Two sets of 8-cylinder quadruple expansion engines
Screws: Twin
Decks: Three
Normal speed: 12 knots
Passenger accommodations: 2,100 in second and third class
Registry: Austria
Maiden voyage: Trieste-Patras-Naples-Ponta Delgada-Quebec-Montreal, arriving on June 29, 1913

Built for the German Hamburg-American Line and christened *Batavia*. Sold to the Austro-Americana Line in 1913 and renamed *Polonia*. Employed mostly for the immigrant trade out of Italy, Greece and the Balkans, with a last call in the Portuguese Azores, she made only a few voyages for the line before being resold to the Hamburg-American Line. She made her last voyage for the Austro-Americana Line on September 21, 1913, when she left Montreal for the last time. Resold in March 1914, she reverted to her original name. Allotted to France as a World War I reparation and placed under the auspices of the "Terre de France." Sold for scrap in Italy in 1924. Note: She and her sister may have only been chartered by the Austro-Americana Line since they made only a few trips and were handed back. Information is sketchy. Photo as *Batavia*.

Sister ship: *Canada*.

Cunard Line

I ALAUNIA

Builder: Scott's Shipbuilding & Engineering Co., Ltd., Greenrock, Scotland
Completed: November 1913
Gross tonnage: 13,405
Dimensions: 538' x 64' Depth: 46' Draft: 28'
Engines: Two 4-cylinder quadruple expansion
Screws: Twin
Watertight bulkheads: Eight
Decks: Four
Normal speed: 14.50 knots
Passenger accommodations: 520 cabins and 1,540 third class
Registry: United Kingdom
Maiden voyage: Liverpool-Queenstown-Portland, Maine-Boston on November 27, 1913

Engaged in the London-Quebec-Montreal service in the summer months and Liverpool-Halifax-Portland-Boston during the winter with calls at Queenstown both east and westbound. On August 27, 1914 she sailed to Canada and did not return to Liverpool until February 14, 1915. Resumed regular services from London to New York on May 11, 1916, with calls at Falmouth and Plymouth eastbound. Sunk by a mine in the English Channel on October 19, 1916, two miles from the lightvessel *Royal Sovreign* after successfully disembarking her passengers at Falmouth, England. The misfortune of the ship cost the loss of two lives. She and her sister ship the *Andania* were the first two ships to be built by Cunard expressly for the Canadian trade, and were the first to inaugurate cabin-class accommodation over the formerly labelled second class.

Sister ships: *Andania* and *Aurania*.

II ALAUNIA

Builder: John Brown & Co., Ltd., Clydebank, Glasgow, Scotland
Completed: July 1925
Gross tonnage: 14,030
Dimensions: 538′ x 65′ Depth: 43′ Draft: 32′
Engines: Four steam turbines double-reduction geared
Screws: Twin
Watertight bulkheads: Eleven
Decks: Four
Normal speed: 15 knots
Passenger accommodations: 633 cabins and 1,040 third class
Officers and crew: 270
Registry: United Kingdom
Maiden voyage: Liverpool-Quebec-Montreal on July 24, 1925

Employed in the Canadian trade on the Southampton-Quebec-Montreal route during the summer and to Halifax and Nova Scotia-New York in the winter months. Made calls at Cherbourg westbound and Plymouth and Le Havre eastbound. The *Alaunia* began her sailings from both Liverpool and London, but by 1926 had made four Liverpool-New York and Halifax trips before settling in the Southampton-Cherbourg-Montreal run westbound and Montreal-Plymouth-Cherbourg-London eastbound with Halifax supplanting Montreal during the winter. And by 1928 was operating out of Southampton exclusively. In August 1933 she was commissioned to transfer gold bullion from Canada to England. Made her last commercial voyage before the war on August 11, 1939, Montreal-Quebec-Plymouth-Le Havre, and was requisitioned by the Admiralty on the 24th. Fitted-out at Gibraltar for troop work, she was sold to the British Admiralty on December 8, 1944 and was rebuilt as a base repair ship for engine room ratings at Devonport, England. Sold to the British Iron and Steel Corporation for scrap on January 5, 1957, and broken up at Blyth, Scotland, on October 9, 1957.

Sister ships: *Ascania* and *Aurania*.

II ALBANIA

Builder: Scott's Shipbuilding & Engineering Co., Ltd. Greenrock, Scotland
Completed: December 1920
Gross tonnage: 12,768
Dimensions: 539' x 64' Depth: 47' Draft: 32'
Engines: Four steam turbines double-reduction geared
Screws: Twin
Watertight bulkheads: Eight
Decks: Two
Normal speed: 15 knots
Passenger accommodations: 38 second and 557 third class
Registry: United Kingdom
Maiden voyage: Liverpool-New York on January 18, 1921.

Engaged in the Liverpool-New York run initially, the *Albania* began a number of Liverpool-Quebec-Montreal trips beginning April 20, 1922. Built for maximum cargo capacity and a limited accommodation for passengers. Staterooms were located on the shelter and 'tween decks. In 1921 she carried only second class passengers and became a cabin class ship in 1924. Transferred to the Hamburg-London-Plymouth-Cherbourg-New York route in January 1923, the unpopularity of the ship caused her to cross on some occasions without passengers. In 1924-25 she became interchangeable on the Southampton-Cherbourg-New York route until she was laid up permanently, completing her last voyage for Cunard on September 12, 1925 from New York to Cherbourg-Plymouth and on to London, where she was sold at the first opportunity. In 1930 the Italian firm of Liberia Triestina purchased the *Albania* and renamed her *California*. Sunk at an Italian port on August 11, 1941, during hostilities.

I ANDANIA

Builder: Scott's Shipbuilding & Engineering Co., Ltd., Greenock, Scotland
Completed: July 1913
Gross tonnage: 13,405
Dimensions: 538' x 64' Depth: 46' Draft: 30'
Engines: Two 4-cylinder quadruple expansion
Screws: Twin
Watertight bulkheads: Eight
Decks: Four
Normal speed: 14.50 knots
Passenger accommodations: 520 second and 1,540 third class
Registry: United Kingdom
Maiden voyage: Liverpool-Quebec-Montreal on July 17, 1913

Engaged in the Liverpool-Quebec-Montreal service in the summer months and to Halifax and Boston during the winter season with calls at Queenstown both east and westbound. The *Andania* was the first of her type to enter service. Built expressly for the Canadian trade, and with her sister the *Alaunia*, were the first cabin-class type liners on the Atlantic run. Called at Portland, Maine in the winter and made three Liverpool-Halifax-Portland-Boston voyages in 1914. Upon her arrival at Boston on April 6, 1914, she became virtually idle making only irregular crossings and was on October 3 requisitioned for service as a Canadian transport until her release on April 17, 1916. On May 2, 1916, she resumed scheduled sailings from London to New York, this occasion being Cunard's first such out of the port of London. An occasional call at Plymouth was incorporated into her new itinerary but the prospects looked dim at the time with the first sailing carrying only 16 passengers. By 1917 she was making some Liverpool-New York sailings in conjunction with four London-Liverpool sailings to Quebec-Montreal and Halifax. On January 27, 1918 she was torpedoed and sunk by a submarine off Rathlin Island, Northern Ireland, with the loss of seven lives.

Sister ships: *Alaunia* and *Aurania*.

II ANDANIA

Builder: R. W. Hawthorn, Leslie & Co., Ltd., Newcastle-on-Tyne, England
Completed: May 1922
Gross tonnage: 13,950
Dimensions: 538′ x 65′ Depth: 43′ Draft: 32′
Engines: Four steam turbines double-reduction geared
Screws: Twin
Watertight bulkheads: Ten
Decks: Four
Normal speed: 15 knots
Passenger accommodations: 486 cabin and 1,187 third class
Officers and crew: 270
Registry: United Kingdom
Maiden voyage: London-Southampton-Quebec-Montreal on June 1, 1922

Engaged in the Hamburg-Southampton-Halifax service in winter; London-Cherbourg-Plymouth-Montreal service during the summer months, with a few Liverpool-Halifax-Boston runs during the winter and proceeding to New York on occasion. Transferred to the Hamburg-Southampton-Cherbourg-New York run westbound and New York-Plymouth-Cherbourg-Hamburg eastbound from 1925 until 1926. In 1927 she was diverted once again to the Liverpool-Quebec-Montreal run in the summer and to Halifax and Nova Scotia in winter with a call at Greenock and Belfast eastbound and westbound throughout the year. With the outbreak of World War II the need for merchant ships necessitated the requisitioning of the *Andania* like many other vessels of her class. Fitted-out as an armed merchant cruiser in September 1939, after completion of her last commercial voyage from Montreal-Quebec-Glasgow-Belfast-Liverpool on the 25th of August. She was torpedoed by submarine UA, seventy miles off Reykjavik, Iceland on June 15, 1940 and sank the next day.

Sister ships: *Antonia* and *Ausonia*.

II ANTONIA

Builder: Vickers Ltd., Barrow-in-Furness, England
Completed: December 1921
Gross tonnage: 13,867
Dimensions: 538' x 65' Depth: 43' Draft: 32'
Engines: Four steam turbines double-reduction geared
Screws: Twin
Watertight bulkheads: Ten
Decks: Four
Normal speed: 15 knots
Passenger accommodations: 607 cabin and 1,040 third class
Officers and crew: 270
Registry: United Kingdom
Maiden voyage: Liverpool-Quebec-Montreal on June 1, 1922

Employed mainly in the London-Cherbourg-Plymouth-Montreal service during the summer and Hamburg-Southampton-Halifax in the winter with some alternating voyages on the Hamburg-London-Plymouth-Cherbourg-New York run. *Antonia* made several voyages from Hamburg to New York but by 1926 was scheduled permanently in the Liverpool-Greenock-Belfast-Quebec-Montreal service in the summer months and to Halifax and Nova Scotia in the winter with a regular call at Greenock and Belfast eastbound throughout the year. *Antonia* also worked in the Liverpool-Queenstown-New York run on occasion when other Cunarders were needed for the heavy traffic on that route. Later on in her career she made a number of Southampton-Cherbourg-New York trips. Made her last commercial voyage for Cunard from Montreal-Quebec-Glasgow-Belfast-Liverpool on the 9th of December 1939, and subsequently laid up. Converted to an armed merchant cruiser in October 1940 and sold to the British Admiralty on March 24, 1942 for conversion to a repair ship and renamed Wayland. Sold for scrap in Scotland in 1948.

Sister ships: *Andania* and *Ausonia*.

AQUITANIA

Builder: John Brown & Co., Ltd., Clydebank, Glasgow, Scotland
Completed: April 1914
Gross tonnage: 45,647
Dimensions: 901′ x 97′ Depth: 55′ Draft: 35′
Engines: Four direct-action Parson steam turbines; three high pressure and one low pressure
Screws: Quadruple
Watertight bulkheads: Ten
Decks: Six
Normal speed: 24 knots
Passenger accommodations: 771 first, 979 second and 1,730 third class
Officers and crew: 550
Registry: United Kingdom
Maiden voyage: Liverpool-New York on May 30, 1914

The *Aquitania* had just completed three round-trip voyages to New York when, upon her arrival at Liverpool on July 17, 1914, her schedule was interrupted by the outbreak of the First World War in August. Converted to an armed merchant cruiser, she was the largest such vessel in the British merchant marine. After incurring some minor damages whilst fitting out, she was paid off by the Admiralty as being too large for practical operations. In the spring of 1915 she was used to transport troops to the Dardanelles, Turkey to fight the suicide brigades of Kemal Atatuk who held the Narrows. She later served as a hospital ship until 1917 in the Mediterranean. Laid up in 1917 and later transported

American troops to France until March 1918. Resumed transatlantic services on February 22, 1919 on the Liverpool-New York run for three voyages before she was diverted to work this route out of the now more convenient port of Southampton on June 14th. Withdrawn from service between December 1919 and July 18, 1920 when she was refitted and converted to oil-firing. Employed regularly on the Southampton-New York run, a call at Cherbourg was added to her itinerary in March of 1923. On occasion the *Aquitania* was used for cruising, a new concept which was then exclusively for the wealthier customer who was not immigrating to the melting pots of America or Canada. Requisitioned once again for troop service on November 21, 1939, this time extending until March 1948 when she was used for transporting American troops after the Second World War. Re-entered passenger service in May 1948 under arrangement with the Canadian Government whereby she made 12 trips to Halifax with her accommodations confined to a single austerity class. Commenced her last voyage for Cunard on November 21, 1949 from Montreal to Southampton via Quebec and arrived on the 1st of December. During her career *Aquitania* steamed over 3,000,000 miles and carried approximately 1,200,000 passengers having crossed the Atlantic some 475 times. An enormous ship to say the least, her propellers weighed 17½ tons each and she was one of the first liners to have a gyro compass fitted. Equipped with Frahm's anti-rolling tanks-fore runners of the modern stabilizers, she was the last of the handsome four-funnelled liners. Sold to the British Iron & Steel Corporation in February 1950. She left for the shipbreaker's yard at Garelock Scotland on December 19, 1949. A very majestic looking ship, she had served Cunard for 35 years and Britain through two world wars without a single incident of misfortune.

II ASCANIA

Builder: W.G. Whitworth & Co., Ltd., Newcastle-on-Tyne, England
Completed: May 1925
Gross tonnage: 14,440
Dimensions: 538' x 65' Depth: 43' Draft: 32'
Engines: Four steam turbines; two high-pressure double-reduction geared and two low pressure.
Screws: Twin
Watertight bulkheads: Ten
Decks: four
Normal speed: 15 knots
Passenger accommodations: 198 first and 506 tourist class*
Officers and crew: 367
Registry: United Kingdom
Maiden voyage: London-Southampton-Cherbourg-Plymouth-Montreal on May 22, 1925

*Originally carried 493 cabin and 664 third class.

Initially employed in the London-Cherbourg-Plymouth-Montreal service during the summer and Hamburg-Southampton-Halifax-New York run in winter, the *Ascania* was diverted to the Southampton-Cherbourg-Quebec-Montreal run in summer and Halifax-New York during the off season with a call at Plymouth and Le Havre eastbound and ending her voyages at London. On two occasions the *Ascania* took part in the search for a disabled vessel. In October 1934 she took part in the search for the disabled British steamer *Millpool*. On the night of December 10-11, 1934 the *Ascania* picked up a distress call from the British steamer *Ulsworth* while caught in a mid-Atlantic gale. Reaching her on the 14th, she was taken in tow to Port Fagal in the Azores 600 miles away. On July 2, 1938 she ran aground on Bic Island, 150 miles off Quebec but was refloated without difficulty. In November 1935 she had the misfortune of being rammed amidships by the Donaldson collier *Norwegian* while moored at a Montreal quay. Requisitioned by the Admiralty for war service on August 24, 1939 she was fitted-out as an armed merchant cruiser. Completing her duty work, she arrived at Southampton on October 5, 1942 when she reconditioned as a troopship and sailed as such on April 21, 1943 until the conclusion of hostilities. Resumed scheduled sailings from Liverpool to Halifax and Nova Scotia on December 20, 1947. After being fully reconditioned in the autumn of 1949, *Ascania* was employed on the Liverpool-Quebec-Montreal run on April 21, 1950. Reallocated to her home port of Southampton in March 1953 after an absence of 14 years and working from this port to Le Havre-Quebec-Montreal in the summer and Halifax-New York in winter. *Ascania* was the last of the Canadian fleet of liners to survive the Second World War. She made her last commercial voyage for Cunard on November 7, 1956 from Montreal-Quebec-Le Havre-Southampton. Withdrawn from service after a one-time trip as a transport to Port Said in November 1956 and laid up in December. Sold for scrap at Newport, Wales leaving for the scrapyards on the 30th of December 1956.

Sister ships: *Alaunia* and *Aurania*.

III AURANIA

Builder: Swan, Hunter & Wigham Richardson Ltd., Newcastle-on-Tyne, England
Completed: September 1924
Gross tonnage: 13,984
Dimensions: 538′ x 65′ Depth: 43′ Draft: 32′
Engines: Four steam turbines double-reduction geared.
Screws: Twin
Watertight bulkheads: Ten
Decks: Four
Normal speed: 15 knots
Passenger accommodations: 633 cabin and 1,040 third class
Officers and crew: 270
Registry: United Kingdom
Maiden voyage: Liverpool-New York in September 1924, arriving at New York on September 24th

Engaged on the Liverpool-New York run until January 23, 1925 when she arrived at Montreal and began making a call at Halifax throughout the winter months while running to Montreal in summer. Simultaneously the call at New York was eliminated. In 1927 the *Aurania* inaugurated a call at Queenstown and by December 1928 was employed in the Southampton-Cherbourg-Halifax-Nova Scotia-New York run with a call at Plymouth and Le Havre eastbound throughout the year and ending her voyages at the port of London on the return crossing. The *Aurania* had originally sailed from Liverpool and London but by 1928 Southampton had become her main port of call in England. Made her last commercial voyage for Cunard on August 18, 1939, Montreal-Quebec-Plymouth-Le Havre-London. Requisitioned for war service, on the 24th of August she was fitted-out as an armed merchant cruiser. In July 1941 she collided with an iceberg while in convoy between Iceland and Halifax but managed to escape serious damage until months later when her demise became a reality. Hit by a torpedo off the coast of Ireland, she managed to make it to Rothesay Bay two days later. When first hit, the *Aurania* listed 20° to port and her number 3 hold was open to the sea with the adjacent number 2 hold flooding as well as the deep tanks. Fortunately, she managed to stay afloat with the remaining watertight compartments closed. Drydocking after the mishap revealed a hole 42′ x 38′. Sold to the Admiralty on March 2, 1942 and converted to a fleet repair ship under the name of *Artifax*. Sold for scrap in Italy in January 1961.

Sister Ships: *Alaunia* and *Ascania*.

II AUSONIA

Builder: W.G. Armstrong, Whitworth & Co., Ltd., Newcastle-on-Tyne, England
Completed: December 1921
Gross tonnage: 13, 912
Dimensions: 538' x 65' Depth: 43' Draft: 32'
Engines: Four steam turbine double-reduction geared
Screws: Twin
Watertight bulkheads: Ten
Decks: Four
Normal speed: 15 knots
Passenger accommodations: 609 cabin and 1040 third class
Officers and crew: 270
Registry: United Kingdom
Maiden voyage: Liverpool-Cherbourg-Quebec-Montreal on June 22, 1922

Employed in the Liverpool-Montreal run during the summer and to Halifax with an occasional call at Boston and New York in the winter season. Transferred to the London-Southampton-Cherbourg-Plymouth-Quebec-Montreal run in May 1923, while working the Hamburg-Southampton-Halifax-Nova Scotia during the winter with a call at Cherbourg westbound and at Plymouth and Le Havre homeward, and ending her trips in London. Her itineraries, like those of her sister ships, varied during the mid-twenties when shipping was at an ebb and ports were often changed. *Ausonia* also continued to make several Liverpool-Halifax-New York trips during this period. Fitted out as an armed merchant cruiser in September 1939 after completing her last commercial voyage for the line on September 1st from Montreal-Quebec-Plymouth-Le Havre. Sold to the Admiralty on June 3, 1942, she was decommissioned in September 1964 and sold to Spanish shipbreakers in August 1965.

Sister ships: *Andania* and *Antonia*.

BERENGARIA

Builder: Vulkan Werkes, Hamburg, Germany
Completed: June 1912
Gross tonnage: 52,101
Dimensions: 919' x 98' Depth: 63'
Engines: Four Curtis-A.E.G.-Vulkan steam turbines
Screws: Quadruple
Watertight bulkheads: Twelve
Decks: Seven
Normal speed: 23.50 knots
Passenger accommodations: 856 first, 799 second and 1,584 third class
Officers and crew: 950
Registry: United Kingdom
Maiden voyage: Southampton-New York arriving at New York on
  July 1, 1921.

Originally built for the Hamburg-American Line and christened *Imperator*. She was ceded to Britain under the treaty of Versailles in 1920 and sold into a joint ownership between Cunard and the White Star Line. She continued to operate under her former name and made ten voyages to New York, her first on the 21st of February 1920, from Liverpool to New York with subsequent voyages on the Southampton-New York track on

June 16, 1920 and called at Cherbourg for first time. Renamed the *Berengaria* June 1921. Employed in the Southampton-New York service year-round, with the call at Cherbourg added in 1923, she was converted to oil-firing from a coal burner while refitted between September 1921 and May 1922. Her daily consumption of oil amounted to 750 tons per day. The *Berengaria* was one of Albert Ballin's great giants of whose running mates were the White Star Line's *Majestic ex Bismark* and U.S. Lines' *Leviathan ex Vaterland*. In August 1929 a stock brokerage office was installed for the convenience of the market traders, but after the Crash and the ensuing Great Depression, she became known as the "Bargain Area" when rates plummeted and travellers were few. Her aft funnel was a dummy serving only for symmetry. The *Berengaria* caught fire twice within a span of ten days. The first time was on March 3, 1938, a day after her arrival at New York, in the third-class section and shortly after that fire was followed by another in her main lounge. Considered to be a fire risk by American authorities, she was put up for sale. Made her last voyage for Cunard in March 1938 from New York to Southampton via Cherbourg and was sold to John Jarvis, shipbreakers at Jarrow, England on November 7th of that year with arrival in December. Work had been held up during the war and she was later towed to the Firth of Forth, Scotland in 1946 and completely dismantled. Though magnificently appointed and handsome in her appearance the *Berengaria* never won the acclaim among the general public as did her consorts *Mauretania* and *Aquitania*.

BRITANNIC

Builder: Harland & Wolff Ltd., Belfast, Ireland
Completed: June 1930
Gross tonnage: 27,778
Dimensions: 712' x 82' Depth 52' Draft 35'
Engines: Two 10-cylinder, 4-stroke, double-acting Burmeister & Wain diesel.
Screws: Twin
Watertight bulkheads: Twelve
Decks: Five
Normal speed: 18 knots
Officers and crew: 485
Passenger accommodations: 429 first and 690 tourist class
Registry: United Kingdom
Maiden voyage: London-Le Havre-Southampton-New York in April 1935

Built for the White Star Line. Passed on to Cunard Line ownership on May 10, 1934 when the two lines consolidated. Engaged in the London-Southampton-New York service with a call at Le Havre homeward, and cruising. Requisitioned for troop work on August 29, 1939, she was attacked by Italian aircraft in the Red Sea in October 1940 and in January 1942 by U-boats and enemy aircraft while in convoy. Miraculously she managed to survive the war unscathed. Decommissioned in March 1947, she resumed commercial sailings from Liverpool to New York via Cobh* on May 22, 1948 after having been refitted entirely. Each year the *Britannic* made a cruise to the Mediterranean, with such voyages lasting sixty days. The ship's fore funnel was a dummy enclosing the wireless room. Her upper bridge was 118' long. *Britannic* was the last ship to sail across the North Atlantic wearing the proud livery of the White Star Line, whose ships were known for elegance rather than the marketing edge, which Cunard promoted—that of speed. In June 1960, she broke one of her crankshafts two days outside of New York westbound. Docked at pier 90, the work was completed on the spot after 3 months of intense work by shipworkers from the Todd shipyards. Commenced her last voyage on November 25, 1960 from New York to Liverpool via Cobh. On December 16, 1960 she left Liverpool under her own power for the shipbreaker's yard at Inverkeithing, Scotland. Quite a dignified way to go to the scrapyard, where the torchers cut away the metal plates for some future usage and that intangible character and soul that ships possess becomes vapor. With the scrapping of the *Britannic* there passed also an elegant standard that was White Star Line. Note: Her B&W engines were the largest ever fitted into a liner to date.

Sister ship: *Georgic.*

*Formerly Queenstown.

CAMPANIA

Builder: Fairfield Shipbuilding & Engineering Co., Ltd., Glasgow, Scotland
Completed: March 1893
Gross tonnage: 12, 884
Dimensions: 622' x 65' Depth: 42'
Engines: Two 3-cylinder triple expansion
Screws: Twin
Watertight bulkheads: Twelve
Decks: Three
Normal speed: 21 knots (She attained a speed of 23.02 knots during her trails)
Passenger accommodations: 394 first, 415 second and 869 third class
Officers and crew: 386
Registry: United Kingdom
Maiden voyage: Liverpool-New York on April 22, 1893

Engaged in the Liverpool-Queenstown-New York run. A very fast steamer, the *Campania* won the Blue Riband from the White Star Line's *Majestic* in May 1893 by making the run from Sandy Hook to Queenstown in 5 days, 17 hours and 27 minutes at a speed of 21.09 knots on her return maiden voyage. She was the first Cunarder to have twin-screws and boasted a promenade deck 370 feet in length. There were 12 main boilers and one single end boiler for port side use. Her 12 furnaces consumed over 20 tons of coal every hour to make her greyhound crossings over the North Atlantic. In 1900 she rammed a sailing vessel in the St. George's Channel, sinking the ship with the loss of her entire crew. Still another mishap occurred in 1905 when an immense wave swept five persons overboard and injured several others. The *Campania* was engaged mainly in the direct Liverpool-New York run, the call at Queenstown now Cobh was innaugurated in January 1900. Made her 250th and last commercial voyage for the Line on May 5, 1914, New York-Liverpool, and withdrawn from service on the 12th of May 1914. However, later on in the year she was placed under the management of the Anchor Line and made five Atlantic crossings under their banner ending on the 15th of October at Liverpool. Sold T.W. Ward in 1914 for scrapping but due to the outbreak of war was resold to the Admiralty and converted to a seaplane carrier with considerable alterations forward and the replacement of her fore-funnel with two others placed side by side. This now gave her three stacks, which look somewhat odd. Broke from her moorings on November 5, 1918 during a storm off Burnt Island and foundered after colliding with the battleship *Revenge* in the Firth of Forth, Scotland. The half-submerged wreck was subsequently blown up as it presented a danger to navigation in the waterway.

Sister ship: *Lucania*

II CARINTHIA

Builder: Vickers Ltd., Barrow-in-Furness, England
Completed: August 1925
Gross tonnage: 20,277
Dimensions: 624' x 74' Depth: 45' Draft: 33'
Engines: Four steam turbines double-reduction geared
Screws: Twin
Collision bulkhead: One
Watertight bulkheads: Nine
Decks: Five
Normal speed: 17 knots
Passenger accommodations: 321 first, 460 second and 950 third class
  (accommodations are limited to 800 when in cruise service)
Officers and crew: 450
Registry: United Kingdom
Maiden voyage: Liverpool-New York on August 22, 1925

Built as a dual-purpose ship, she was employed in the Liverpool-Queenstown-New York run and cruising for which she is well remembered. Refitted in December 1932 and converted to a cabin tourist class ship. The *Carinthia* left New York on January 7, 1933 for a world cruise that covered over 40,000 miles and with calls at 40 ports. Transferred to the New York-West Indies cruise service in January 1936 after having been in the London-Channel ports-New York run for two years prior. In 1937 one could cruise to Nassau and Havana out of New York through the winter months for as little as $85 for a nine-day holiday. The Carinthia made a world cruise every year between 1925 and 1933. Made her last commercial voyage for the Line on September 2, 1939 from New York to Liverpool, after having been requisitioned by the Admiralty the day before her departure. Torpedoed off the Ulster coast, Ireland by submarine U46 on June 6, 1940. Fortunately the *Carinthia* managed to stay afloat for 30 hours but foundered on June 8th. Upon impact of the torpedo, two officers and two ratings were killed. *Carinthia's* promenade deck was a full 390 feet long and her exquisite amenities made her and her sister *Franconia* very popular liners. When cruising was just making its debut in the twenties, one could take a 9-day cruise from New York to Nassau and Havana, the gambling havens of the times, for as little as $64. If one opted for a 14-day voyage around the Caribbean, the prices were in the vicinity of $115.

Sister ship: *Franconia*.

III CARINTHIA

Builder: John Brown & Co., Ltd., Clydebank, Glasgow, Scotland
Completed: June 1956
Gross tonnage: 21,947
Dimensions: 608' x 80' Depth: 46' Draft: 29'
Engines: Four steam turbines double-reduction geared
Screws: Twin
Collision bulkhead: One
Watertight bulkhead: Nine
Decks: Five
Normal speed: 20 knots
Passenger accommodations: 180 first, 888 tourist class.
  (accommodations are combined into one class when pleasure cruising)
Officers and crew: 461
Registry: United Kingdom
Maiden voyage: Liverpool-Greenock-Quebec-Montreal on June 27, 1956

Engaged in the Liverpool-Cobh or Greenock-Halifax-New York run in the winter with sailings from Liverpool to Greenock-Quebec and Montreal during the summer months and cruising. Equipped with motion stabilizers all public rooms were fully air-conditioned. A very good looking ship in her outward design the *Carinthia* and *Sylvania* one of her sister ships were designed in traditional Cunard conservative style whereas the other two sisters *Carmania* and *Franconia* were somewhat ostentatious in their decor. The *Carinthia* in fact was furnished with chairs taken from the old *Aquitania* in her first class dining room. The *Carinthia* along with her three sister ships were painted white in the winter of 1966-67 and sent cruising when the Canadian trade had diminished considerably. *Carinthia* ended her career on that run on November 25, 1966, when she made her last voyage from Montreal to Liverpool via Quebec City-Halifax-Cobh and Greenock. Laid up pending her sale which came about in January 1968, to the Italian Sitmar Line and placed under Liberian registry. Passed back under British ownership when P&O Lines purchased the ship in 1988 and renamed her *Fair Princess* for their subsidiary Princess Cruises. Presently in their service. Renamed *Fairland*; *Fairsea*, 1971.

Sister ships: *Carmania*, *Franconia* and *Sylvania*.

I CARMANIA

Builder: John Brown & Co., Ltd., Clydebank, Glasgow, Scotland
Completed: November 1905
Gross tonnage: 19,566
Dimensions: 678′ x 72′ Depth: 42′ Draft: 33′
Engines: Three direct-action Parson steam turbines
Screws: Triple
Watertight bulkheads: Twelve
Decks: Five
Normal speed: 17.50 knots (attained a speed of 20.04 knots on her trials)
Passenger accommodations: 425 cabin, 365 tourist and 650 third class*
Registry: United Kingdom
Maiden voyage: Liverpool-New York on December 2, 1905

*Original complement was for: 400 first class, 653 second class, 2,380 third class passengers.

Employed in the Liverpool-Queenstown-New York run during the summer months and in the New York-Mediterranean service in winter. The *Carmania* began operating to the Mediterranean and Adriatic on January 16, 1908. By 1912 she made only one such voyage on March 2 and the following year remained on the New York-Liverpool run. Throughout her extensive career she worked nearly every service of Cunard at some time. In 1919 she inaugurated a call at Halifax westbound and later called at Boston from time to time. Caught fire at Liverpool on June 4, 1912 but was not seriously damaged. On October 9, 1913 she rescued a number of persons from the Uranium Line's emigrant ship *Volturno*, ablaze in the mid-Atlantic. Fitted-out as an armed merchant cruiser on August 15, 1914, she engaged the Hamburg-South American liner-cruiser *Cap Trafalgar* off Trinidad on the 14th of September. The *Carmania* performed heroically under the command of Captain J. C. Barr sinking the German liner after sustaining 79 hits from the vanquished ship. As the

Cap Trafalgar sank, fresh smoke appeared on the horizon and four funnels soon came into view. The *Carmania*, with her guns and the ship herself damaged extensively, stoked her holds and steamed southwest by the sun and wind. Later it was learned that the four-stacker approaching the scene had been the *Kronprinz Wilhelm*, the famous North German Lloyd raider coming to the aid of her consort. The *Carmania* is the only armed merchant cruiser ever to have defeated and sunk a similarly outfitted merchant vessel as was the *Cap Trafalgar*. Decommissioned in 1916 she reverted back to her owners and resumed sailings on November 9, 1916. Maintained services during the war from Liverpool to Halifax and New York beginning on December 21, 1918 via Queenstown and the other U.K. ports year-round. Reallocated to the Liverpool-Boston-New York run in April 1923 and converted to oil firing in the same year. Finishing her refit she made the changeover to a cabin tourist and third class* ship. Diverted to still another run she worked the Liverpool-Quebec-Montreal service in summer and by 1926 was servicing the London-Southampton-New York route with calls at Plymouth and Le Havre eastbound and interchangeable with the Liverpool-Boston-New York run. In 1927 she worked mainly out of Southampton with some Liverpool-New York runs. The winter months could usually find her cruising from New York to Havana when that port was the main attraction of the warmer waters. Made her last voyage for Cunard on August 7, 1931, New York-Cherbourg-Southampton-Plymouth-Le Havre-London. Laid up at Tilbury dock until sold to shipbreakers at Blyth, Scotland in April, 1932. *Carmania* was the first Cunarder to be driven by direct action Parson steam turbines, then a revolutionary step forward in ship engineering. The *Carmania* had a promenade deck 353 feet long and was often referred to, along with her sister *Caronia*, as "The Pretty Sisters".

Sister ship: *Caronia*.

*Later, to tourist-cabin in 1926.

II CARMANIA

Builder: John Brown & Co., Ltd, Clydebank, Glasgow, Scotland
Completed: August 1954
Gross tonnage: 21,370
Dimensions: 60' x 79' Depth 46' Draft: 29'
Engines: Four steam turbines double-reduction geared
Screws: Twin
Collision bulkhead: One
Watertight bulkheads: Nine
Decks: Five
Normal speed: 20 knots
Officers and crew: 457
Passenger accommodation: 120 first and 929 tourist class
 (accommodations are reduced to a single class when in cruise service)
Maiden voyage: Liverpool–Quebec–Montreal on September 2, 1954

Originally christened *Saxonia*, she was renamed in 1962. Employed in the Liverpool–Cobh or Greenock–Quebec–Montreal service she was the largest ship built to date for the Cunard Line's Canadian service. Reverted to the Southampton–LeHavre–Cobh–Quebec–Montreal route on June 19, 1957 and to Halifax and New York in winter. Refitted between October 1962 and April 1963 when she was renamed, the *Carmania* went through an extensive refitting for employment in warmer waters since the Canadian trade was not bringing in the revenues needed to operate her and her three sister ships profitably. The public rooms were restyled in a manner more indicative of warm weather cruising and private plumbing was installed throughout the vessel; a swimming pool replaced the aft cargo hatches and her black hull was covered with several coats of gleaming white. Re-entering service on the 8th of April 1963 she sailed from Southampton to Montreal via Rotterdam in an attempt to attract more European travelers. Now a dual-purpose ship she cruised out of New York and Port Everglades in the winter. The *Carmania* ran aground on

January 14, 1969 on the island of San Salvador in the Bahamas while on a cruise with 471 passengers aboard. Damaged only slightly with some minor leakage, she was refloated four days later and repaired at Newport News, Virginia. At the time of the mishap her passengers were picked up by a Costa Line ship and disembarked where they could make other travel arrangements. Not long after, she was involved in a collision with a Soviet tanker off Gibraltar in May. She incurred further under-the-waterline damage by grounding in the Caribbean the following year, when she was positioned permanently at Port Everglades in January 1970, where she cruised to Nassau and the West Indies making one transatlantic voyage a year for drydocking. Made her last transatlantic crossing on March 13, 1971 from Port Everglades to Southampton via New York and LeHavre. Refitted upon her arrival, she re-entered service in July 1971 on a cruise service out of Southampton to the Canary Islands, Iberian ports and calls in the Mediterranean as far as Piraeus. Since both the Canadian trade had dried up and the Caribbean afforded little before this market had been fully developed some years later, a last attempt at an even older market would seal the fate of the *Carmania* and her sisters. Making her last voyage on August 1, 1971 from Southampton to Villefranche, the *Carmania* returned to her home port on October 31st, after making a charter cruise from Villefranche to other Mediterranean ports. Subsequently laid up pending the ratification of a British trade union's blocking the employment by Cunard of cheaper foreign labour. The existing regulations upheld, Cunard was forced to lay up the ship in Cornwall's River Fal. Sold in August 1973 through a pseudo-Liberian company, the Nikreis Maritime Corporation of Liberia, who acted as agents for the sale to the Soviet owned Black Sea Steamship Company. Renamed *Leonid Sobinov* she is presently in their service.

Note: Photo as *Saxonia*.

Sister ships: *Carinthia, Franconia,* and *Sylvania.*

I CARONIA

Builder: John Brown & Co., Ltd., Clydebank, Glasgow, Scotland
Completed: February 1905
Gross tonnage: 19,782
Dimensions: 678' x 72' Depth: 53' Draft: 32'
Engines: Two 4-cylinder quadruple expansion engines
Screws: Twin
Watertight bulkheads: Twelve
Decks: Five
Normal speed: 18 knots (attained a speed of 19.62 knots on her trials)
Passenger accommodations: 524 cabin, 365 tourist and 650 third class.*
Registry: United Kingdom
Maiden voyage: Liverpool-Queenstown-New York on February 25, 1905

*Original complement: 409 first, 615 second, 2,557 third class.

Employed in the Liverpool-Queenstown-New York service and New York-Mediterranean ports during the winter. Made a couple of trips to Boston prior to her commandeering as a transport in July 1914. Released from government service in 1918 when she resumed her regular route on January 19, 1919 and called at Halifax westbound. Shifted to the New York-Cherbourg-Plymouth-London-Hamburg run on April 8, 1922 until November 4, when she returned to her original run. In early 1924 she began calling at Boston on her eastbound trip and from then after westbound mostly. By 1926 she carried cabin and tourist cabin accommodations and worked the London-Southampton-New York run with a call at Plymouth and Le Havre eastbound with cruising from New York to Havana during the winter months. She later became interchangeable in 1927 working the Liverpool Cobh-Boston-New York route in winter and the Southampton-Le Havre-New York route during summer. Both the *Carmania* and her sister ship *Caronia* were fitted with Stone-Lloyd hydraulic doors which could be operated from the bridge to shut the watertight compartments in case of emergency. The *Caronia's* promenade deck was 353 feet long. In 1928 she was settled permanently on the Southampton-New York route. Made her last commercial voyage for the Line on September 25, 1931, from New York to Southampton and subsequently laid up. Sold to Hughes Bolchow, shipbreakers in 1932 for £20,000 sterling with delivery in July of that year. Resold to Japanese shipbreakers in 1932 for £39,000 and sailed to Japan under the name of *Taiseiyo Maru*, which means "The Great Oceanship". A well-earned calling for one of Cunard's loveliest liners. Scrapped by June 1933.

Sister ship: *Carmania*.

II CARONIA

Builder: John Brown & Co., Ltd., Clydebank, Glasgow, Scotland
Completed: December 1948
Gross tonnage: 34,172
Dimensions: 715' x 91' Depth: 53' Draft: 33'
Engines: Six steam turbines; high-pressure, double-reduction geared; intermediate pressure and low pressure single-reduction geared
Screws: Twin
Collision bulkhead: One
Watertight bulkheads: Nine
Decks: Six
Normal speed: 22 knots
Passenger accommodations: 581 first, and 378 cabin class. (accommodations are combined into a single class of 600 when pleasure cruising)
Officers and crew: 600
Registry: United Kingdom
Maiden voyage: Southampton-Cherbourg-New York on January 4, 1949

Built as a dual-purpose ship, but mostly for cruising, the *Caronia* was the first Cunarder to be fitted with toilet facilities in all cabins. Geared for the American cruise market, she was painted in three shades of green, which earned her the nickname of "Green Goddess" Unfortunately she was plagued by steering problems, and her large funnel often exacerbated the situation by spouting carbon on her uppermost deck, she being the largest single funnelled liner in the world at the time of construction. On one occasion, while on a world cruise, she was taken by the wind and rammed a light house while entering Yokohama harbour, pushing it into the sea. She had a promenade deck 495 feet in length, and was one of the first liners to make use of six of its 45-feet launches to carry passengers ashore where docking, for the large ship presented a problem. On January 6, 1951 she left New York on a hundred-day cruise, which covered more than 8,200 miles, and the average fare ranged in the vicinity of $25,000. Engaged in a cruise service to ports all over the world, the *Caronia* usually worked out of New York and made about three transatlantic crossings from Southampton via Le Havre each year around the high season. The *Caronia's* general pattern of cruises was to cross to New York in January via the Caribbean then up to New York for a ninety-day world cruise, in the Pacific or around Africa; to the Mediterranean and the Black Sea area in spring, the North Cape and Scandinavia in summer, and back to the Mediterranean in the autumn before her annual overhaul. Made her last voyage for the Line on November 18, 1967, New York-Southampton without passengers. Sold to the Greek-owned Universal Lines and renamed to *Columbia* in 1968; *Caribia* in late 1968. Following bankruptcy, she was laid up at pier 86 in June 1970; later at anchor when a lien by the City of New York was issued for unpaid harbour dues. Sold for scrap in April 1974 in Taiwan for $3,500,000. Left New York under tow by an ocean tug, the vessel sought refuge at Guam while caught in a tropical storm. Her incongruity of design and maneuverability were to befall her for the last time and the ship broke loose while entering the harbour. Ramming into the breakwater rock pilings, her hull was torn open below the waterline and she was later dismantled where she lay. A sad ending for a handsome ship. One of her most celebrated patrons was a lady from New York who lived aboard the *Caronia* for what aggregated nearly a decade and a half in travel, and spending close to £8,000,000 sterling in fares.

CARPATHIA

Builder: Swan Hunter Ltd., Newcastle-on-Tyne, England
Completed: February 1903
Gross tonnage: 13,603
Dimensions: 558' x 64' Depth: 41' Draft: 31'
Engines: Two 4-cylinder quadruple expansion
Screws: Twin
Watertight bulkheads: Eight
Decks: Three
Normal speed: 14 knots
Passenger accommodations: 204 first and 1,500 third class*
Registry: United Kingdom
Maiden voyage: Liverpool-Queenstown-Boston on May 5, 1903

*Originally held: 274 first, 382 second, 2,273 third class.

Engaged in the Liverpool-Queenstown-New York run until January 12, 1904, when she entered into the Mediterranean trade from New York for a few voyages while maintaining some voyages to New York out of her home port. By October 1905 she was scheduled almost entirely in the Fiume-Trieste-Messina-Palermo-Naples-Gibraltar-Funchal-New York service with occasional calls at the Azores and Lisbon. Between 1911-1913 she made an occasional call at Boston on her Atlantic run and added a call at Patras or Piraeus on her Mediterranean route. The *Carpathia* attained great fame for herself and her master captain Rostron when she answered the White Star Liner *Titanic's* distress calls on April 14, 1912, after she had collided with an iceberg at 11:40 p.m. off the banks of Newfoundland on her maiden voyage from Southampton to New York. The *Titanic* had reported she was sinking by the head when the *Carpathia*, sailing for the Mediterranean picked up the S.O.S. signal and altered her course. Steaming full speed ahead, she arrived on the scene where the *Titanic* had gone down around 4:00 a.m. on the following morning. The *Carpathia* rescued the survivors, which amounted to 498 passengers and 207 crew members out of the original 2,208 persons aboard that fateful night when the so-called "unsinkable" *Titanic* went down at 2:20 a.m. in latitude 41° 46' longitude 50° 14'. The *Carpathia*, resuming her regular services after sailing for New York, made only two more voyages to the Mediterranean in 1915 after settling in the Liverpool-New York service by July 17, 1915 for the next two years. By February 25, 1917 she was sailing out of the port of London for New York and other U.K. ports because of the war. The *Carpathia* made her last commercial voyage for Cunard across the Atlantic on January 20, 1918, from Halifax, and on the 17th of July she became a war casualty when she was sunk 170 miles from Bishop Rock when hit by three torpedoes. Five men were lost when the torpedoes struck, trapping them in the boiler room.

CUNARD ADVENTURER

Builder: Rotterdamsche Droogdok Maats Co., Rotterdam, Netherlands
Completed: 1971
Gross tonnage: 14,151
Dimensions: 486' x 69' Depth: 41' Draft: 19'
Engines: Four 12-cylinder, single-action Stork-Werkspoort diesel engines
  plus a bow thruster with controllable pitch propeller athwartship
  forward
Screws: Twin
Decks: Five
Normal speed: 21.50 knots
Passenger accommodations: 806 passengers in a single class
Officers and crew: 300
Registry: United Kingdom
Maiden voyage: Southampton-Barcelona-Naples-Palma-Gibraltar-
  Southampton on October 9, 1971*

*Positioning voyage November 19, 1971, Southampton-Lisbon-Madeira-
  Las Palmas-Antigua-Martinique-St. Thomas-San Juan.

Launched on February 2, 1971. Purchased by the Cunard Line from Overseas National Airways while still on the stocks, she was the first liner to be christened with a name not ending with the suffix ia. The only other exception being the Cunarder *Royal George*, a vessel purchased by the Line and not built expressly for the company. Originally Cunard owned 50% of the ship and ONA 50%. The *Adventurer* incurred engine room trouble on her maiden voyage when a crack was discovered on her starboard shaft bearings. For hours, she drifted in the Bay of Biscay on November 20, 1971. Repaired at Lisbon on the 22nd. Originally based to work out of Southampton to the Canary Islands and various Mediterranean ports that changed with almost each voyage, she was later reallocated to work out of San Juan beginning December 4, 1971, and working a cruise itinerary to La Guaira-Grenada-Martinique-Antigua-St. Thomas. Fully air-conditioned and equipped with two Brown-AEG fins for stabilizing the ship in rough weather. The *Adventurer*, like most modern vessels of today, has controllable pitch propellers and bow thrusters athwart. Reallocated to work out of Port Everglades to San Juan-Nassau-St. Thomas-Martinique-Antigua service in mid-1975. She also worked out of Vancouver to Alaska during the summer. On the 14th of February 1976 she was involved in a collision with the Costa Line's Carla C in San Juan harbour with minor damages. The innovative conception of the seventies with fly and cruise packages has proven to be a success financially for many shipping lines. And one can arrange their lifestyle schedule around these cruises, which like the Adventurer, sailed every Saturday. The Cunard *Adventurer* also marked the beginning of the cruise age with the sleek look in ship design, which many new liners were to follow suit. Made her last voyage for the Line on September 25, 1976, San Juan-Madeira-Rotterdam and laid up pending her sale. Sold to the Norwegian-Caribbean Line in February, 1971 for about $12,000,000 and renamed *Sunward II*. Sold to the Greek Epirotiki Lines in mid-1991 and renamed *Pallas Athena*. Presently in their service.

Sister ship: *Cunard Ambassador.*

CUNARD AMBASSADOR

Builder: N.V. Machienbau & Schips P. Smit, Jr. Rotterdam, Netherlands
Completed: March 1972
Gross tonnage: 14,160
Dimensions: 486' x 72' Depth 41' Draft 19'
Engines: Four 12-cylinder, single-acting diesels plus a bow thruster with controllable pitch propeller athwartship forward
Screws: Twin
Decks: Five
Normal speed: 24 knots
Passenger accommodations: 831 first class
Officers and crew: 309
Registry: United Kingdom
Maiden voyage: Lisbon-Las Palmas-Barbados-St. Lucia-Martinique-St. Thomas-San Juan on October 26, 1972

Built expressly for the Cunard Line, she was one of the first ships ordered outside of the British Commonwealth. Her unconventional name fell out of order with Cunard tradition as well. Her avant garde design was, however, to set a new style for cruise ships of the future, which over the years bloomed into more modern concepts. The *Cunard Ambassador* had four lounges and a unique sky lounge as well. A new feature aboard the ship was a shopping arcade, which other lines soon adopted. Equipped with motion stabilizers and fully air-conditioned. She had 17,000 square feet of open deck space and her cinema sat 100 persons. Built at a cost of $17 million dollars. The *Cunard Ambassador* was positioned to work out of San Juan on October 26, 1972 for a series of cruises to the Caribbean during the off seasonal months from New York to Bermuda beginning June 2, 1973 until October 13th when she reverted to the winter schedule. When revenues did not meet up to Cunard expectations she was chartered out to Bahama Cruise Line. On September 12, 1974, while enroute from Port Everglades to New Orleans where she was to pick up passengers for Vera Cruz, a fire began when fuel spewed from a ruptured fuel line and ignited when it hit the hot diesel engines. The fire, which broke out just after dawn, raged for two days and burned its way through six decks via the air-condition ducts and she began to list heavily. The tragic event had occurred while just 35 miles off Key West in the Gulf of Mexico. Her passengers and crew with the exception of 53 crew members were evacuated for fear she might roll over and sink to the U.S. Naval tanker *Tallalah* within two hours of the blaze. The fire extinguished, all were taken to Fort Lauderdale and the ship towed to Key West on the 14th. Declared a total loss she was later sold to the Danish firm of C. Clausen Steamship Company for £1,250,000 pounds and converted to a livestock carrier for carrying sheep. She was towed to Denmark on March 17, 1975. Rebuilt and renamed *Linda Clausen*. Resold in December 1980 to the Lembu Shipping Corp., of Panama and renamed *Procyn*. Resold to the Qatar Transport & Marine Services Company in 1983 and renamed *Raslan*. Sold for scrap to Hai Tai Iron & Steel Co., arriving at Kaohsiung, Taiwan on September 9, 1984. Breaking up commenced on September 26th. I recall the event of the fire quite well since I was having tea talking over the sale of a seat on the Boston Stock Exchange with the managing director of Trafalgar House Ltd. (Cunard Line's parent company), Victor Mathews when the event was brought to his attention at the Berkeley St. office in London.

Note: The *Cunard Ambassador* seemed to have been cursed from the beginning since fire had broken out again in her engine room under the ownership of her former two owners after Cunard and in the control room under her last owner.

Sister ship: *Cunard Adventurer.*

CUNARD COUNTESS

Builder: Burmeister & Wain Skibsbygeri, Copenhagen, Denmark
Completed: May 1975
Gross tonnage: 17,593
Dimensions: 535′ x 72′ Depth: 49′ Draft: 19′
Engines: Four single-acting, 7-cylinder diesels with controllable pitch
   propellers plus two bow thrusters athwartship forward
Watertight bulkheads: Thirteen
Decks: Six
Normal speed: 18.50 knots
Passenger accommodations: 800 in a single class
Officers and crew: 350
Registry: Bahamas
Maiden voyage: San Juan-Caribbean on August 7, 1976*

*Positioning voyage was La Spezia-Barcelona-Las Palmas-Antigua-San
 Juan on July 25, 1976.

Built expressly for the Cunard Line. She was fitted-out at La Spezia, Italy
May 28, 1975–July 1976 by the Industrie Navali Mechaniche Affini.
Originally registered in the United Kingdom, the *Countess* was
transferred to Bahamian registry for tax purposes. This of course
diminishes the image most of the travelling public have for the venerable
Cunard Line name and its British calling. Economics has also forced the
construction of these ships in foreign yards just as two earlier
predecessors were constructed in Dutch shipyards back in 1971. The
Cunard Countess has 380 staterooms of which 259 are situated outside.
Her potential cruising capacity is for 950 berths but much of this space is
occupied by the entertainment and host staff. Twenty-six cabins are
deluxe. Fully air-conditioned and equipped with motion stabilizers, the
Countess' public facilities include a night club, casino, four bars, a
theatre, swimming pool, library, beauty parlour, shopping arcade, sauna.
Her dining room seats 500. Refurbished in 1979. On October 15, 1980 her
British crew went on strike off the Bahamas with 708 passengers on board
upon learning the ship's registry would be changed from British to
Bahamian allowing for lower wage foreign labour. Taken over by the
British government in 1982 with the outbreak of the Falklands War and
converted to a troopship. Decommissioned in 1983, she was refurbished
in Malta and returned to her normal run out of San Juan to Tortola-St.
Maarten-Guadeloupe-St. Lucia-St. John's year-round on 7-day cruises.
Minimum fare begins at $1,099. Refurbished in May, 1983 at Malta, at a
cost of $7,500,000, added, an indoor-outdoor theatre-in-the-round as well
as a disco. A jacuzzi whirlpool was added, the gymnasium enlarged, and a
video arcade for the youngsters. Ports may vary and include LaGuaira-
Grenada-Barbados-Martinique.

Sister ship: *Cunard Princess.*

CUNARD PRINCESS

Builder: Burmeister & Wain Skibsbygeri, Copenhagen, Denmark
Completed: March 1977
Gross tonnage: 17,496
Dimensions: 535′ x 72′ Depth: 49′ Draft: 19′
Engines: Four B & W 4-stroke single-acting, 7-cylinder diesels with
  clutches, flexible couplings and single-reduction gearing in reverse with
  controllable pitch propellers, plus 2 bow thrusters athwartship-forward
Screws: Twin
Watertight bulkheads: Thirteen
Decks: Five
Normal speed: 18.50 knots
Passenger accommodations: 947 in a single class
Officers and crew: 280
Registry: Bahamas
Maiden voyage: La Spezia-Barcelona-Madeira-New York on
  March 15, 1977

Built expressly for Cunard she was launched in December 1974, as the *Cunard Conquest*. Fitted out by the Navale Mechaniche Industrie. La Spezia, Italy between November 6, 1975–April 14, 1976. A small fire broke out while she was being fitted-out in her galley caused by a short circuit, delaying her delivery to New York where renaming took place on March 29, 1977 by the late Princess Grace of Monaco. The *Cunard Princess* holds the distinction of being the first vessel to be christened in New York harbour. The event itself seems ironical with former Cunard tradition but in line with the constant aberrations Cunard has undergone over recent years, i.e., changes in registry of ships; abandonment of the ia suffix in their ships' names, etc. Modelled on the lines of two earlier Cunarders, the *Cunard Adventurer* and *Cunard Ambassador*, the *Cunard Princess* with her flush naval type stern is more of an economical feature of construction rather than the result of aesthetic design. Despite this she is a good looking ship outwardly. I had the occasion to see the ship at Balboa in the Panama Canal and she looked quite the lady all lit up at night with a crimson lit sign with the words CUNARD just above her boat deck. However enamoring the name may be to many, Cunard, ever since the company became part of a British conglomerate, has exploited its past historical significance to the American public with success. Ever since her debut, the *Cunard Princess* has operated on several routes. After the abandonment of the New York-Bermuda route in the mid-1980s, she operated on the Los-Angeles-Cabo San Lucas-Maxaitan-Puerto Vallarta-Manzanillo-Acapulco route and for a time before ran from Acapulco-Panama Canal Transit-Montego Bay-Grand Cayman-Cozumel-Fort Lauderdale. During the off-seasonal months she works the Alaska route in summer out of Vancouver and Whittier to Alert Bay-Ketchikan-cruising around Tracy Arm-Juneau-Skagway-Yakutat Sound-Hubbard Glacier-Prince Edward Sound-Columbia Glacier and College Fjord. She was refurbished in 1985 at a cost of $1,500,000. Routes in the future may vary. She also makes 10-day cruises out of Acapulco and terminates in Fort Lauderdale.

Sister ship: *Cunard Countess.*

DORIC

Builder: Harland & Wolff Ltd., Belfast, Ireland
Completed: May 1923
Gross tonnage: 16,484
Dimensions: 602' x 68' Depth: 41' Draft:
Engines: Four steam turbines single-reduction geared
Screws: Twin
Decks: Four
Normal speed: 16 knots
Passenger accommodations: 600 cabin and 1700 third class
Officers and crew: 400
Registry: United Kingdom
Maiden voyage: For White Star Line Liverpool-New York arriving on
   February 5, 1924

Built for the White Star Line and passed under Cunard Line ownership when the two companies consoldiated on May 10, 1934. The merger came about as a result of the severity of the Great Depression and the exhortation of the British Government. Used solely for cruising while under Cunard-White Star ownership. She was damaged in a collision while in a fog off Cape Finisterre, Portugal with the Compagnie des Transport's *Formigny* on September 5, 1935 in the early hour of 3:30 a.m. The damage incurred was a 10-foot hole in the side of her hull just 3 feet above her waterline. The P & O liner *Viceroy of India* and the Orient Line's *Orion* answered her S.O.S. and embarked her passengers by 7:30 a.m. that morning. The *Doric* was the only turbine-driven liner ever built for the White Star Line and was a very handsome liner. During her career as a White Star liner she became amorously known as "Cupid's Ship" due to the many singles who she brought together on her many romantic cruises. Sold to John Cashmore shipbreakers at Newport, Wales for £35,000 sterling. Left Tilbury dock, London on October 7, 1935 for the breaker's yard.

I FRANCONIA

Builder: Swan, Hunter & Wigham Richardson Ltd., Newcastle-on-Tyne, England
Completed: January 1911
Gross tonnage: 18,150
Dimensions: 625' x 71' Depth: 40' Draft: 30'
Engines: Two four-cylinder quadruple-expansion
Screws: Twin
Watertight bulkheads: Ten
Decks: Four
Normal speed: 16.50 knots
Passenger accommodations: 444 first, 659 second, and 1,992 third class
Registry: United Kingdom
Maiden voyage: Liverpool-Queenstown-Boston-New York on February 25, 1911

Employed in the Liverpool-Queenstown-Boston run during the summer months and Liverpool-Queenstown-New York-Mediterranean services in the winter. *Franconia* was the first Cunarder to have a gymnasium installed. On June 4, 1913 she made a call for the first time at the port of Portland, Maine and called at Halifax on the eastbound trip on November 30, 1914 for the first time. The same summer she began calling at Greek ports while on the Mediterranean run. Made her last commercial voyage for Cunard on February 6, 1915, New York-Queenstown-Liverpool. She was requisitioned for troop work upon her arrival on February 15 and fitted-out as a transport in Quebec. Sunk by a German submarine 200 miles northeast of Malta on October 4, 1916. Before sinking, she listed heavily to starboard as she went down, taking a toll of 12 lives with her.

Sister ship: *Laconia*.

II FRANCONIA

Builder: John Brown & Co., Ltd., Clydebank, Glasgow, Scotland
Completed: June 1923
Gross tonnage: 20,341
Dimensions: 624' x 74' Depth: 45' Draft: 33'
Engines: Six Brown & Curtis double-reduction geared turbines
Screws: Twin
Collision bulkhead: One
Watertight bulkhead: Nine
Decks: Five
Normal speed: 16.50 knots
Passenger accommodations: 253 first and 692 tourist class (one class when cruising)*
Officers and crew: 434
Registry: United Kingdom
Maiden voyage: Liverpool-Queenstown-New York on June 23, 1923

*Original complement: 319 first, 557 second and 1,009 third class

Built as a dual-purpose ship, the *Franconia* was engaged in the Liverpool-Queenstown-New York run and cruising. On occasion she made some Southampton-Cherbourg-New York voyages. She made a world cruise almost every January from 1924 onward and a North Cape Cruise during mid-year. She was the first tourist class Cunarder to call Copenhagen when she called there on July 26, 1925. In 1931 she was chartered to the Furness-Bermuda Line for five months of the summer season and for a shorter time the following year. Transferred to the London-Channel ports-New York service in 1934, she reverted back to her original run the following year. On December 24, 1938 she left Southampton on a world cruise that covered 41,727 miles and called at 37 ports. Requisitioned for troop service on September 30, 1939 she carried over 149,000 troops and steamed 320,000 miles. In 1945 she was used as the headquarters at the Yalta conference in the Black Sea. During the course of her services as a transport she was damaged on her first trip out when the Royal Mail steamer *Alcantara* collided into her side on October 5, 1939, smashing six of the *Franconia's* lifeboats. Responsibility lay with the *Alcantara's* poor method of zig-zagging while in convoy. On June 16, 1940, the Franconia met with another close call when she was damaged by enemy bombers off the coast of Brittany. Luckily none of the bombs made a direct hit, but some came so close they managed to derange her main auxiliary machinery. She then took on a heavy list and lost her lighting. Decommissioned in August 1948, after carrying displaced persons from Hamburg to Canada. The *Franconia* resumed sailings from just below Quebec in June 1949. Ran aground on Orleans Island near Quebec in 1950 and remained there for four days until she was refloated. Made her last voyage for the Line on November 16, 1956 from New York to Liverpool via Cobh. *Franconia's* promenade deck was 419 feet long. Throughout her career she had earned herself the endearment of many travellers. Sold for scrap at Rosyth, Scotland, where she arrived from Liverpool on December 18, 1956.

Sister ship: *Carinthia.*

III FRANCONIA

Builder: John Brown & Co., Ltd., Clydebank, Glasgow, Scotland
Completed: June 1955
Gross tonnage: 21,406
Dimensions: 608' x 80' Depth: 46' Draft: 29'
Engines: Four steam turbines double-reduction geared
Screws: Twin
Collision bulkhead: One
Watertight bulkhead: Nine
Decks: Five
Normal speed: 20 knots
Passenger accommodations: 118 first and 900 tourist class
(accommodations are combined into one class when in cruise service)
Officers and crew: 456
Registry: United Kingdom
Maiden voyage: Greenock-Quebec-Montreal on July 1, 1955

Originally christened *Ivernia*, she was renamed *Franconia* in 1963. Engaged in the Southampton-Le Havre-Halifax-New York service in winter and to Quebec and Montreal in summer with a call at Cobh eastbound. In 1956 she worked on the Liverpool-Greenock-Quebec-Montreal run in summer and Halifax-New York service in winter and also made five New York-Halifax-Le Havre-London trips beginning on December 20. Reallocated to the Southampton-Le Havre-Quebec-Montreal run on April 17, 1957. The following year she was calling at both London and Southampton outbound. Equipped with Denny-Brown motion stabilizers and fully air-conditioned. The *Franconia* had received her new name after she was refitted at John Brown's between October 1962-June 1963, when she emerged as a dual-purpose vessel, her hull painted white for cruising. Positioned to work out of New York and Port Everglades with cruises to the West Indies in the summer of 1963. Reallocated to a weekly New York-Bermuda run in 1968 between the months of March and September and from October to March out of Port Everglades to the West Indies with one transatlantic crossing each year for overhauling. Made her last commercial voyage for Cunard on November 21, 1970, eastbound out of Port Everglades to London calling at Cobh-Cherbourg-Le Havre and Southampton. Laid up in the River Fal, Cornwall, England, in May 1972, pending sale. Sold to a corporate shell, the Nekreis Maritime Corp. in August 1973, Panama for ultimate delivery to the Union of Soviet Socialist Republics, who renamed the ship *Fedor Shalyapin*. Both she and her sister ship *Carmania* were sold for approximately £1,000,000. They had sailed together on the same routes; were laid up together and sold as a pair. Retrospectively, the price of these two lovely ships was a mere pittance. Presently in service for the Russian Far East Steamship Company.

Note: Photo as *Ivernia*.

Sister ships: *Carinthia, Carmania* and *Sylvania*.

GEORGIC

Builder: Harland & Wolff Ltd., Belfast, Ireland
Completed: June 1932
Gross tonnage: 27,469
Dimensions: 712' x 82' Depth: 53' Draft: 35'
Engines: Two Burmeister & Wain ten-cylinder, four-stroke, double-acting diesel
Screws: Twin
Watertight bulkheads: Twelve
Decks: Five
Normal speed: 18 knots
Passenger accommodations: 429 first and 564 tourist class
Officers and crew: 485
Registry: United Kingdom
Maiden voyage: London-New York on May 3, 1935

Built for the White Star Line. Passed on to Cunard ownership on May 10, 1934 when the two companies consolidated. Engaged in the London-Channel ports-New York service, with cruises from New York to the West Indies during the winter months. Requisitioned for troop work on March 1940 and was gutted by fire off Tewfik in the Suez Canal when fired upon by enemy aircraft at 2:00 a.m. on July 14, 1941. She ran aground with her engine room flooded 18 feet high. Refloated on October 27 and sailed from the Suez under tow on December 28, arriving at Port Sudan on January 10, 1942, where she was repaired temporarily. Towed to Karachi, Pakistan on March 31 for further work and sailed under her own power at a speed of 10-11 knots on December 11 for Bombay, where she arrived two days later. Repaired and sailed on January 20, 1943, at a speed of 16 knots, for Liverpool. She was taken to Harland & Wolff and rebuilt as a permanent transport with one mast and her aft-funnel gone. She was then sold to the Ministry of Transport and was, after December 1944, chartered by the Cunard Line. Chartered by Cunard for six round trips from Liverpool to Cobh and New York on May 4, 1950, and for seven or so similar trips each year until her last voyage from New York to Halifax, Cobh, Le Havre and Southampton on October 19, 1954. Chartered by the Australian Government in May 1955, and sold for scrap in January 1956, where she arrived at Faslane, Garelock, Scotland on February 1, 1956.

Sister ship: *Britannic*.

HOMERIC

Builder: F. Schichau, Danzig, Germany
Completed: 1920
Gross tonnage: 34,351
Dimensions: 776' x 83' Depth: 49'
Engines: Two 4-cylinder triple expansion
Screws: Twin
Watertight bulkheads: Fourteen
Decks: Five
Normal speed: 19.50 knots
Passenger accommodations: 523 first, 841 cabin, and 314 third class*
Officers and crew: 625
Registry: United Kingdom
Maiden voyage: Maiden voyage for White Star Line Southampton-New
York arriving at New York on February 24, 1922

*Passenger accommodations White Star figures: first 487, second 434,
tourist cabin 452, and third class 366.

Built for the North German Lloyd and was to be called *Columbus*.
Launched as the *Columbus* on December 17, 1913. Construction was held
up during World War I and she was not completed until 1920. Ceded to
Great Britain in 1920 and sold to the White Star Line by the British
Shipping Controller and renamed *Homeric*. Acquired by the Cunard Line
on May 10, 1934 when the Cunard and White Star Lines merged to form
the Cunard White Star Line. Used solely for pleasure cruising while under
Cunard ownership she was withdrawn from service in September 1935,
and laid up at Ryde, England. Sold for scrapping in February 1936 and
arrived at Inverkeithing, Scotland in March.

Note: The *Homeric* was partially fitted-out in 1920 by her German
builders. She was altered considerably by the White Star Line and was
completed by them in 1922 when she entered their service in February of
that year. She was the largest ship in the world with twin-screws at the
time of her construction and was notably one of the most plush liners of
her time, of which the word plush had been a by-word with most of the
White Star fleet.

I IVERNIA

Builder: Swan & Hunter Ltd., Wallsend-on-Tyne, England
Completed: March 1900
Gross tonnage: 14,278
Dimensions: 600′ x 65′ Depth: 42′ Draft: 32′
Engines: 4-cylinder quadruple expansion
Screws: Twin
Watertight bulkheads: Ten
Decks: Four
Normal speed: 15 knots
Passenger accommodations: 485 cabin and 978 third class*
Officers and crew:
Registry: United Kingdom
Maiden voyage: Liverpool-Queenstown-New York on April 14, 1900

*Original passenger accommodations: 392 first, 434 second, and 2,072 third class (944 with cabins).

Engaged in the Liverpool-Queenstown-Boston service. Between 1903-05 she made 11 Liverpool-Queenstown-New York trips. Struck Daunt's Rock while headed eastbound, just outside of Queenstown on May 24, 1911 and did not return to service until October 17, 1911. The following month she was placed in the New York-Mediterranean trade on November 30. During her lay-up she had been converted to a cabin class ship while still maintaining some trips on her old run to Boston. By March, 1912, however, she was settled in Cunard's Hungarian-American service out of Fiume, with calls at Trieste-Messina-Palermo-Naples-Funchal and on to New York carrying mostly immigrants. In 1914 she added Patras, Greece to her ports of call. The *Ivernia's* daily fuel consumption was some 152 tons of coal to keep her engines running. She was one of the first vessels to feature the new thermotank ventilation system, which enabled passengers to control the ventilation of air in their cabins—a forerunner to air conditioning. Made her last voyage for the Line from the Mediterranean arriving at New York on August 21, 1914. Requisitioned for service as a Canadian transport the following month she sailed to Quebec where she was fitted-out and completed as such by October 3rd. For a period the *Ivernia* was used as a prison ship for officers during the war and was stationed just off Southend in southeastern England. Sunk by the German submarine U47 on New Year's Day 1917, 58 miles off Cape Matapan, Greece with the loss of 200 of the 2,800 troops aboard plus 22 crew members. The *Ivernia* had been under the command of Captain W. T. Turner, who was master of the *Lusitania* at the time she was sunk.

Sister ship: *Saxonia*

I LACONIA

Builder: Swan, Hunter & Wigham Richardson Ltd., Newcastle-on-Tyne, England
Completed: January 1912
Gross tonnage: 18,099
Dimensions: 625' x 71' Depth: 44' Draft: 30'
Engines: Two 4-cylinder quadruple expansion
Screws: Twin
Watertight bulkheads: Ten
Decks: Four
Normal speed: 16.50 knots
Passenger accommodations: 661 first, 898 second and 2,136 third class
Officers and crew:
Registry: United Kingdom
Maiden voyage: Liverpool-Queenstown-New York on January 20, 1912

Employed in the Liverpool-Queenstown-Boston run during the summer months and to New York from the Mediterranean during the winter. The *Laconia* made her first cruise to the Med on February 15, 1913, and inaugurated a call at Halifax westbound on June 18, 1913. She was the first Cunarder to be equipped with Frahm's anti-rolling tanks—forerunner of the modern gyro stabilizers. In 1914 she began calling at the Greek port of Patras while working on her winter schedule. Made her last peacetime voyage for the Line from Boston to Liverpool via Queenstown on October 13, 1914. Refitted as an armed-merchant cruiser upon her return. Operated as such until September 1916, when she was used as a base ship in the Rufuji River, Tanzania, Africa for operations against the German cruiser *Konigsberg*. Returned to regular Liverpool-Boston service on September 9, 1916, with a number of sailings to New York. The *Laconia* left New York for the last time headed eastbound on February 17, 1917. While 160 miles off Fastnet, Ireland, she was sunk by a German submarine at 10:00 p.m. on the night of February 25, while carrying passengers. Most survived the disaster but there was a loss of 12 lives.

Sister ship: *Franconia*.

II LACONIA

Builder: Swan, Hunter & Wigham Richardson Ltd., Newcastle-on-Tyne, England
Completed: January 1922
Gross tonnage: 19,695
Dimensions: 624' x 74' Depth: 45' Draft: 33'
Engines: Six steam turbines double-reduction geared
Screws: Twin
Watertight bulkheads: Ten
Decks: Five
Normal speed: 16 knots
Passenger accommodations: 375 first, 526 second and 1,117 third class
Registry: United Kingdom
Maiden voyage: Liverpool-Queenstown-New York on May 25, 1922

Engaged in the Liverpool-Cobh-New York and Boston service, sometimes calling at Halifax westbound or Boston in either direction. She made five voyages from New York beginning on June 7, 1923, to Hamburg via Cherbourg-Plymouth and London. Nearly every year the *Laconia* made a Mediterranean cruise one of her first on January 31, 1925, and several world cruises in the years that followed out of New York. She became very well known as a cruise ship with many long cruises lasting 52 days and longer. Made her last commercial voyage for the Line on August 25, 1939, from New York to Liverpool via Boston-Galway-Cobh-Dublin and Belfast. Converted to a liner-cruiser on September 2, 1939 and later did some trooping. On September 12, 1942 while some 700 miles southwest of Freetown, Africa, she was hit by two torpedoes from the German U-boat U-156, mastered by Captain Werner Hartenstein. The first torpedo struck at 8:15 p.m. the second followed 15 minutes after. The *Laconia* foundered with 1,800 Italian prisoners of war from North Africa along with a number of British Colonial civil servants from a total complement of 2,732 souls. The survivors were later picked up by a trio of U-boats. The perpetrator U-156 picked up 260 people and later transferred them to the U-506. Another 157 people were rescued by the U-507. Many of the survivors filled the decks of the U-boats and others were taken in tow in the lifeboats until an American bomber appeared, circled, and departed. The same plane later returned dropping 5 bombs on U-156. The U-boat was then forced to return his survivors to the water after sustaining damage. On September 18 the U-boats rendezvoused with the French cruiser *Gloire* after the Germans had notified the Vichy French at Dakar, Senegal that the survivors were awaiting rescue in their lifeboats. The British were taken to Casablanca, Morocco. The Italians who had survived the ordeal were taken at the time the U-506 arrived, and not only gained their lives but their freedom as well.

Sister ships: *Samaria* and *Scythia*.

LANCASTRIA

Builder: William Beardmore & Co., Ltd., Glasgow, Scotland
Completed: June 1922
Gross tonnage: 16,243
Dimensions: 578′ x 70′ Depth: 43′ Draft: 31′
Engines: Six steam turbines double-reduction geared
Screws: Twin
Watertight bulkheads: Ten
Decks: Five
Normal speed: 16.50 knots
Passenger accommodations: 235 first, 388 second, and 1,256 third class
Registry: United Kingdom
Maiden voyage: Glasgow-Quebec-Montreal on June 13, 1922

Built for the Anchor Line, the ship was transferred to the Cunard Line while still on the stocks and christened *Tyrrhenia*. Renamed *Lancastria* in March 1924, she became a cabin class ship with accommodations for cabin and third class; cabin and tourist cabin in 1926. Engaged in the Liverpool-Quebec-Montreal run in summer and to Boston and New York in the winter when she entered service. In 1923 she was transferred to the Hamburg-Southampton-Halifax-New York run with calls at London-Plymouth and Cherbourg from time to time. The following year she made a number of trips from Liverpool to New York via Halifax and in 1925 three voyages from Southampton-Liverpool-Boston. 1926 found her working out of the port of London-Le Havre-New York run with a call at Plymouth homeward. The *Lancastria* undoubtedly worked every service of the Line from the British Isles to America. On July 1, 1925 she had made a Mediterranean and a North Cape Cruise, and from the thirties onward was used mostly in the Mediterranean for cruising. She ran aground near

Egremont outside of Liverpool on October 19, 1936, when returning from a Mediterranean cruise. She was refloated in 8 hours undamaged. The *Lancastria* was based out of New York in the summer of 1939 where she cruised to Nassau. She made her last such voyage on September 3 before reverting to her original run. After the outbreak of war she commenced her last commercial voyage for Cunard from London-Le Havre-Cobh-Southampton-Cherbourg-New York where she arrived on the 27th of December 1939. Laid up pending her disposition, she was requisitioned by the British Government on March 5, 1940 for troop work. The *Lancastria* was to become one of the British Merchant Marine's worst war disasters. On June 17, 1940, the day France had accepted Hitler's terms of surrender, *Lancastria* along with hundreds of other sea-going craft, participated in the evacuation of allied troops at Dunkirk. Just as the *Lancastria* had finished with her complement of over 5,300 men, women and children at St. Nazaire, her bunkers filled to the top with fuel, she was attacked by seven or eight German Junkers and Dorniers who landed four direct hits on her. The first went right down her funnel and exploded in the engine room. The others exploded in her number 2 and 3 holds blowing out the sides of the ship, according to her Captain Rudolph Sharp's eyewitness account. The majority of those aboard drowned. The bombs had hit with such a simultaneous force that the *Lancastria* nearly jumped out of the water and foundered within 20 minutes after impact. The appalling loss of life in this disaster climbed way above 3,000. The great loss of life may have been lessened had the 1,400 tons of oil fuel dispersed after the bombing not covered the water's surface thus preventing the swimmers from making the shore. Seven hours after the event, survivors were picked up by the anti-submarine trawler *Cambridgeshire* around 11:00 p.m., while under enemy gunfire. The sinking of the *Lancastria* had been so tragic that the news had been hushed almost throughout the war before it was released to the general public.

LAURENTIC

Builder: Harland & Wolff Ltd., Belfast, Ireland
Completed: November 1927
Gross tonnage: 18,724
Dimensions: 603′ x 75′ Depth: 41′
Engines: Two 4-cylinder triple-expansion engines and one low-pressure turbine.
Screws: Triple
Decks: Five
Normal speed: 16.50 knots
Passenger accommodations: 594 cabin, 401 second and 500 third class
Officers and crew: 510
Registry: United Kingdom
Maiden voyage: Liverpool-Quebec-Montreal, where she arrived on July 14, 1934

Built for the White Star Line, she passed on to Cunard White Star Line ownership on May 10, 1934 when the two companies merged. Used almost entirely for pleasure cruising while under Cunard, after having made only two trips to Canada and subsequently laid up in the River Fal, Cornwall,

England. Sent cruising once again on the night of August 18, 1935, the Blue Star Liner *Napier Star* rammed into the *Laurentic* off the Skerries in the Irish Sea during a fog. The *Napier Star* crashed into the *Laurentic's* bow and starboard side, killing six of her crew. Laid up at Millbrook, Southampton in December 1935 but did some troop work to Palestine in September 1936. Laid up once again in April 1938 in the River Fal until commissioned as an armed merchant cruiser on August 24, 1939 and fitted with seven 5.5-inch guns and three 4-inch guns on her upper decks. She was sunk by submarine U99 300 miles off Bloody Foreland on the West coast of Ireland on November 4, 1940.The U99, under the command of Lieutenant Otto Kretschener, fired the first torpedo at the *Laurentic* at 9:50 p.m. on the night of November 3rd. Hitting her first under her aft funnel at a range of 1,500 yards. The *Laurentic* immediately sent out an S.O.S. signal that she had been torpedoed in the engine room. The German submarine then fired two more torpedoes, sinking the ship. The *Laurentic*, all her lights lit, began to fire starshells to light up the sky and locate the U-Boat. The second torpedo had hit the liner near the fore-funnel area. At 4:00 a.m. the next morning the U-Boat surfaced and fired a fourth torpedo at the ship. Hitting her 5.5′ guns and three 4′ aftwards the *Laurentic's* struggle ended and sank in location 54° 09′ N-13° 44′ west. There was a loss of 49 people. The *Laurentic* was the last of the coal-firing liners and the last to be driven by reciprocating engines.

LUCANIA

Builder: Fairfield Shipbuilding & Engineering Co., Ltd., Glasgow, Scotland
Completed: July 1983
Gross tonnage: 12,952
Dimensions: 622' x 65' Depth: 42'
Engines: Two 3-cylinder triple expansion
Screws: Twin
Watertight bulkheads: Twelve
Decks: Three
Normal speed: 21 knots
Passenger accommodations: 386 first, 381 second, and 885 steerage
Officers and crew: 415
Registry: United Kingdom
Maiden voyage: Liverpool-New York on September 2, 1893

Employed in the Liverpool-Queenstown-New York run. The *Lucania* won the Blue Riband from her sister ship *Campania* in May 1894 when she made the run from Sandy Hook to Queenstown in 5 days, 8 hours and 38 minutes at a speed of 21.95 knots. On October 10, 1903 she earned fame by being one of the first liners to be in touch with the Marconi stations at Cape Breton, Nova Scotia and Poldhu, England by wireless. This opened the gateway of communications between land and sea as well as from ship to ship and fostered a new era in oceanic journalism with Cunard's newly published *Daily Bulletin,* which recorded the most important events on both sides of the Atlantic. Moreover, it was to set a milestone in the safety of ships at sea. The *Lucania* and her sister ship were the first Cunarders to have pole masts and *Lucania* one of the first to have refrigeration equipment installed. Made her last voyage for the line on July 7, 1909, New York-Liverpool and withdrawn from service. Damaged severely by fire at Huskisson dock at Liverpool on August 14, 1909, she was subsequently sold to Wards of Sheffield for scrap at Swansea, Wales. Despite her damages she ran to the shipbreaker's yard at a speed of 17 knots. Completely dismantled by 1910. The *Lucania's* design marked the end of a transitionary period when liners still embodied the lines of a sailing ship vis-a-vis the modern liner of the turn of the century.

Sister ship: *Campania.*

LUSITANIA

Builder: John Brown & Co., Ltd., Clydebank, Glasgow, Scotland
Completed: August 1907
Gross tonnage: 30,396
Dimensions: 790' x 88' Depth: 61' Draft: 36'
Engines: Four direct-action Parson steam turbines; two high pressure and two low pressure
Screws: Quadruple
Watertight bulkheads: Eleven
Decks: Six
Normal speed: 24.50 knots
Passenger accommodations: 605 first, 607 second and 1,405 third class
Officers and crew: 1,800
Registry: United Kingdom
Maiden voyage: Liverpool-Queenstown-New York on September 7, 1907

Engaged in the Liverpool-Queenstown-New York service. She recaptured the Blue Riband from the North German Lloyd's *Kaiser Wilhelm II* on her second voyage out in October 1907 by making the run from Queenstown to Sandy Hook in 4 days, 19 hours and 52 minutes at a speed of 23.39 knots. Yet still, her best time was made on her 41st voyage westbound on May 18, 1910 with a passage of 4 days, 7 hours and 55 minutes at a mean speed of 25.37 knots. To attain such high speeds, the *Lusitania* consumed 850 tons of coal every 24 hours. Inactive between December 30, 1912 and August 23, 1913, she was commissioned by the Admiralty in August 1914, but was soon released back to Cunard in September. On May 1, 1915 the *Lusitania* sailed out of New York on her eastbound voyage with a total of nearly 1,700 passengers and crew. At 2:10 p.m. on May 7, while off the Old Head of Kinsale, Ireland, she was hit without warning* by a torpedo just ahead of her first funnel, from the German U20. Immediately afterward there was a second explosion, which has given credence to the theory that the *Lusitania* was hit by two torpedoes. (After divers dove on the wreck fifty years later, it was revealed that there was an outward explosion due to the periphery of the mangled hull, which faced outwards. This, of course,

disclosed the fact that the ship was carrying contraband to Britain.) Following the impact, the *Lusitania* listed 15 degrees to starboard and made it impossible to launch her port-side lifeboats. With a gaping hole in the side of her hull the sea rushed in taking the *Lusitania* down by the bow within 21 minutes. On board were 1,254 passengers of which 124 were Americans who lost their lives in the tragedy and paved the way for America's entry into the First World War. All counted, 798 passengers and 400 crew members died. An attempt to salvage what gold was aboard had been made by the salvage ship *Orphir* in October 1935, but being that she lay some 315 feet below, the project was soon abandoned. On November 6, 1935 a memorial was held aboard the *Orphir* just over the scene of the wreck with a number of the survivors attending the service. The *Lusitania* had been the first quadruple-screw steamer ever built; her loss one of the most disastrous events of World War I. She was familiarly known as the "Lucy." Some note should be made that it had been rumored for some years that the British Government had forbidden diving on the wreck because the ship had been carrying contraband illegally under international law, it being forbidden for a passenger vessel to be carrying such dangerous cargo. Any revelation of this would have been very embarrassing to world opinion at the time.

Sister ship: *Mauretania.*

*__*Note:__ To some extent there was a warning by the German Embassy, which had placed an ad in the travel section of most New York newspapers warning the public that a state of war existed between Germany and the United Kingdom and that anyone travelling in the war zone did so at their own risk.

Note: On November 29, 1985 an Admiralty Court judge ruled that the British Government could not claim any goods salvaged from the ship. In 1982 a British team had retrieved about $3.4 million dollars worth of treasure from the *Lusitania*. The government's case had been premised under a 14th century law that gave claim to any salvaged material brought to England.

MAJESTIC

Builder: Blohm & Voss, Hamburg, Germany
Completed: March, 1922
Gross tonnage: 56,599
Dimensions: 956′ x 100′ Depth: 58′
Engines: Eight direct-action Parson turbines
Screws: Quadruple
Watertight bulkheads: Eleven
Decks: Seven
Normal speed: 23.50 knots
Passenger accommodations: 589 tourist cabin and 544 third class*
Registry: United Kingdom
Maiden voyage: Southampton-Cherbourg-New York with arrival on
   July 4, 1934

*Passenger accommodation originally for 860 first, 736 second and 850
   third class.

Built jointly for the Cunard & White Star Lines but launched as the *Bismark* on June 20, 1914 for the Hamburg-American Line. Construction was held up during World War I and she was not completed until March, 1922. She had, meanwhile, been ceded to Britain in 1919 under the treaty of Versailles and was sold by the British Shipping Controller to a joint ownership between the Cunard and White Star Lines and renamed *Majestic*. Later passed on to completed White Star ownership but later under the Cunard White Star Line, when the two companies merged on May 10, 1934. The Cunard Line had held 62 percent of the stock in the new company. Employed in the Southampton-Cherbourg-New York run for Cunard White Star Line. The *Majestic* was well known as the "Queen of the Western Ocean" and was the largest ship afloat when built, up until the French Line's *Normandie*. Her funnels were 180 feet high from the furnace bars and she was the first liner to show sound motion pictures. Made her last transatlantic voyage for the Line on February 20, 1936, from New York to Southampton, via Cherbourg. Laid up in March 1936, and sold to T. W. Ward on May 15, 1936 for the sum of £115,000 and was, in turn, resold to the Admiralty for conversion to a boys' training ship and renamed *Caledonia* in 1937. Gutted by fire and sank at Rosyth, Scotland, on September 29, 1939. Sold once again to Ward's in March 1940. Refloated on July 17, 1943 and taken to Inverkeithing, Scotland for breaking up. She was the largest ship yet sold for scrap.

I MAURETANIA

Builder: Swan, Hunter & Wigham Richardson Ltd., Wallsend-on-Tyne, England
Completed: October 1907
Gross tonnage: 30,696
Dimensions: 790' x 88' Depth: 61' Draft: 36'
Engines: Four direct-action Parson steam turbines; two high pressure and two low pressure
Screws: Quadruple
Watertight bulkheads: Eleven
Decks: Six
Normal speed: 25.50 knots (attained a speed of 27.04 knots on her trial runs)
Passenger accommodations: 563 first, 464 second, and 1,138 third class
Officers and crew: 1,266
Registry: United Kingdom
Maiden voyage: Liverpool-Queenstown-New York on November 16, 1907

The *Mauretania* won the Blue Riband from her sister the *Lusitania* in November 1907, after making the run from Ambrose Lighthouse to Queenstown in 4 days, 22 hours, and 29 minutes at a speed of 23.69 knots. She lost the title back to the *Lusitania* but regained it permanently in July 1909, eastbound with a crossing of 4 days, 17 hours, and 20 minutes at a super speed of 25.89 knots. Commissioned as a transport in November 1914, she was renamed *Tudor Rose*. Later on, she was used mostly as a hospital ship and laid up at Greenock, Scotland between 1916 and 1917. In 1917 she was used to transport American Troops in the latter part of the year. Returning to her regular service in October 1918, she was reallocated to the Southampton-New York run in February 1919, and added a call at Halifax westbound beginning May 9th. Damaged by fire at Southampton on July 25, 1921, she was repaired and fitted-out for burning fuel oil. Re-entered service on March 22, 1911, from Southampton to New York with a call at Cherbourg outbound; a call at Plymouth was added in late 1924, eastbound. The *Mauretania* made a Mediterranean cruise almost every February: Her first on February 7, 1923, until 1927. In 1931 her hull was painted white and she was sent cruising extensively, making only 5 transatlantic crossings the following year. On September 26, 1934, the day the *Queen Mary* was launched, the *Mauretania* made her last voyage from New York to Southampton via Plymouth and Cherbourg and was withdrawn from service in October. Sold to Metal Industries on April 2, 1935 for scrapping, the *Mauretania* left Southampton on July 1, 1935 for Rosyth, Scotland to be broken up — her departure being broadcast over the radio. The *Mauretania* had been through the years the most popular ship amongst the general public to sail on the North Atlantic Ferry, both in England and America. She had held the Blue Riband for 22 years, her speed increasing as she aged, with a record speed of 27.65 knots in 1929. She was well known as "The Grand Old Lady." The *Mauretania* held an eminence that no other liner could ever assume since her long mourned absence. It was a shame she could not have had a more regal passing, such as scuttling at sea, a demise many would have endorsed. Today one may view her ship's bell on display along with a 17-foot model of the liner at Lloyd's Register of Shipping in London. Her promenade deck was 452 feet in length and B-deck stretched 584 feet. The *Mauretania* had inaugurated Cunard's first sailing out of the port of Southampton. It should be noted that despite the general popularity of the replacement, the *Queen Mary* and her consort the *Queen Elizabeth* both these ships were products of the Great Depression constructed to carry thousands of passengers across the Atlantic. And though more likely than not it was their immense size rather than their elegance that had captured the minds of many. Whereas the vintage of ship to which the *Mauretania* belonged marked the zenith in class, sleekness, decor, and clientele.

Sister ship: *Lusitania*.

II MAURETANIA

Builder: Cammell, Laird & Co., Ltd., Birkenhead, England
Completed: June 1939
Gross tonnage: 35,655
Dimensions: 772′ x 54′ Depth: 54′ Draft: 31′
Engines: Six steam turbines, single-reduction geared
Screws: Twin
Decks: Six
Normal speed: 23 knots
Passenger accommodations: 475 first, 418 cabin and 404 tourist class (700 when cruising)
Officers and crew: 593
Registry: United Kingdom
Maiden voyage: Liverpool-New York on June 19, 1939

Following her debut, the *Mauretania* made only four trips to New York and was laid up at New York from December 16, 1939 until requisitioned for troop work on March 1, 1940. She left New York on the 20th of March for Sydney, Australia via Balboa, Panama and Honolulu. After carrying over 350,000 troops and steaming 542,000 miles on 48 voyages, she arrived at Liverpool on May 30, 1945, having completed her war services. Overhauled between September 1946 and April 1947 at Birkenhead, she re-entered service on April 26, 1947, sailing from Liverpool to New York. Engaged in the Southampton-Le Havre-Cobh service with cruises during the quarter of each year mostly out of New York. She was given full air-conditioning throughout the ship in 1957. Due to a severe lull in transatlantic travel, she was sent cruising in October 1962, her hull repainted in light cruising green for the more temperate waters. Her reallocation to the New York-Gibraltar-Cannes-Genoa-Naples run proved to be unsuccessful and she was often laid up at Southampton for a lack of passengers. In search of revenue, Cunard often chartered her out. Made her last voyage for Cunard from New York to the Mediterranean on a 56-day cruise on September 15, 1965. Withdrawn from service on November 10, 1965 upon her arrival at Southampton. Sold for scrap at Wards, Inverkeithing, Scotland, where she arrived on November 23, 1965. She was broken up by March 1966.

MEDIA

Builder: John Brown & Co., Ltd., Clydebank, Glasgow, Scotland
Completed: August 1947
Gross tonnage: 12,345
Dimensions: 531' x 70' Depth 46' Draft 30'
Engines: Four steam turbines double-reduction geared
Screws: Twin
Watertight bulkheads: Ten
Decks: Four
Normal speed: 18 knots
Officers and crew: 189
Cargo capacity: 422,430 cubic feet of general and insulated space
Passenger accommodations: 251 in one class
Registry: United Kingdom.
Maiden voyage: Mersey-New York on August 20, 1947

Employed in the Liverpool-New York run with occasional calls at Boston-Newport News, and Norfolk, Virginia outbound and Cobh-Greenock eastbound. Equipped with motion stabilizers and all public rooms air-conditioned. In 1960 her route was strictly Liverpool-New York calling at Cobh or Greenock on the eastbound voyage on occasion. The *Media* was originally designed for the Brocklebank Line, a subsidiary of Cunard, originally to carry only 12 passengers. The accommodations were enlarged and she became the first building order contracted for by Cunard after the Second World War. Built with six holds she was classified as a cargo-passenger liner. The *Media* was not very steady at sea and she was the first Cunarder to be fitted with motion stabilizers in 1952. The ship's post war design had rendered her and her sister ship *Parthia* nearly obsolete in less than a decade and a half. Commenced her last voyage for the Line on September 22, 1961 from New York to Liverpool. Sold to the Cogedar Line in October 1961 and renamed *Flavia*. Resold to the Costa Line in 1968 without a change in name. Resold once again in early 1982 to The Flavian Shipping S.A. of Hong Kong. Renamed *Flavian* and placed under Panamanian registry. Laid up in Hong Kong on October 25, 1982. Damaged by collision with an unknown vessel in the Western anchorage during Typhoon Ellen. Resold once again to Chinese owners under the name of the Lavia Shipping S.A. in 1986 and renamed *Lavia*. Presently in their service. Note: Under her last two ownerships she has been managed by Virtue Shipping Enterprises Ltd., of Hong Kong.

Sister ship: *Parthia*.

OLYMPIC

Builder: Harland & Wolff Ltd., Belfast, Ireland
Completed: June 1911
Gross tonnage: 44,439
Dimensions: 882' x 92' Depth: 59'
Engines: Two 4-cylinder triple-expansion engines and one low-pressure turbine
Screws: Triple
Watertight bulkheads: Fifteen
Decks: Seven
Normal speed: 21.50 knots
Passenger accommodations: 668 first, 474 second, 204 tourist cabin, and 350 third class
Officers and crew: 853
Registry: United Kingdom
Maiden voyage: Southampton-Cherbourg arriving at New York on July 17, 1934

Built for the White Star Line, she passed on to Cunard ownership on May 10, 1934 when the two companies amalgamated. Employed mostly as a cruise ship while under Cunard White Star, as the new company came to be known. The *Olympic* did make some voyages to New York. On one unfortunate trip, she rammed and sunk the *Nantucket* lightship while in a dense fog off the New England coast of America on the night of May 16, 1934. All seven of the lightship's crew were lost. The United States Government brought suit against the Line for a half-million dollars. Withdrawn from service shortly after the incident in March 1935, and sold to John Jarvis shipbreakers in September of that year. The *Olympic* left Southampton for the last time on October 11, 1935, steaming for the scrapyards at Jarrow, England. Broken up by March 1936. The *Olympic's* promenade deck was 495 feet long.

Sister ships: *Britannic, Titanic.*

II PARTHIA

Builder: Harland & Wolff Ltd., Belfast, Ireland
Completed: April 1948
Gross tonnage: 13,362
Dimensions: 531' x 70' Depth: 46' Draft: 30'
Engines: Four steam turbines double-reduction geared
Screws: Twin
Watertight bulkheads: Ten
Decks: Four
Normal speed: 18 knots
Passenger accommodations: 251 first class passengers
Officers and crew: 189
Cargo capacity: 422,430 cubic feet of general and insulated space
Registry: United Kingdom
Maiden voyage: Liverpool-New York on April 10, 1948

Employed in the Liverpool-New York run with calls at Boston and Newport News and Norfolk, Virginia westbound. Occasionally a call at Cobh or Greenock was made eastbound. Equipped with motion stabilizers and all her public rooms with air-conditioning. In 1960 her route was limited to Liverpool-New York with the calls at Cobh or Greenock on occasion. Made her last voyage for the Cunard Line from Liverpool to New York, arriving on the 30th September 1961. Sold to the New Zealand Shipping Company on November 1, 1961 and renamed *Remuera*. Resold to the Eastern and Australian Steamship Company in January 1965 and renamed *Aramac*. Sold for scrap to the Chin Ho Fa Steel & Iron Co., Ltd. in Taiwan in November 1969. She arrived there on November 22 and was broken up between March 5th and May 31, 1970.

Sister ship: *Media.*

QUEEN ELIZABETH

Builder: John Brown & Co., Ltd., Clydebank, Glasgow, Scotland
Completed: February 1940
Gross tonnage: 82,998
Dimensions: 1,031' x 119' Depth: 74' Draft: 39'
Engines: Sixteen steam turbines single-reduction geared.
Screws: Quadruple
Watertight bulkheads: Fifteen
Decks: Ten
Normal speed: 29 knots
Passenger accommodations: 882 first, 668 cabin and 798 tourist class
Officers and crew: 1,296
Registry: United Kingdom
Maiden voyage: Southampton-New York on October 16, 1946

The *Queen Elizabeth* was for some time the largest ship in the world with a promenade deck that extended 724 feet — two to three times longer than the traditional liner. Her forward funnel was 71 feet high and each propeller weighed 32 tons, her anchors 16 tons. Employed in the Southampton-Cherbourg-New York run, with a call at Plymouth eastbound, and some cruising. The *Elizabeth* made an unannounced crossing from the Clyde to New York on February 27, 1940, to the surprise of many who saw her suddenly steaming up the Hudson that March. Laid up until November 3, 1940, when she left New York for Sydney to be fitted-out as a transport. Fitted-out to carry 2,000 armed troops, she ferried 811,324 wartime passengers during the Second World War. Decommissioned on March 6, 1946, after having steamed 492,635 nautical miles. Overhauled at Gourock

at the mouth of the Clyde at a cost of $5,000,000, she re-entered service in October of 1946, though a number of tickets were issued for as low as $200 before her reconditioning. Fitted with motion stabilizers in March 1955. The *Elizabeth* began cruising out of New York in February 1963 to Nassau after a refit in 1965-66, which included full air-conditioning and an outdoor pool, but by the end of the decade both cruising and the transatlantic ferry were at a nadir. Operating at a loss of £750,000 annually, it was decided to sell the *Queen Elizabeth*. The purchaser turned out to be an unusual entity, that of the City of Fort Lauderdale, Florida. The price was set at $7,750,000 and the contract was consummated on April 5, 1968. The *Elizabeth* left berth 107 at Southampton for the last time on November 29 and was, upon her arrival at Port Everglades, converted like her running mate, the *Queen Mary,* to a hotel and nightclub. Throughout her long career she had made 907 Atlantic crossings covering over 3,470,000 miles and carried more than 2,300,000 people excluding her war service. Affirmed the largest ship in the world, she lacked the graceful lines of the lesser-sized liners. Her sale to the City of Fort Lauderdale provided for an 85 percent share in the profits to Cunard. Unfortunately, due to mismanagement the ship lay idle for two years and was finally resold to Mr. C.Y. Tung in mid-1970 for his Orient Overseas Line for the sum of $3,200,000. Renamed *Seawise University* and insured for $8,000,000, she was anchored in Hong Kong harbour. Caught fire at 10:30 a.m. on January 9, 1972 between A and B decks. After pouring tons of water onto the ship she listed 17 degrees. She keeled over and sank on her starboard side. Her twisted hull half submerged in 120 feet of water was later scrapped.

Note: A maritime court at Hong Kong ruled out 'probable arson' despite the fact that the conflagration had broken out at three different locations on the ship simultaneously.

QUEEN ELIZABETH 2

Builder: John Brown & Co., Ltd., Upper Clyde, Glasgow, Scotland
Completed: April 1969
Gross tonnage: 67, 139*
Dimensions: 96′ x 105′ Depth 56′ Draft: 33′
Engines: Nine M.A.N. diesels**; Her propellers are equipped with lips;
 variable pitch controlling and vane wheels; Plus 2 Stone Kamewa bow
 thrusters athwartship
Screws: Twin
Collision bulkhead: One
Watertight bulkheads: Fourteen
Decks: 13
Normal speed: 32.50 knots
Officers and crew: 906
Passenger accommodation: 575 first and 1,302 tourist class
 (accommodations are limited to 1,740 when in cruise service)
Registry: United Kingdom
Maiden voyage: Southampton–Le Havre–Cobn–New York on May 2, 1969

*Original tonnage: 65,863 g.t.
**Formerly driven by four steam turbines double-reduction geared.

Employed in the Southampton-Le Havre-New York run with a call at Cobh
on occasion and cruising. The port of Cherbourg later supplanted the stop
at Le Havre beginning on April 21, 1972 and the call Cobh was eliminated
in November 1971. The QE2 as she has come to be known called at Boston
Eastbound for the first time on October 1, 1971. One of the last liners on
the old transatlantic ferry and as flagship of the fleet has had a varied career
to date. Being a dual-purpose ship she worked out of New York and Port
Everglades to the Caribbean in winter and has made some trips to Nassau
since 1972. Transferred passengers and crew from Mustique, Barbados after
French Lines *Antilles* was abandoned off Mustique in the Caribbean on
January 8, 1971, when she caught fire. Commenced her first world cruise
out of New York on January 10, 1975 with prices ranging from $4,800 to
$86,240 for the 80-day cruise. Victimized by a bomb scare on May 19, 1972
by a caller who demanded a $350,000 ransom from Cunard, the British
Defense Ministry dispatched a military bomb disposal team to the ship then
somewhere around the Azores eastbound. After searching the liner, no
explosives were found. The QE2 broke-down while on a cruise with 1,648
passengers when one of the three boilers exploded while the ship lay 270
miles south of Bermuda on April 1, 1974. Passengers were transferred to the
Norwegian Flagship Cruises' *Sea Venture* and landed at Hamilton on the
4th. After drifting for 48 hours, the QE2 was towed to anchorage one mile
off the Bermudian coast on the 7th for repairs. Underwent an extensive refit
at Bayonne, New Jersey in December 1978 at a cost to her owners of
$2,600,000. Added were special accommodations such as the prefabricated
Queen Mary and Queen Elizabeth suite the latter accommodation of which
was available on her 1985 world cruise for a cool $310,000. On May 3, 1982
the QE2 was requisitioned for troop service in Britain's brief war with
Argentina. She was given a fast coat of war grey and ferried 3,200 troops to
the South Atlantic via Ascension on May 12th. The British Government paid
Cunard $225,000 per diem for the use of the ship. Refitted and conditioned
for normal service she returned to service in August of that year. The ship
has 4,500 square feet of open deck space, 2 discos, 3 jacuzzis, 4 restaurants,
4 pools (2 indoors and 2 outdoors), 2 grand ballrooms, a sauna, 7 shops, a
casino; an IBM computer center, and even a branch of the London
department store Harrods. Thirty public rooms in all. Her promenade deck
is 750 feet long. Keel to funnel base is 134 feet; keel to masthead is 204 feet.
Fully air-conditioned and equipped with motion stabilizers. She has nine
cocktail lounges and a theatre seating 530 persons. There are 1,877 berths
and 24 lifts. The Cunard Line's flagship. The problem of fuel cost had
necessitated a decision in October 1985 to re-engine the ship. The QE2
entered the Lloyd Werft Shipyards in Bremerhaven, Germany on November
1, 1986 for a six-month period to fit the ship with nine M.A.N. diesel
engines at a cost of some $130,000,000. Made a call at the Port of Baltimore
on May 5, 1985 for the first time while on a Caribbean cruise out of New
York, she is mainly cruising when not running on her regular transatlantic
serivce between mid April and late October. Presently in service.

Note: When the QE2 had been delivered to Cunard from her builders she
was refused because of numerous faulty problems with her turbines and
her original maiden voyage had been cancelled. Built at a cost of
$80,000,000. Her re-engining cost more than one-and-a-half this figure.
The QE2 has a bulbous bow.

QUEEN MARY

Builder: John Brown & Co., Ltd., Clydebank, Glasgow, Scotland
Completed: May 1936 (she was laid down on December 27, 1930; work was suspended from December 1931, until April 1934, due to the depression and was not completed until May 1936)
Gross tonnage: 81,237
Dimensions: 1,020′ x 119′ Depth: 74′ Draft: 39′
Engines: Sixteen steam turbines single-reduction geared
Screws: Quadruple
Watertight bulkheads: Eighteen
Decks: Ten
Normal speed: 30 knots (attained a speed of 32.84 knots on her trials)
Passenger accommodations: 711 first, 763 cabin and 577 tourist class
Officers and crew: 1,285
Registry: United Kingdom
Maiden voyage: Southampton-Cherbourg-New York on May 27, 1936

Engaged in the Southampton-Cherbourg-New York run with a call at Plymouth eastbound. The *Queen Mary* won the Blue Riband from the French Line's *Normandie* by making the run from Bishop Rock to Ambrose Lighthouse in an amazing 4 days, 27 minutes, at a speed of 30.14 knots. She soon lost the title back to the French liner the next year but recovered it in 1938 with an outward crossing of 3 days, 21 hours, and 48 minutes at a speed of 30.99 knots. Laid up at New York on September 5, 1939, she left for fitting-out as a transport on March 21, 1940, sailing for Sydney and calling at Capetown, South Africa enroute three weeks after having been commissioned. The *Mary* left Sydney on her first voyage on the 5th of May. On the night of October 2, 1942, the *Queen Mary* was in convoy. Escorted by the British Navy, the anti-aircraft cruiser *Curacao* attempted to clear the bow of the *Queen Mary* while in convoy. Unfortunately her timing and speed were retarded in the clearance and the *Mary* severed her stern like a knife cutting through butter. There was an appalling loss of 338 of the men aboard the *Curacao* when the incident came about just north of Bloody Foreland, Ireland. On September 27, 1946, the *Queen Mary* returned to Southampton from Halifax on her last trooping voyage and a few days later was sent to John Brown's for reconversion to a passenger ship. Nearly one year later she commenced her first post-war sailing from Southampton to New York via Cherbourg on the 31st of July, 1947. During her service as a

transport she carried about 810,000 wartime personnel including repatriated troops after the war with their war brides to Canada and America. Both she and her running mate, the *Queen Elizabeth*, carried whole divisions plus to various battle fronts and together helped shorten the war in Europe. Some of the outstanding features of the *Mary* are her 750 foot long promenade deck. Her rudder weighs some 140 tons and her anchors each of 16 tons with 166 fathoms of chains. Her aft funnel rises 78 feet above the boat deck. Because of her immense size she was unable to dock at Cherbourg and passengers were taken to and from the ship by tender. On a cold day in January, 1949, she had the misfortune of running aground just outside the port and had to return to Southampton, where they poured tons of cement into her damaged stern to prevent her from rupturing her steel plates. Fare on the *Queen Mary* averaged $312 one way fare in first class as opposed to $192 for cabin class; $142 for tourist class in 1949. Fitted with stabilizers in 1958, she made her first cruise from Southampton-Las Palmas in December 1963. Operating at a loss of about £2,000,000 annually due to the heavy traffic by air and newer liners on the Atlantic run, Cunard decided to sell the aging liner. After her regular 1966 transatlantic run and a few cruises, she was put up for sale in May 1967. On September 26 an agreement was reached with the City of Long Beach, California for the sum of $3,450,000. Just four days earlier the Mary had made her last transatlantic voyage for the line from New York to Southampton where she arrived for the last time on the 27th — completing her thousandth voyage for Cunard. Commenced her last voyage for the Line on October 3, 1967, Southampton-Lisbon-Las Palmos-Rio de Janeiro-Valparaiso-Callao-Balboa-Acapulco-Long Beach. Upon arrival the famous liner was given a tumultuous welcome. Reconstructed over a period of four years to serve the purposes of her new owners who converted the ship to a maritime museum, hotel, and convention center on May 10, 1971. Resold to Wrather Port Properties in 1982, the *Queen Mary* serves in a more aesthetic sense as a symbol of a bygone era, just as an earlier predecessor the *Cutty Sark* in Greenwich, England salutes the age of the clipper ship.

Note: In following with Cunard tradition by ending their ships with the ia suffix, when it came time for christening the ship Cunard's director Lord Roydon asked King George V, "Would he mind if the ship be named after the most illustrious queen of England?" The King replied, "That is the greatest compliment that has ever been made to me or my wife." And so the intended Queen Victoria became the *Queen Mary*.

ROYAL GEORGE

Builder: Fairfield Shipbuilding & Engineering Co., Ltd., Glasgow, Scotland
Completed: November 1907
Gross tonnage: 11,146
Dimensions: 541' x 60' Depth: 30' Draft: 26'
Engines: Three direct action steam turbines
Screws: Triple
Decks: Three
Normal speed: 18 knots
Passenger accommodations: 473 first, 319 second, and 799 third class
Registry: United Kingdom
Maiden voyage: Liverpool-Halifax-New York on February 8, 1919

Built for the Egyptian Mail Steamship & Engineering Co., Ltd. and christened *Heliopolis*. Sold to the Royal Line in 1910 and renamed *Royal George*. Resold to the Cunard Line in February 1919, and retained her name. Engaged in the Liverpool-Halifax-New York run until July 26, 1919, when she was placed in the New York-Le Havre-London route eastbound and Southampton-New York run from August 14, 1919. The call at Halifax was incorporated into her westbound itinerary the next month and a call at Cherbourg added westbound in 1920. She was later used as a depot ship at Cherbourg for a time. Made her last commercial voyage for the Line on June 25, 1920, New York-Southampton and was laid up at Falmouth, England in 1921. The *Royal George* had been purchased to make up for loss tonnage during World War I. She had acquired the name of "Rolling George" because of her exceedingly unsteadiness at sea. Sold for scrap at Wilhelmshaven, Germany in September 1922.

SAGAFJORD

Builder: Forges & Chantiers de La Mediterranee, La Seyne, France
Completed: May 1965
Gross tonnage: 24,108
Dimensions: 617' x 79' Depth: 53' Draft: 27'
Engines: Two, 9-cylinder, 2-stroke, single-acting Sulzer diesels plus a bow thruster athwartship forward
Screws: Twin
Decks: Six
Normal speed: 20 knots
Passenger accommodations: 509 in a single class
Officers and crew: 350
Registry: Bahamas
Maiden voyage: Oslo-Kristiansand-Copenhagen-New York on October 2, 1965*

*MV for NAL.

Built for the Norwegian-America Line and christened *Sagafjord*. Passed on to Cunard Line ownership in May 1983, when the former company was bought out** but retained her name. Built as a dual purpose ship for liner service and extensive cruising her present owners concluded on capitalizing on her former reputation by not changing the ship's name. It is a dishonour, however, to see that they have elected to register the ship under a flag of convenience and insulting both British and Scandinavian prestige. Of course, Cunard Line has been living on the laurels of their illustrious past. So much for a name . . . . I got a glimpse of this lovely ship in Rio de Janeiro in April 1987 and was able to admire her well-designed hull. Unfortunately, no visitors were allowed because of tighter security worldwide in the wake of terrorism aboard ships as well as aircraft. The *Sagafjord* underwent a refurbishing in 1983 and her new owners lavished the ship with an additional 24 deluxe suites and a two-deck high nightclub featuring indoor and outdoor theatre-in-the-round at a cost of $15,000,000. Completely air-conditioned and equipped with motion stabilizers. Almost ninety percent of her 311 staterooms have private tub and shower. Cabins have ship-to-shore telephones and there are four elevators within the ship. The new suites also have television with VHS video systems. There is an indoor and an outdoor swimming pool, gymnasium with sauna. Her dining room accommodates all passengers in a single sitting as well as her grand salon. Food is attractive as any other cruise ship. Pricing of cruises makes this ship more attractive to an older crowd and the mood is very relaxed. The *Sagafjord* continues to make her annual world cruise each January and cruises between Fort Lauderdale and Los Angeles via the Panama Canal on 14-day cruises from mid-April to mid-June when she is repositioned to the Vancouver/Anchorage to Alaska route on 10-day cruises. By mid-September she returns to the southerly route but has and does make several unique cruises to all parts of the world. Minimum fare on one of her Alaskan cruises begin at $2,250 for 10 or 11 days. Longer cruises of 20 and 21 days are also available on her positioning voyages from Fort Lauderdale to Vancouver or 14-day cruises from San Juan to Los Angeles.

**Both the *Sagafjord* and the *Vistafjord* were sold for a reported $83,000,000 along with the goodwill of the company.

II SAMARIA

Builder: Cammell, Laird & Co., Ltd., Birkenhead, England
Completed: August 1921
Gross tonnage: 19,848
Dimensions: 624' x 74' Depth: 45' Draft: 32'
Engines: Six steam turbines double-reduction geared
Screws: Twin
Watertight bulkheads: Ten
Decks: Five
Normal speed: 16 knots
Passenger accommodations: 248 first and 641 tourist class* (one class while cruising)
Officers and crew: 434
Registry: United Kingdom
Maiden voyage: Liverpool-Boston on April 19, 1922

*Original complement: 287 first, 564 second, and 1,456 third class.

Engaged in the Liverpool-Queenstown-Boston and New York service with some cruising. On January 26, 1924 she made a six-month world cruise out of New York. In 1934 she made ten consecutive cruises out of London. Requisitioned for troop work in 1941 and was not decommissioned until August 1948, when she carried Canadian troops and their families from Cuxhaven and Le Havre to Quebec City or Halifax until September. Following this service she worked out of London to Quebec and Montreal in 1950 before being re-routed to her home port of Liverpool to Quebec service June 14, 1951, following a refit in the autumn of 1950. Placed in the Southampton-Le Havre-Quebec run on July 12, 1951. The *Samaria* ran aground just below Quebec in 1952 but was refloated without difficulty. On June 15, 1953 she represented the Cunard Line at the Coronation Review at Spithead, England. Made her last voyage for the Line Montreal-Quebec-Le Havre-Southampton on November 23, 1955. Sold for scrap at Inverkeithing, Scotland in January 1956.

Sister ships: *Laconia* and *Scythia*.

I SAXONIA

Builder: John Brown & Co., Ltd., Clydebank, Glasgow, Scotland
Completed: April 1900
Gross tonnage: 14,197
Dimensions: 600' x 64' Depth: 42' Draft: 32'
Engines: Two 4-cylinder quadruple expansion
Screws: Twin
Watertight bulkheads: Ten
Decks: Four
Normal speed: 15 knots
Passenger accommodations: 500 second and 1,254 third class*
Registry: United Kingdom
Maiden voyage: Liverpool-Queenstown-Boston on May 22, 1900

*Original complement: 427 first, 382 second and 2,178 third class.

Engaged in the Liverpool-Queenstown-Boston service. Beginning December 4, 1909, she ran from New York to the Mediterranean, returning to the Boston service in the summer. By April 25, 1912 she had been scheduled almost permanently in the Line's Hungarian-American service from Fiume to Trieste-Messina-Palermo-Naples-Funchal-New York, and began calling at Greek ports in 1914. The *Saxonia's* single funnel was 106 feet high from her uppermost deck and she had a coal capacity of 1,430 tons. Requisitioned for war services, she was fitted-out at Quebec and became a Canadian transport on October 3, 1914, when she was ready for service. Retained until May 1, 1915, when she resumed service from Liverpool to New York as a second and third class ship. Maintaining irregular service on this run, she made some London-New York trips beginning January 13, 1917 and in mid-1919 was calling at the ports of Le Havre and Halifax outbound. By January 1, 1920 she worked the New York-Cherbourg-Plymouth-London route calling at Halifax westbound and on occasion homeward. Later on in her career she worked the New York-Hamburg route in April 1920. Made her last commercial voyage for Cunard on November 15, 1924, from New York to London via Cherbourg and Plymouth. Laid up at Tilbury dock prior to her sale to Dutch shipbreakers in January 1925.

Sister ship: *Ivernia.*

II SCYTHIA

Builder: Vickers Ltd., Barrow-in-Furness, England (*Scythia* was completed at Rotterdam, Holland owning to a labour strike in England)
Completed: December 1920
Gross tonnage: 19,930
Dimensions: 624' x 74' Depth: 45' Draft: 30'
Engines: Six steam turbines double-reduction geared
Screws: Twin
Watertight bulkheads: Ten
Decks: Five
Normal speed: 16 knots
Passenger accommodations: 248 first and 707 tourist class*
Officers and crew: 434
Registry: United Kingdom
Maiden voyage: Liverpool-New York on August 20, 1921

*Original passenger complement: 469 first, 390 second and 1,365 third class.

Engaged in the Liverpool-Queenstown-Boston and New York service with some cruising. In 1923, '24, '25 she made a cruise to the Mediterranean. By 1927 she had abandoned the call at Boston and worked directly to the port of New York westbound. Her accommodations were limited to a single class when cruising and reduced from her regular service complement. Requisitioned for troop service on August 27, 1939, she was almost sunk by an aerial torpedo in Algiers harbour on November 23, 1942. Damaged, she was towed to Gibraltar for repairs and later made it to New York on June 9, 1943 for further repairs, which took over ten weeks. Thereafter, she transported American troops to Britain in September and October of 1943. After being decommissioned in September 1948, she carried displaced persons from Cuxhaven and Le Havre to Quebec or Halifax with ten trips terminating in October 1949. Refitted in November of that year, she re-entered service from Liverpool to Quebec on August 17, 1950, and from London to Quebec and Montreal on September 14, 1950. On April 10, 1951 she was re-routed to sail from Southampton-Le Havre-Quebec-Montreal in summer and Southampton-Halifax-New York during winter with some Liverpool-Cobh-New York trips. The *Scythia* had the misfortune of colliding with the Canadian collier *Wabana* 35 miles south of St. Anne de Montes in the St. Lawrence River on June 5, 1952. The *Scythia* sheered off 32 feet of the *Wabana's* starboard side while travelling at a speed of 14 knots. There was no loss of life, but both vessels were found at fault when a formal investigation revealed that neither ship had made proper and diligent use of their radar. She commenced her last voyage for the Line on October 5, 1957 from Liverpool to New York via Cobh. She was then chartered by the Canadian Government for three voyages carrying Canadian service personnel from Montreal-Quebec-Rotterdam-Southampton. Made her last such voyage on December 10, 1957. Withdrawn from service and sold for scrap. She left for the breaker's yards at Inverkeithing, Scotland on January 1, 1958.

Sister ships: *Laconia* and *Samaria*.

SLAVONIA

Builder: James Laing & Sons Ltd., Sunderland, England
Completed: May 1903
Gross tonnage: 10,606
Dimensions: 526' x 59' Depth: 33' Draft: 22'
Engines: Two 3-cylinder triple expansion
Watertight bulkheads: Eight
Decks: Three
Normal speed: 13.50 knots
Passenger accommodations: 133 first, 187 second, 800 third class*
Registry: United Kingdom
Maiden voyage: Sunderland-Trieste on March 17, 1904

*Original complement of passengers: 40 Saloon, 87 second and 2,116 third class.

Engaged in the New York-Gibraltar-Naples-Palermo-Messina-Trieste-Fiume run. The *Slavonia* made some Liverpool-Fiume trips after yearly drydocking. Wrecked two miles southward of Flores Island in the Azores on June 10, 1909, she sank on the 11th with no loss of life. Before going down, her C.O.D., then the equivalent of an S.O.S., was picked up by the North German Lloyd *Prinzess Irene,* then 280 miles away. She arrived on the 10th and began taking off her 100 first class passengers, which took all night to accomplish due to the rough seas. Leaving the scene, she sailed for Gibraltar where she arrived on the 14th. The Hamburg-American liner *Batavia* had also arrived and taken off 256 third-class passengers leaving only the crew, who later abandoned the ship on the 11th when the sea had completely filled her hull, the ship a total wreck.

Sister ship: *Pannonia.*

II SYLVANIA

Builder: John Brown & Co., Ltd., Clydebank, Glasgow, Scotland
Completed: June 1957
Gross tonnage: 22,017
Dimensions: 608' x 80' Depth: 46' Draft: 29'
Engines: Four steam turbines double-reduction geared
Screws: Twin
Collision bulkhead: One
Watertight bulkheads: Nine
Decks: Five
Normal speed: 20 knots
Passenger accommodations: 177 first and 780 tourist class
Officers and crew: 460
Registry: United Kingdom
Maiden voyage: Greenock-Quebec-Montreal on June 5, 1957

Engaged in the Liverpool-Greenock-Quebec-Montreal run. Reallocated to the Liverpool-Cobh-New York service in January 1961 and to Quebec and Montreal in summer. The *Sylvania* made calls at Halifax in the winter westbound and eastbound on occasion with calls at Greenock homeward in place of Cobh. In 1962 she worked year-round to New York and three years later had begun making calls at Boston eastbound. In February of 1965 she made a Mediterranean cruise, which was the first such cruise for Cunard since January, 1939. In 1967 she was based at Gibraltar for a service of cruises to the Mediterranean. Equipped with motion stabilizers, all her public rooms are air-conditioned. The *Sylvania* made her last voyage for Cunard on December 11, 1967 from Montreal to London via Quebec, Halifax and Cobh. Laid up subsequently at Southampton pending her sale. After a short life of only a decade with the Line she was sold to the Italian Sitmar Line in the spring of 1968 and renamed *Fairwind*. Renamed *Sitmar Fairwind* in 1988. She passed back under British ownership when she ws sold to the P&O Lines in 1988 and renamed *Dawn Princess* for their subsidiary, Princess Cruises. Presently in their service.

Sister ships: *Carinthia, Carmania* and *Franconia.*

ULTONIA

Builder: Swan & Hunter Ltd., Wallsend-on-Tyne, England
Completed: October 1898
Gross tonnage: 10,402
Dimensions: 513' x 57' Depth: 37' Draft: 29'
Engines: Two 3-cylinder triple expansion engines
Screws: Twin
Watertight bulkheads: Eight
Decks: Three
Normal speed: 13 knots
Passenger accommodations: 119 second and 2,111 third class
Registry: United Kingdom
Maiden voyage: Liverpool-Queenstown-Boston on February 28, 1899

Built for the British India Steam Navigation Company and was to be named *Yamuna*. Sold to the Cunard Line after her launching and renamed *Ultonia*. Engaged in the Liverpool-Queenstown-Boston service with an occasional trip to New York. In May 1904 she was reallocated to the Fiume-Trieste-Messina-Palermo-Naples-Gibraltar-New York service, making an occasional New York or Boston-Queenstown-Liverpool voyage. Made some trips from Liverpool to Canada in 1912. In April of 1912 she was converted from a three class ship to two classes and re-entered her regular service on September 14, 1912 while still maintaining some London-Southampton-Quebec-Montreal trips. The *Ultonia* added the port of Patras to her Hungarian-American line service as well as other Greek ports in 1914. Made her last commercial voyage for the Line on July 25, 1913, New York-Gibraltar. Requisitioned for troop service on September 10, 1914, she was sunk by a German submarine 350 miles southwest of Land's End, England on June 27, 1917, with the loss of one life.

VISTAFJORD

Builder: Swan Hunter Shipbuilders, Ltd., Wallsend-on-Tyne, England
Completed: 1973
Gross tonnage: 24,116
Dimensions: 627′ x 82′ Depth: 53′ Draft: 27′
Engines: Two Sulzer 2-stroke single acting, 9-cylinder diesels plus an
  athwartship controllable pitch propeller forward
Screws: Twin
Decks: Six
Normal speed: 20 knots
Passenger accommodations: 670 in a single class
Officers and crew: 350
Registry: Bahamas
Maiden voyage: Oslo-New York on May 22, 1973*

*MV for NAL

Built for the Norwegian-America Line, she passed on to Norwegian America Cruises and Cunard Line ownership when the latter bought out the company in mid-1983 for approximately $83,000,000 along with her running mate the *Sagafjord*. The names of the ships were retained since they were popularly known amongst the public by the prestigious name of Norwegian-America Line. The *Vistafjord's* new livery of course is in the Cunard colours but this seems incongruent given her Nordic name; the registry of the ship throws things off even more. Company executives, however, are keen on dollars and not tradition. You won't find too many British officers on the ships either. I had the opportunity of making a transatlantic crossing on the *Vistafjord* back in May 1980, from New York to London and had a lovely cabin. The ship is probably the last liner to have been built on British soil and she has returned to a British company. Cruising capacity for the ship is usually 635 — the remaining berths being appropriated for cruise staff. Completely air-conditioned and equipped with motion stabilizers. Many of the cabins are furnished with a bathtub. Staterooms are also fitted with ship-to-shore telephones, radio and individually controlled thermostats. Public facilities include both an indoor and an outdoor swimming pool. There is a sauna and gymnasium, library with writing room, card room, beauty salon, barber shop, gift shop, laundry and dry cleaning service. There are six elevators. Refurbished in the winter of 1983-84 at a cost of $7,000,000. Twenty-four new deluxe staterooms, some with private verandas were added. The casino was enlarged as was the dining room. Improvements were made on the indoor-outdoor theatre-in-the-round. Her grand ballroom seats 700 persons. There is a large disco and several bars. Cabins are spacious throughout the vessel. The *Vistafjord* sails from Port Everglades on alternating itineraries to the Caribbean on 14-day cruises during the winter. Her ports of call include Santo Domingo-Aruba-La Guaria-Grenada-Barbados-Martinique-Antigua-St. Thomas or Playa del Carmen-Cozumel-Grand Cayman-Montego Bay-Guadeloupe-St. Kitts-Nevis-St. Martin-Tortola-St. Thomas-Port Everglades. Throughout the spring she sails across the Atlantic in April for the Mediterranean, then sails north for Scandinavian ports and the North Cape around October. There are 294 cabins situated outside with only 46 located inside. There are a total of 404 cabins. The new cabins feature double-size beds and a small refrigerator. She consumes 72 tons of fuel per day.

Sister ship: *Sagafjord.*

French Line

II ANTILLES

Builder: Arsenal de Brest, Brest, France
Completed: 1952
Gross tonnage: 19,828
Dimensions: 599' x 80' Depth: 46' Draft: 26'
Engines: Eight steam turbines, double-reduction geared
Screws: Twin
Watertight bulkheads: Nine
Decks: Five
Normal speed: 23 knots
Passenger accommodations: 404 first, 285 cabin and 89 tourist class
Officers and crew: 360
Registry: France
Maiden voyage: Le Havre-Lisbon-Tangiers-Algiers in March 1953

Employed in the Le Havre-Southampton-West Indies trade. Fully air-conditioned and equipped with motion stabilizers, the *Antilles* made an occasional voyage to New York, usually as a leg on a cruise. Fondly known as the "Aunt Tilly" she was built expressly for the cruise market trade to the French Colonies of the West Indies. On the evening of January 8, 1971, at approximately 5:00 p.m. the *Antilles* went aground on an uncharted submerged reef a half mile north of the island of Mustique in the Caribbean. Bursting into flames when a fuel tank ruptured on impact, her boiler room was quickly flooded by the oil. At one point the fire-fighting team appeared to have the conflagration under control but the intensity of the flames grew to such a high temperature all attempts to extinguish the inferno became futile. Just twenty-two minutes after the fire broke out, the *Antilles'* distress call was picked up at the nearby island of Barbados where merchant vessels were sent out to rescue the passengers and crew of the stricken liner. All 635 passengers and crew were disembarked safely at Mustique by the French Line's banana boat *Point Allegre*, and the *Suffren* along with other smaller craft. Some 500 passengers were later picked up at Mustique by Cunard Line's *QE2* and brought to the island of Barbados where they were able to make other arrangements for their destinations. The last report of the *Antilles* came the following day when the lovely liner had rolled over on her side, still engulfed in flames. Designated a total loss, she had been valued at some $14,400,000. A terrible misfortune for the French Line and to the many travellers who came to know this charming intermediate liner. Sold for scrap on March 12, 1971.

BRETAGNE

Builder: Barclay, Curle & Co., Ltd., Glasgow, Scotland
Completed: September 1922
Gross tonnage: 10,108
Dimensions: 472′ x 59′ Depth: 45′ Draft: 27′
Engines: Four Curtiss steam turbines, double-reduction geared
Screws: Twin
Watertight bulkheads: Seven
Decks: Four
Normal speed: 14.50 knots
Passenger accommodations: 440 in a single first-class capacity
Registry: France
Maiden voyage: France-West Indies in 1937

Built for the Royal Holland Lloyd and christened *Flandria*. Sold to the French Line in 1937 and renamed *Bretagne*. Engaged in the St. Nazaire-Colon-Mexico-West Indies trade and later worked out of Le Havre-English ports-West Indies service. The *Bretagne's* tonnage was later reduced to 8,119 gross tons and she was sunk by a German submarine on October 14, 1939, while enroute to England.

CHAMPLAIN

Builder: Chantiers & Ateliers de St. Nazaire, Penhoet, France
Completed: 1932
Gross tonnage: 28,124
Dimensions: 645′ x 83′ Depth: 46′
Engines: Six Parson steam turbines, single-reduction geared
Screws: Twin
Watertight bulkheads: Ten
Decks: Five
Normal speed: 20 knots
Passenger accommodations: 548 cabin, 318 tourist and 134 third class
Registry: France
Maiden voyage: Le Havre-New York on June 18, 1932

Engaged in the Le Havre-Southampton-New York service calling at Plymouth eastbound and cruising during the off seasonal months. The *Champlain* had a promenade deck 350 feet long and a dining room two decks high and 65 feet long. Struck an acoustic mine off La Pallice, France, on June 17, 1940, and sank within a quarter of an hour while she had been working out of Bordeaux since the German invasion. The *Champlain* lived a regretfully short time for a liner as did her consorts *Lafayette* and *Normandie*.

CHICAGO

Builder: Chantiers de L'Atlantique de St. Nazaire, Penhoet, France
Completed: 1908
Gross tonnage: 10,502
Dimensions: 508' x 58' Depth: 39'
Engines: Two 3-cylinder triple expansion
Screws: Twin
Watertight bulkheads: Fourteen
Decks: Four
Normal speed: 15.50
Passenger accommodations: 383 second and 1,354 third class
Registry: France
Maiden voyage: Le Havre-New York on May 30, 1908

Engaged mainly in the Le Havre-New York run until 1918 when she was transferred to the Bordeaux-New York service. Returning to her original service out of Le Havre in 1919, a call at Halifax was added westbound the following year. Converted to a cabin and third-class liner in 1923 with an added call to Vigo, Spain eastbound; both directions by 1926. Operating on the various routes of the French Line she also made a trip to New Orleans out of Bordeaux on January 2nd, and to Newport News, Virginia on May 1, 1926. That same year she made only three Le Havre-New York voyages. Settled in the Bordeaux-Vigo-Halifax-New York run in March 1927, until she was reconstructed and renamed in 1928 to *Guadeloupe* with a new service from St. Nazaire to the West Indies. Commenced her last voyage for the French Line on June 28, 1928, New York-Vigo-Bordeaux. Sold for scrap at St. Nazaire, France in 1936 and broken up by 1937.

Note: Photo as *Guadalupe*.

COLOMBIE

Builder: Ateliers et Chantiers de France, Dunkirk, France
Completed: September 1931
Gross tonnage: 12,803
Dimensions: 509' x 67' Depth: 42'
Engines: Six steam turbines, single-reduction geared
Screws: Twin
Watertight bulkheads: Eight
Decks: Five
Normal speed: 16 knots
Passenger accommodations: 192 first, 140 cabin and 246 tourist class
Registry: France
Maiden voyage: Le Havre-Colon-West Indies on November 1, 1931

Launched on July 18, 1931. Employed in the Le Havre-English ports-Côte Ferme Cristobal service. Called at Copenhagen on June 10, 1937, for the first time. Commissioned as a transport in 1939 and seized by the United States at Martinique, West Indies in December 1942 and utilised as a transport. In 1946 she was used as a hospital ship under the name of *Aleda F. Lutz*. Returned to the French Line and recovered her original name and on April 11, 1946, after being rebuilt by DeSchelde at Vlissingen, Holland, and resumed regular sailings. Withdrawn in late 1948 to undergo a complete reconstruction lasting two years at Flushing, Netherlands. She emerged as a single-funnelled ship, which replaced her former two, and with many interior modifications. Resumed service on October 12, 1950, on the Le Havre-Southampton-Point a Pitre-Roseau-Fort de France-St. Lucia-Trinidad-Barbados westbound and Barbados-Fort de France-Point a Pitre-Plymouth-Le Havre eastbound service. Engaged in this route until December 1962, when she was settled to permanent cruising to the Antilles. Sold to the Greek Typaldos Lines in March 1964 and renamed *Atlantic; Atlantica*. Sold to Nemo A.E. at Perama, Greece for scrap in 1970 and partially broken up by September of that year. The remaining hulk was sold to Desgasa in May 1974 and towed to Barcelona, Spain.

CUBA

Builder: Swan, Hunter & Wigham Richardson, Ltd., Wallsend-on-Tyne, England
Completed: 1923
Gross tonnage: 11,337
Dimensions: 495' x 62' Depth: 35'
Engines: Four Rateau steam turbines, double-reduction geared
Screws: Twin
Decks: Four
Normal speed: 16 knots
Passenger accommodations: 448 in a single first-class capacity
Registry: France
Maiden voyage: St. Nazaire-Havana-Vera Cruz in May 1923

Engaged in the St. Nazaire-Vera Cruz-West Indies-Central American trade. Made her first trip to New York in August of 1929 from Le Havre via Plymouth. Taken over by the British Ministry of War in December 1941 and converted to a transport with management under the auspices of the Cunard Line. Sunk in the English Channel on April 6, 1945, while enroute to Le Havre, France.

I DE GRASSE

Builder: Cammell, Laird & Co., Ltd., Birkenhead, England
Completed: 1924
Gross tonnage: 19,665
Dimensions: 572' x 71' Depth: 42' Draft: 30'
Engines: Four steam turbines, single-reduction geared
Screws: Twin
Watertight bulkheads: Twelve
Decks: Five
Normal speed: 16.50 knots
Passenger accommodations: 536 cabin and 410 tourist class*
Registry: France
Maiden voyage: Le Havre-New York on August 24, 1924

*Original passenger accommodations were 542 first, 377 second and 184 third class.

The *De Grasse* was laid down in 1918 but work was suspended until 1923 because of the war. She was later towed to St. Nazaire for completion when a British labour dispute threatened further delay. Ordered as *Suffren*, but altered to *De Grasse* when the French Line purchased the Hamburg-American liner *Bluecher* and gave her the name of *Suffren* in 1923. Engaged in the Le Havre-New York trade with a call at Plymouth eastbound. During the mid-thirties she did some work in the Mediterranean area and was transferred to the Bordeaux-New York run 1937. Withdrawn from service in 1940 and sunk by German gunfire on the Bordeaux estuary on August 30, 1933. Refloated on August 30, 1945, and reconditioned and replacement of her former two stacks by a single squat type. *De Grasse* inaugurated the Line's first voyage after the war and sailed from Le Havre to New York on July 12, 1947, calling at Southampton east- and westbound. Reallocated to the West Indies service on April 24, 1952, out of Le Havre and was sold to the Canadian-Pacific Line in February 1953 to become the *Empress of Australia*. Resold to the Grimaldi-Siosa Line in February 1956 and renamed *Venezuela*. Stranded in March 1962 outside of Cannes and broken up at La Spezia, Italy in December 1962.

II DE GRASSE

Builder: Swan, Hunter & Wigham Richardson Ltd., Wallsend-on-Tyne, England
Completed: May 1956
Gross tonnage: 18,739
Dimensions: 578' x 72' Depth: 47' Draft: 28'
Engines: Two 8-cylinder, 2-stroke, double-acting diesels
Screws: Twin
Watertight bulkheads: Ten
Decks: Seven
Normal speed: 20 knots
Passenger accommodations: 581 in single class
Officers and crew: 285
Registry: France
Maiden voyage: Le Havre-West Indies on November 12, 1971

Built for the Norwegian-America Line and christened *Bergensfjord*. Sold to the French Line in March 1971 and renamed *De Grasse*. She had been purchased to replace the loss of their cruise ship *Antilles*. Though a lovely ship the *De Grasse* did not generate the revenues expected by the French Line. Coupled by the oil crisis in 1973 the ship was sold to the Norwegian Thoresen & Co., Ltd., in November 1973 and renamed *Rasa Sayang*. Resold to the Greek Sunlit Cruises Ltd. in mid-1978 and renamed *Golden Moon*. Resold once again to Greek owners in July 1980 and regained her former name. Engulfed by fire on August 27, 1980 at Perama, Greece while being refitted, she was towed to open waters and deliberately beached near Kynoscoura in shallow water. A total loss, part of her port side remained above the water.

ESPAGNE

Builder: Chantier & Ateliers de Provence, Port-de-Bouc, France
Completed: August 1910
Gross tonnage: 11,155
Dimensions: 545' x 60' Depth: 36'
Engines: Two 4-cylinder, triple expansion
Screws: Twin
Watertight bulkheads: Thirteen
Decks: Four
Normal speed: 18 knots (attained a speed of 19.48 knots during her trials)
Passenger accommodations: 310 first, 389 second and 621 third class
Registry: France
Maiden voyage: St. Nazaire-West Indies on October 5, 1910

Employed primarily in the St. Nazaire-Vera Cruz-West Indies trade, the *Espagne* made two voyages from Bordeaux to New York in 1911, her first in February arriving on the 19th. She also made two similar voyages in 1912 and 1914. In the spring of 1915 she worked mostly on the Bordeaux-New York route beginning in April until August 1919, thereafter reverting to her original route to the Caribbean. Sold for scrap at St. Nazaire, France in April 1934.

II FLANDRE

Builder: Ateliers & Chantiers de France, Dunkirk, France
Completed: 1952
Gross tonnage: 20,477
Dimensions: 600' x 80' Depth: 46' Draft: 26'
Engines: Eight Rateau double-reduction geared turbines
Screws: Twin
Watertight bulkheads: Nine
Decks: Five
Normal speed: 23 knots
Passenger accommodations: 232 first and 511 tourist class*
Officers and crew: 360
Registry: France
Maiden voyage: Le Havre-New York on July 23, 1952

*Original passenger accommodations were 407 first, 389 cabin and 97 tourist class.

Engaged in the Le Havre-Southampton-New York run with a call at Plymouth eastbound between April and November and to the West Indies during the winter months. The *Flandre's* maiden voyage to New York was marred while enroute when electrical faultiness and fuel pump disorders caused the ship to break down just outside New York. Towed into New York harbour to her pier, she was still greeted with the traditional fireboat showering and horns from smaller craft but the incident had earned her a not so becoming nickname, "The Flounder". Returning to her builders at Dunkirk for repairs, she did not re-enter service until April 17, 1953. Reconditioned in early 1955 she had her passenger accommodations changed to the present figure. Resuming service on April 29, 1955, she made a number of Le Havre-Vigo-New Orleans-Galveston, Texas voyages in late 1955 and the early part of 1956. Reallocated to the West Indies trade in the fall of 1962 shortly after the debut of the *France*. She returned to the North Atlantic trade briefly in the summer of 1967 when she made two trips from Le Havre to Quebec City and Montreal for Expo '67. Sold to the Italian Costa Line in February 1968 and renamed *Carla Costa; Carlac* in 1986. Chartered by Princess Cruises between December 1967-1968, she ran as the *Princess Carla*. Presently in their service.

Sister ship: *Antilles*.

II FRANCE

Builder: Chantiers & Ateliers de St. Nazaire, Penhoet, France
Completed: January 1912
Gross tonnage: 23,769
Dimensions: 720' x 76' Depth: 48'
Engines: Four direct-action steam turbines
Screws: Quadruple
Watertight bulkheads: Sixteen
Decks: Five
Normal speed: 23.50 knots (attained a speed of 25.09 knots on her trials)
Passenger accommodations: 535 first, 549 second and 1,486 third class
Officers and crew: 600
Registry: France
Maiden voyage: Le Havre-New York on April 20, 1912

Laid down as *La Picardie* but changed to *France* shortly after. Employed in the Le Havre-New York trade. Laid up in October 1914, soon after the outbreak of World War I. Between March and May of 1915 she transported troops under the name of *France IV*. Laid up and commissioned as a hospital ship in November 1915 until May 1917. In March 1918 she carried American troops until the end of the year. Resuming scheduled sailing under her original name from New York on January 4, 1919. She was France's first turbine liner and was constructed with a double bottomed hull. Her coal consumption was 720 tons per day. Reconditioned in March 1919, she resumed service that August. Completely overhauled between August 1923 and May 1924 and converted to oil-firing, she re-entered service on May 10th. In January of 1926 the *France* added a call at Plymouth to her itinerary. Made three cruises to the Mediterranean out of New York in 1928-29. Commenced her last voyage for the French Line on September 9, 1932, from New York to Le Havre via Plymouth and subsequently laid up. Among the notable amenities aboard the *France* was the first bowling lane situated on her boat deck along with the more familiar recreational pastimes such as shuffleboard and skeet shooting. During the course of her career the *France* seemed to have a streak of bad luck. Of course the most feared of all mishaps that might befall a ship is that of fire. The *France* had more than her share. In 1912 she had a fire break out in her coal bunkers during her sea trials; in 1919 there was an explosion aboard which killed nine men; another in 1933 while moored at her dock and once again in 1935 when she was being dismantled. Sold for scrap in November 1934, she left for the shipbreaker's yard at Dunkirk on April 15, 1935, and was broken up by June of that year.

III FRANCE

Builder: Chantiers de L'Atlantique, St. Nazaire, France
Completed: November 1961
Gross tonnage: 66,348
Dimensions: 1,034' x 109' Depth: 81' Draft: 34'
Engines: Sixteen steam turbines, single-reduction geared.
Screws: Quadruple
Watertight bulkheads: fourteen
Decks: Ten
Normal speed: 31 knots (attained a speed of 34.13 knots on her trials)
Officers and crew: 1,006
Passenger accommodations: 622 first and 1,619 tourist class (1,300 when in cruise service)
Registry: France
Maiden voyage: Le Havre-Canary Islands on January 19, 1962*

*Maiden crossing to New York from Le Havre via Southampton on February 3, 1962.

Launched on May 11, 1960 she was employed in the Le Havre-Southampton-New York service with cruises on occasion to the West Indies and distant ports around the world. One such trip was a 40-day cruise to the West Indies, South America and South Africa from New York on January 6, 1971. On January 4, 1974 she made a 90-day world cruise. Built at a cost of $30,000,000, she is the longest ship in the world. Equipped with motion stabilizers and fully air-conditioned, her superstructure is constructed of aluminum. Unlike most ships which provided in the early years of travel the fore and aft end of the promenade deck for their tourist class passengers, the France provided a special promenade deck for tourist class. She had the largest theatre seating of 664 persons and her tourist class dining room seating of 828 was also the

largest of any other liner. Her actual berth capacity is for 2,400, including 38 deluxe suites and 2 super deluxe suites. Her holds could carry 94 cars and she had a library with well over 600 volumes in several languages, yes, including English. She was the flagship of the French Line and is the last of those liners built specifically for prestige as messengers of good will between nations. A visage of the past, she evoked the memory of the elegant *Normandie* but only from afar. Inside the ship had a rubberized matting instead of teak decking in her enclosed promenade deck and much of the tourist class area was somewhat harsh in color schemes which gave a more sterile mood to the rooms. Built primarily for the North Atlantic trade with an indoor pool and little outside deck space for passengers, she did not succeed as a cruise ship and the oil crisis of 1973-74 impeded her operation even on the route for which she was intended. The French Government, which has always subsidized the French Line, decided to retire the great liner in the autumn of 1974 when she made her last voyage for the line on September 5, 1974 from New York to Le Havre via Southampton. Before the voyage was completed her crew mutinied on the 12th just three miles outside of Le Havre, insisting that the government maintain the subsidy of $1,880,000 which had been appropriated each year to fund operation of the ship. A final announcement was made six days later to retire the ship. She was officially withdrawn on October 25, 1974 . Laid up at Le Havre pending sale for nearly five years. She was to be sold to a Saudi Arabian, Akram Ojjeh, for $22,000,000 on July 9, 1979 for conversion to a floating casino and French culture centre off Daytona Beach, Florida. This never materialized and she was resold to Norwegian Caribbean Lines* the following month for $18,000,000 and renamed *Norway*. Presently in their service. I booked a westbound ticket on the *France* in August 1973 in the London office and was given a lovely crystal perpetual calendar of the Line's fleet and services by Mr. Richer, the last director of that office.

*Now Norwegian Cruise Lines.

ILE DE FRANCE

Builder: Chantiers de St. Nazaire, France
Completed: 1926
Gross tonnage: 44,356
Dimensions: 793' x 92' Depth: 56'
Engines: Four direct-acting Parson steam turbines
Screws: Quadruple
Watertight bulkheads: Fifteen
Decks: Seven
Normal speed: 23 knots
Passenger accommodations: 448 first, 637 cabin and 509 tourist class
Officers and crew: 700
Registry: France
Maiden voyage: Le Havre-Plymouth-New York on June 22, 1927

Employed in the Le Havre-Plymouth-New York service, she inaugurated a call at Southampton on January 30, 1935, with the call at Plymouth eastbound only. Perhaps one of the most famous liners to ever work the North Atlantic Ferry, the *Ile de France* was the first ship to carry a small seaplane for the expediting of mail. She was the first liner on the Atlantic to be fitted with Welin gravity davits for her lifeboats. The entrance to her grand vestibule was four decks high, and to keep the optimistic investor of the twenties well informed, a stock ticker was among her many amenities. The *Ile de France* left New York on May 1, 1940, headed for the Orient after having been converted to a transport. On July 19, 1940, she was seized by the British at Singapore and placed under the auspices of the British Ministry of Transport with management under Cunard Line. Decommissioned on September 22, 1945, but maintained to carry displaced persons until April 16, 1947, as well as transport French troops to fight North Vietnamese troops in French Indo-China. In the course of her war services she carried over 300,000 troops and plied over 500,000 miles. Reverting back to her owners she underwent a complete rebuilding and refurnishing. Resuming transatlantic sailings on July 21, 1949, her

outward appearance had been changed dramatically with the replacement of her three slender smoke stacks by two broader funnels. Though most of her splendid interior remained intact there were some vivid changes. Her once varnished deck chairs had been painted in a bright red. Gone were the young debutantes off to Paris to catch the latest fashions. They were replaced by cigar wielding businessmen of the garment industry off to copy the latest fashions for mass production in a newly-created material called polyester. In the early morning hours of July 26, 1956, the *Ile de France* headed eastbound picked up the distress call of the sinking Italian Line's ship *Andrea Doria* after she had collided with the Swedish-American liner *Stockholm* off the Nantucket Shoals. Upon arrival the *Ile de France* rescued over 700 people from the sinking liner. Shortly afterwards she was nearly disabled when she was caught in an Atlantic storm which mangled some of her superstructure and flooded several cabins. In February 1957 she ran aground off Martinique during a cruise. Her passengers taken ashore where they could make other arrangements for transportation, the *Ile de France* was towed to far off Newport News, Virginia where her hull was repaired. With the transatlantic travel at a lull it was concluded to retire the ship the next season. Commenced her last voyage for the French Line on November 10, 1958, New York-Plymouth-Le Havre and was subsequently laid up. Sold to Japanese shipbreakers on January 12, 1959, she left Le Havre headed for Osaka on February 26th sailing under the name of *Furansu Maru*, which means "The French Ship." A courtesy well-deserved for an elegant ship whose popularity was known on both sides of the Atlantic. Her name will always be counted with those splendid ships that were said to have possessed a soul. Broken up by September 1959.

Note: The *Ile de France's* ending was not as dignified as her sailing out of Le Havre for the last time. The Japanese who had purchased the ship for scrap later chartered her out to a Hollywood production company for the making of a film, "The Last Voyage." And before she was broken up in the traditional manner several of her lounges and suites were blown up, her fore funnel torn from its base and sent careening into the deckhouse.

II LAFAYETTE

Builder: Chantiers & Ateliers de Provence, Marseilles, France
Completed: 1915
Gross tonnage: 12,220
Dimensions: 546′ x 64′ Depth: 35′
Engines: Two 4-cylinder quadruple expansion engines and two Parson low-pressure steam turbines
Screws: Quadruple
Watertight bulkheads: Thirteen
Decks: Four
Normal speed: 16.50 knots (attained a speed of 18.09 knots on her trial runs)
Passenger accommodations: 336 first, 158 second and 830 third class
Registry: France
Maiden voyage: Bordeaux-New York on November 3, 1915

Originally to be named *Ile de Cuba* for the West Indies trade but changed to *Lafayette* after launching. Engaged in the Le Havre-New York service. Converted to a hospital ship in October 1916 and resumed transatlantic sailings in November 1919. Following the war her route was to New York between June and October and between November and May she sailed to the Caribbean. In November of 1920, however, she was stationed permanently on the southern route. In February 1927 she made one voyage to New York. Renamed *Mexique* in 1928, she was maintained on her southerly route but worked out of St. Nazaire to Vera Cruz and the West Indies. As *Mexique* she made two voyages to New York in 1928. She had been built especially for the West Indies trade. Sunk by a mine in the Gironde Estuary, France on June 19, 1940.

III LAFAYETTE

Builder: Chantiers & Ateliers de St. Nazaire, Penhoet, France
Completed: 1929
Gross tonnage: 25,178
Dimensions: 613′ x 78′ Depth: 45′
Engines: Four MAN, 6-cylinder, 2-stroke, double-acting diesels
Screws: Quadruple
Watertight bulkheads: Seventeen
Decks: Five
Normal speed: 17 knots
Passenger accommodations: 591 cabin, 334 tourist and 142 third class
Officers and crew: 472
Registry: France
Maiden voyage: Le Havre-Plymouth-New York on May 17, 1930

Engaged in the Le Havre-Plymouth-New York service with some cruising. In March 1934 she ran into a gale while on a North Atlantic crossing. Heaving for almost five hours many of her windows were broken and sustained heavy damage to her upper works. Quite similar to her running mate the *Champlain* in appearance, the *Lafayette* was the French Line's first motorship. Made her last voyage for the Line on April 20, 1938, New York-Le Havre. Destroyed by fire while in drydock at Le Havre on May 4, 1938. The remaining hulk was later sold to shipbreakers at Rotterdam, Netherlands and broken up by June of that year.

LA LORRAINE

Builder: Compagnie Generale Transatlantique, St. Nazaire, France
Completed: 1900
Gross tonnage: 11,372
Dimensions: 580' x 60' Depth: 36'
Engines: Two 4-cylinder, triple expansion
Screws: Twin
Watertight bulkheads: Eighteen
Decks: Four
Normal speed: 20 knots (attained a speed of 21.80 knots on her trial runs)
Passenger accommodations: 338 first, 307 second and 866 steerage
Officers and crew: 410
Registry: France
Maiden voyage: Le Havre-New York on August 11, 1900

Employed in the Le Havre-New York trade year-round. She and her sister ship *La Savoie* were the first French liners to have wireless telegraphy installed. The *Lorraine* had 18 main boilers and 190 stokers to man the stokeholds. Mobilized as a transport at the outbreak of World War I in August 1914 and renamed *Lorraine II*. She was later converted to an armed-merchant cruiser in April 1917, and resumed regular sailings in April 1918 under her original name. The *La Lorraine* and her sister became well known steamers on the Atlantic ferry in their time. Made her last voyage for the Line on October 14, 1922, New York-Le Havre and was sold for scrap at St. Nazaire, France in December of that year.

Sister ship: *La Savoie*.

LA PROVENCE

Builder: Chantiers & Ateliers de St. Nazaire, Penhoet, France
Completed: 1906
Gross tonnage: 13,753
Dimensions: 627′ x 65′ Depth: 38′
Engines: Two 4-cylinder, triple expansion
Screws: Twin
Watertight bulkheads: Twenty-one
Decks: Four
Normal speed: 21 knots (attained a speed of 23 knots during her trials)
Passenger accommodations: 358 first, 339 second and 898 third class
Registry: France
Maiden voyage: Le Havre-New York on April 21, 1906

Employed in the Le Havre-New York run year-round. In 1907 she transported over 107,000 immigrants to the port of New York. Made her last commercial voyage from New York to Le Havre on June 17, 1914. Converted to an armed-merchant cruiser in December 1914 and renamed *Provence II*. Torpedoed and sunk while enroute from Toulon, France to Salonica, Greece with an estimated 1,700 colonial infantry troops by U-35 in the Aegean Sea on February 26, 1916. The disaster took the lives of 830 of those aboard.

LA SAVOIE

Builder: Compagnie Generale Transatlantique, St. Nazaire, France
Completed: 1901
Gross tonnage: 11,168
Dimensions: 580' x 60' Depth: 35'
Engines: Two 4-cylinder, triple expansion
Screws: Twin
Watertight bulkheads: Eighteen
Decks: Four
Normal speed: 20 knots
Passenger accommodations: 400 cabin, 184 tourist-cabin and 101 third class*
Officers and crew: 410
Registry: France
Maiden voyage: Le Havre-New York on August 31, 1901

*Original accommodations: 322 first, 304 second and 850 steerage

Engaged in the Le Havre-New York run year-round. The *La Savoie* and her sister *La Lorraine* were appointed with the usual plush designs of French decor for which they both became renowned and remembered. Like her sister she had 18 main boilers and 190 stokers to man her burning stokeholds. Converted to an armed-merchant cruiser in August 1914 with the outbreak of war and renamed *Savoie II*. Returned back to her regular service towards the end of April 1919. In 1923 she was converted to a cabin and third class ship and returned to service that spring. In May 1925 some tourist-cabin accommodations were fitted. Made her last voyage for the Line on October 7, 1927, New York-Le Havre and subsequently sold for scrap in November to shipbreakers at Dunkirk, France. Broken up by December.

Sister ship: *La Lorraine.*

LIBERTÉ

Builder: Blohm & Voss, Hamburg, Germany
Completed: March 1929
Gross tonnage: 51,839
Dimensions: 937′ x 102′ Depth: 48′
Engines: Twelve turbines, single-reduction geared
Screws: Quadruple
Watertight bulkheads: Fourteen
Decks: Seven
Normal speed: 24.50 knots
Passenger accommodations: 555 first, 545 cabin and 450 tourist class
Registry: France
Maiden voyage: Le Havre-New York on August 17, 1950

Built for the North German Lloyd and christened *Europa*. Allotted to the French Government in May 1946 as a World War II reparation and transferred to the French Line in July. Though the name *Lorraine* had been contemplated she was eventually renamed more appropriately *Liberté*. On the night of December 8, 1946, the *Liberté* broke loose from her moorings during a severe gale and rammed into the sunken hulk of the *Paris* which lay in Le Havre harbour, damaging her starboard side extensively. Scuttled to prevent her from capsizing, she was refloated on April 15, 1947, and taken to St. Nazaire in November. Reconditioned and rebuilt extensively at a cost of about $19,000,000. Re-entering service in the summer of 1950, she was a splendid example of late Art Deco interiors with an array of elegant first-class suites and even apartments. Placed in the Le Havre-Southampton-New York run with a call at Plymouth eastbound. Her funnels were replaced in 1954, giving her a somewhat incongruent appearance due to their height. With the construction of the new *France* she was retired from service making her last voyage for the French Line on November 10, 1961, from New York to Le Havre via Plymouth. Sold to the Bei Terrestre Marittima shipbreakers at La Spezia on December 30, 1961, and arrived there on January 30, 1962.

Note: Originally offered to the United States, she was eventually given to France by the United Nations Reparations Commission as compensation for the loss of the *Normandie*, but only because the United States did not particularly wish to repair a number of serious fractures in her hull.

NORMANDIE

Builder: Chantiers & Ateliers de St. Nazaire, Penhoet, France
Completed: 1935
Gross tonnage: 83,423
Dimensions: 1,027' x 118' Depth: 58'
Engines: Four steam turbines connected to four electric motors
Screws: Quadruple
Watertight bulkheads: Eleven
Decks: Ten
Normal speed: 30 knots (attained a speed of 31.95 knots on her trial runs)
Passenger accommodations: 848 first, 670 tourist and 454 third class
Officers and crew: 1,320
Registry: France
Maiden voyage: Le Havre-Southampton-New York on May 29, 1935

A most appropriate name for this most elegant example of Gallic elegance and stately majesty, the name *President Doumer* had initially been considered. Engaged in the Le Havre-Southampton-New York trade, the *Normandie* won the Blue Riband from the sleek Italian Line's *Rex* on her maiden voyage by making the run from Bishop Rock to Ambrose Lighthouse in 4 days, 3 hours, and 14 minutes at a speed of 29.94 knots. The *Normandie's* main dining room was three decks high and 270 feet long with a seating capacity of 1,000 — a lavish hall unequaled to date.

Built with a bulbous bow to increase her speed. Her funnels were 160 feet in circumference and rose 145 feet in height. Her swimming pool, the largest ever built on a liner, measured 100 feet in length with a width of 30 feet. In March 1936 her superstructure was enlarged to give her the present tonnage and was acclaimed to be the largest ship in the world at the time. Her bronze propellers weighed 23 tons each and measured 15 feet in diameter. The outbreak of hostilities forced her to be laid up in New York making her last transatlantic crossing in August arriving at New York on the 28th. Seized by the United States on December 16, 1941, for conversion to a transport with renaming to *Lafayette*. Caught fire by a worker's acetylene torch which had ignited some bedding brought aboard prematurely at 2:35 p.m. on February 9, 1942. As the fire raced through the great liner raging out of control, fireboats poured tons of water while fire engines dockside pumped tons of water into the inferno. Becoming top-heavy because of the great intake of water, she keeled over on her port side at the French Line quay in 50 feet of water. Refloated by the Americans on August 9, 1943, at a cost of $4,000,000. Anticipating further costs for reconstruction she was sold to Lipsett Incorporated for a miniscule $161,680. Scrapped at Port Newark, New Jersey in September 1946. A truly tragic demise for perhaps the most elegant superliner. She was the pride of France when she made her debut, lost in the hands of strangers. Rumors circulated following the disaster that the ship had been sabotaged. The pressing question was by whom? The Germans were too convenient a scapegoat.

PARIS

Builder: Chantiers & Ateliers de St. Nazaire, Penhoet, France
Completed: 1921
Gross tonnage: 34,569
Dimensions: 763' x 85' Depth: 59'
Engines: Four direct-action Parson steam turbines
Screws: Quadruple
Watertight bulkheads: Fourteen
Decks: Five
Normal speed: 22 knots (attained a speed of 22.44 knots on her trials)
Passenger accommodations: 340 first, 163 tourist and 409 third class*
Officers and crew: 664
Registry: France
Maiden voyage: Le Havre-New York on June 15, 1921

*Original passenger accommodations: 584 first, 698 second and 857 third class.

Launched on September 12, 1916, her construction was held up during World War I and the hull was later towed to Quiberon, France where it remained until brought back to St. Nazaire in 1921 and completed. Employed in the Le Havre-New York service with a call at Plymouth eastbound. Her passenger accommodations were burnt-out at Le Havre in August 1929, and she did not resume transatlantic sailings until January 1930. The *Paris* had an enclosed promenade deck that extended 423 feet in length. Her grand dining hall could accommodate 540 persons each sitting. Commenced her last voyage for the French Line, New York-Le Havre on April 8, 1939. Ten days later she caught fire at Le Havre, keeled over and sank in the outer harbour. Her charred hulk remained for many years and was not removed until the Line's *Liberté* broke from her moorings and rammed into the wreck in December 1946. A favourite to the many who sailed with her, she was a paragon of French elegance and stately design.

ROCHAMBEAU

Builder: Chantiers de L'Atlantique de St. Nazaire, Penhoet, France
Completed: August 1911
Gross tonnage: 12,678
Dimensions: 559' x 64' Depth: 43'
Engines: Two 4-cylinder triple expansion engines and two BP turbines
Screws: Quadruple
Watertight bulkheads: Thirteen
Decks: Four
Normal speed: 15.50 knots (attaining a speed of 17.50 knots on her trial runs)
Passenger accommodations: 477 in second and 1,546 third class*
Registry: France
Maiden voyage: Le Havre-Bordeaux-New York arriving at New York on September 25, 1911

*Original passenger accommodations: 628 in second and third class, 1,248 steerage.

Employed in the Le Havre-Channel ports-New York run until 1915 when she was based out of Bordeaux. The *Rochambeau* maintained commercial sailings throughout the First World War and later was used to repatriate American troops in 1919 from France. Decommissioned in 1920 when she returned to regular service in 1923, she was converted to a cabin and third class ship. Her large passenger lists of the early twenties began to dwindle as the years increased and in the late twenties she carried as little as two to three hundred passengers across. When the Great Depression hit she carried as few as one hundred. Made her last voyage for the French Line from New York to Le Havre via Vigo, Bordeaux and Plymouth on July 25, 1933. Laid up upon her return, she was sold for scrap to Gosselin & Dumouries at Dunkirk, France in May 1934.

SUFFREN

Builder: Blohm & Voss, Hamburg, Germany
Completed: May 1902
Gross tonnage: 11,948
Dimensions: 527' x 62' Depth: 36'
Engines: Two 4-cylinder quadruple expansion
Screws: Twin
Watertight bulkheads: Thirteen
Decks: Four
Normal speed: 15 knots
Passenger accommodations: 432 cabin and 719 third class
Officers and crew: 252
Registry: France
Maiden voyage: Le Havre-New York on May 8, 1923

Built for the Hamburg-American Line and christened *Bluecher*. Seized by the Brazilian Government at Recife on October 26, 1917, and renamed *Leopoldina*. Chartered to the French Line in 1920, she made her first voyage under the tri-color on March 12, 1920 from New York to Le Havre. Laid up in December 1921, she remained out of service until purchased by the French Line in March 1923. Renamed *Suffren,* she re-entered service in May 1923 as a cabin and third class ship. Employed in the Le Havre-New York trade until she made her last voyage for the French Line on October 10, 1928, from New York to Le Havre. Withdrawn from service and sold for scrap in Genoa, Italy in May 1929.

II VILLE D'ALGER

Builder: Chantiers & Ateliers de St. Nazaire, Penhoet, France
Completed: 1935
Gross tonnage: 10,172
Dimensions: 492′ x 63′ Depth: 35′ Draft: 22′
Engines: Six steam turbines, single-reduction geared
Screws: Twin
Watertight bulkheads: Seven
Decks: Three
Normal speed: 21 knots
Passenger accommodations: 156 first, 422 tourist and 950 fourth class
Registry: France
Maiden voyage: Marseilles-Algiers on September 2, 1935

Engaged in the Marseilles-Algiers-North African ports trade. Requisitioned for troop service during World War II and scuttled by the Germans at Port de Bouc, France in August, 1944. Refloated and reconstructed after the war with the elimination of her former two funnels by a new single one of modern design and a reduction in tonnage to 9,890 gross tons. Re-entered service on her regular route in 1948. Sold to the Typaldos Lines in 1966 and renamed *Poseidon*. Sold for scrap at Spezia, Italy, where breaking up commenced on June 20, 1969.

Sister Ship: *Ville D'Oran*.

VILLE D'ORAN

Builder: Societe Provencale de Constructions Navales, La Ciotat, France
Completed: 1936
Gross tonnage: 10,172
Dimensions: 492' x 63' Depth: 35' Draft: 22'
Engines: Six Parson steam turbines, single-reduction geared
Screws: Twin
Watertight bulkheads: Seven
Decks: Three
Normal speed: 24 knots
Passenger accommodations: 149 first, 334 tourist and 671 fourth class
Registry: France
Maiden voyage: Marseilles-Oran on October 17, 1936

Employed in the Marseilles-Oran-North African ports trade. Requisitioned by the British Ministry of Transport during World War II and managed by the Cunard Line. Decommissioned in June 1946 and reconstructed with her two funnels replaced by a single one of modern design. Re-entered service in 1954. The *Ville D'Oran* was the fastest ship engaged in the Mediterranean. Sold to the Typaldos Lines in June 1965 and renamed *Mount Olympos*. Sold for scrap at Trieste, Italy, she arrived in tow on December 15, 1969. Breaking up commenced on July 1, 1970. Broken up by September of that year.

Sister ship: *Ville D'Alger.*

Greek Line

ARKADIA

Builder: Vickers, Armstrong Ltd., Newcastle-on-Tyne, England
Completed: November 1931
Gross tonnage: 20,648
Dimensions: 590′ x 84′ Depth: 43′ Draft: 26′
Engines: Two steam turbines connected to four electric motors
Screws: Quadruple
Collision bulkhead: One
Watertight bulkheads: Eleven
Decks: Five
Normal speed: 19.50 knots
Passenger accommodations: 55 first and 1,331 tourist class*
Officers and crew: 456
Registry: Greece
Maiden voyage: Bremerhaven-Southampton-Liverpool-Greenock-Quebec-
  Montreal on May 22, 1958

*Originally carried 150 first and 1,150 tourist class.

Built for the Furness-Bermuda Line and christened *Monarch of Bermuda*. Sold to the British Ministry of Transport during the war years and managed by Shaw, Savill & Albion Company from 1949 under the name *New Australia*. Resold to the Greek Line in December 1957 and renamed *Arkadia*. Engaged in the Bremerhaven-Amsterdam-London-Le Havre-Cobh-Quebec-Montreal service but also made calls at such ports as Cherbourg-Southampton-Liverpool-Belfast-Dublin whenever the situation arose to fill her passenger lists. During the winter months she cruised out of Southampton to the Baltic and made some cruises out of New York and Boston with a call at Halifax westbound on the positioning voyage. She made her first and only transatlantic crossing to New York in 1959 when she arrived on January 20th. Refitted at Blohm & Voss, Hamburg in 1960, a ten-foot section was added to her bow thus increasing her overall length; she then worked mainly out of Southampton on cruises to Tenerife-Las Palmas-Madeira-Casablanca-Gibraltar and Lisbon between December and March. Made her last voyage for the Line on August 16, 1966, Bremen-Montreal. When the Canadian immigrant trade had petered-out in the mid-sixties she was laid up in the River Fal, Cornwall, England on November 21, 1966. A most odd looking ship while under Greek Line colours, the *Arkadia* had originally been constructed with three stacks. After her rebuilding she emerged with a single stack and a foremast that also emitted smoke from down below. At a distance it sometimes appeared as if she were on fire. Sold to the Desguaces Maritimos, Spanish shipbreakers on December 9, 1966, and arrived in Valencia on the 19th. Later taken to Castellon, she was broken up between January and March 1967.

LAKONIA

Builder: Nederlandsche Scheepsbouw, Maats, Amsterdam, Netherlands
Completed: 1930
Gross tonnage: 20,314
Dimensions: 609' x 75' Depth: 36' Draft: 27'
Engines: Two 10-cylinder, 2-stroke, single-acting diesel engines
Screws: Twin
Decks: Five
Normal Speed: 17 knots
Passenger accommodations: 693 in a single first-class capacity
Officers and crew: 335
Registry: Greece
Maiden voyage: Southampton-Madeira-Tenerife-Las Palmas-Tangiers-
  Lisbon-Le Havre-Southampton on April 24, 1963

Built for the Nederland Royal Mail Line and christened *Johan van Oldenbarnevelt*. Sold to the Greek Line in early 1963 for $1,200,000 and renamed *Lakonia*. Engaged in the Southampton-Tenerife-Las Palmas-Madeira-Iberian ports-Le Havre cruise service. At 10:50 p.m. on Sunday evening, December 22nd, while on her eighteenth cruise, the *Lakonia* caught fire enroute to Madeira. The fire, which began in the ship's hair dressing salon, spread rapidly through the old ship. Unable to put out the flames, her passengers and crew were ordered to abandon ship. Rescue calls were immediately sent out as she lay about 180 miles north of Madeira. Among the first vessels to arrive was the Argentine ship *Salta*. She was joined by the British *Montcalm*, the American *Rio Grande* and the Pakistani *Mehdi*. Her passengers and crew rescued, she was taken in tow but keeled over and sank 250 miles west of Gibraltar on the 29th. At the Greek inquest it was brought to light that a poor boat drill had been executed on the following day out of Southampton as required by international law, and that an ill-trained crew had been employed to operate the ship. The liner's inexperienced fire fighting team had contributed to the loss of 132 lives of the 1,028 on board. Serious indictments had also been brought against the ship's Captain M. Zarbis. Loss of this newly acquired vessel had been a severe setback to the marketing and goodwill of the Greek Line in the United Kingdom plus the cancellation of 26 cruises which had been scheduled for the following year by the *Lakonia*.

NEPTUNIA

Builder: Nederlandsche Scheepsbouw, Maats, Amsterdam, Netherlands
Completed: February 1920
Gross tonnage: 10,519
Dimensions: 523' x 59' Depth: 38' Draft: 29'
Engines: Two 3-cylinder triple expansion
Screws: Twin
Watertight bulkheads: Ten
Decks: Three
Normal speed: 16 knots
Passenger accommodations: 44 first and 803 tourist class
Registry: Greece
Maiden voyage: Piraeus-Genoa-New York arriving New York on May 18, 1949

Built for the Nederland Royal Mail Line and christened *Johan De Witt*. Sold to the Greek Line on December 15, 1948, and renamed *Neptunia*. Engaged in the Piraeus-Mediterranean ports-New York service she was later reallocated to work out of Bremerhaven-Le Havre-Southampton-Halifax-New York service with an occasional call at Boston eastbound, her first on March 30, 1951. Beginning December 26, 1952, she made a few 9-day New York-Nassau-Havana cruises. Diverted once again to a new route on April 15, 1955, to the Bremerhaven-Southampton-Cherbourg-Quebec-Montreal service. The *Neptunia* had a varied career working many routes for Greek Line including some New York-Vigo-Bordeaux voyages, but her main itinerary alternated between the Bremerhaven-Le Havre-Southampton-Liverpool-Belfast-Dublin-Cobh-Quebec-Montreal run in summer and to Halifax and New York in winter. On occasion Cherbourg was substituted for Le Havre. Originally constructed with two smoke stacks, she had been reconstructed with a single funnel. Made her last voyage for the Line on October 25, 1957, Boston-Cobh-Bremerhaven. Enroute she had the misfortune of striking Daunt's Rock just outside of Cobh, Ireland on November 2, 1957, after having called at Cobh. Beached on Whitegate Roads, seriously damaged below the waterline, she was refloated on December 2 but beached once again. Sold to Simons Scheepss-Loperij for £66,500 and scrapped at Hendrik Ido Ambacht where she arrived in tow at the New Waterway on March 7, 1958.

NEW YORK

Builder: Fairfield Shipbuilding & Engineering Co., Ltd., Glasgow, Scotland
Completed: September 1922
Gross tonnage: 16,991
Dimensions: 579' x 70' Depth: 39' Draft: 29'
Engines: Six steam turbines, double reduction geared
Screws: Twin
Watertight bulkheads: Ten
Decks: Four
Normal Speed: 16 knots
Passenger accommodations: 77 first and 1,208 tourist class*
Registry: Greece
Maiden voyage: Piraeus-Valetta-Naples-Lisbon-New York on May 19, 1939

*Originally carried 179 first, 404 cabin and 1,399 tourist class.

Built for the British Anchor Line and christened *Tuscania*. Sold to Greek Line in April 1939 and renamed *Nea Hellas: New York* in March 1955. Engaged in the Piraeus-Valetta-Naples-Lisbon-Halifax-New York run westbound with a call at Lisbon-Naples and Piraeus eastbound. She made occasional calls at Boston and Ponta Delgada in the Azores homebound.

Requisitioned by the British Ministry of Transport in December 1940, she sailed in convoy on the 18th. Throughout the war she was managed by her former owners, the Anchor Line. On October 12, 1944, she ran aground off King George V dock in Glasgow and swung around broadside facing the incoming and outgoing traffic. Refloated soon after. During the course of the war she acquired the name "Nelly Wallace" as she had come to be known by the British troops. Reconditioned, she returned to regular service and sailed from Istanbul-Piraeus-Naples-Genoa-Lisbon-New York where she arrived on August 8, 1947. Eight years later she was reallocated to the Bremerhaven-Le Havre-Cherbourg-London-Liverpool-Belfast-Dublin-Cobh-New York route on March 24, 1955. Though at times she called at all these ports it later was contingent upon the passenger traffic and certain ports supplanted others. During winter she made a westbound call at Halifax and occasionally made some high season Quebec-Montreal voyages. She often included an eastbound call from Boston. Reverted back to the Mediterranean route on September 17, 1959. On October 13 she made a round-trip to Canada calling at Quebec-Halifax-Naples-Piraeus-Odessa-Istanbul-Piraeus — her last transatlantic trip — and was placed in a cruise service out of Southampton to Madeira and the Canary Islands. Withdrawn from service on November 14, 1960, and sold to Japanese shipbreakers for £312,000 sterling. She left Piraeus for Onomichi, Japan on August 19, 1961, arriving at the breaker's yards in October. She was broken up by December of that year.

OLYMPIA

Builder: Alexander Stephen & Sons, Ltd., Glasgow, Scotland
Completed: October 1953
Gross tonnage: 17,434
Dimensions: 611' x 79' Depth: 47'
Engines: Four steam turbines, double-reduction geared
Screws: Twin
Collision bulkhead: One
Watertight bulkheads: Ten
Decks: Five
Normal speed: 21 knots
Passenger accommodations: 1,037 in a single class*
Officers and crew: 350
Registry: Greece
Maiden voyage: Glasgow-Belfast-Liverpool-Southampton-Cherbourg-Cobh-Halifax-New York on October 15, 1953

*Originally carried: 197 first and 1,348 tourist class (650 when cruising)

Engaged in the Bremerhaven-Southampton-Cherbourg-Cobh-New York service. The *Olympia* had no sooner entered service when she went aground on December 14th at Southampton due to the fouling of a rudder cable. Repairs took 9 days before she returned to service. The *Olympia* began some initial cruising in January 1954, and was reverted to the Mediterranean run from Piraeus-Messina-Naples-Lisbon-Ponta Delgada-New York on March 26, 1955. She also made occasional calls at Halifax westbound and Boston eastbound. Around 1959 the *Olympia* began her voyages at Haifa, Israel and included a call at Limassol, Cyprus before calling at Piraeus outbound. She also called at Genoa and Valetta, Malta from time to time. Built at a cost of $15,000,000, she was refitted in

Genoa in November 1961 at a cost of $2,000,000. Many improvements were made and full air-conditioning installed and anti-rolling tanks. She re-entered service on January 29, 1962. Placed in a weekly cruise service out of New York to Bermuda and Nassau and 3-day cruises to "nowhere" in the late sixties when the transatlantic service had been driven to a low point by the airlines, the *Olympia*, like many other lines were operating marginally before the great boom in cruising came the following decade. Refitted once again in Genoa in 1970 to fit the new trend, her two classes were combined into one. A lido section was built at her stern and all cabins fitted with private facilities. The $4,000,000 facelift seemed to insure a new lease on life but the oil crises deterred the prospects. Following the refit, which took five and a half months, she re-entered the cruise service out of New York. After making her annual transatlantic voyage on March 11, 1974, New York-Naples-Messina-Piraeus. The *Olympia* resumed a most precarious future cruising out of New York, the company financially in dire straits. Reverting to a cruise service out of Piraeus on April 5, 1974, to Istanbul-Izmir-Haifa-Limassol-Rhodes until November, when she was laid up at Perama, Greece due to the skyrocketing fuel costs which had jumped from $35 a long ton to as much as $120. After the closing down of the Greek Line in January 1975, she was finally put up for sale in September 1977, when all hopes for re-entry into service had faded. Taken over by the Industrial Bank of Greece. Sold to the Finnish-owned Commodore Cruise Lines in 1982 for $1,200,000 and renamed *Caribe: Caribe I* in 1982. Presently in their service.

Note: The *Olympia* was the largest ship ever launched without a name. For a number of years disputes between her Greek owners and the several incumbent Greek governments over certain hiring policies, registry and the naming of the ship. Registered in Liberia, she finally hoisted the Greek flag on September 27, 1968. Prior to her official maiden voyage she made a promotional cruise to Dublin, Ireland.

QUEEN ANNA MARIA

Builder: Fairfield Shipbuilding & Engineering Co., Ltd., Glasgow, Scotland
Completed: March 1956
Gross tonnage: 21,716
Dimensions: 640' x 82' Depth: 48' Draft: 29'
Engines: Six steam turbines, double reduction geared
Screws: Twin
Collision bulkhead: One
Watertight bulkheads: Ten
Decks: Five
Normal speed: 21 knots
Passenger accommodations: 141 first and 1,165 tourist class
Officers and crew: 464
Registry: Greece
Maiden voyage: Genoa-Messina-Naples-Lisbon-Halifax on March 24, 1965

Built for the British Canadian-Pacific Line and christened *Empress of Britain.* Sold to the Greek Line in February 1964 for $9,000,000 and refitted for an additional $6,000,000 between November and March 1965 in Genoa. Renamed *Queen Anna Maria,* she was Greek Line's flagship. Engaged in the Piraeus-Messina-Naples-New York service with an occasional call at Halifax. Eastbound her itinerary often included a call at Boston with calls at Ponta Delgada in the Azores-Lisbon-Valetta-Malta-Piraeus-Limmasol, Cyprus and Haifa eastbound. As the transatlantic trade dwindled she was often cruising out of New York to Bermuda and Nassau on a weekly basis, often calling at Boston, Baltimore and Norfolk. In addition weekend cruises to "nowhere" for three days were often incorporated into her schedule. This new form of marketing cruises familiarized the general public many who hitherto had never been on a cruise. With fares as low as $93 including port taxes, impetus was given to the transition to cruise ships for many of the older liners. Equipped with motion stabilizers and fully air-conditioned, she was the last liner to sail under the Greek Line house-flag. Victimized by the severe oil crisis in the early seventies, she made her last eastbound crossing on November 12, 1974, New York-Boston-Ponta Delgada-Lisbon-Valetta-Piraeus-Haifa. On the night of December 11, 1974, she slipped out of New York without passengers to avoid liens on the vessel by creditors. Laid up at Piraeus on January 22, 1975, she was sold to the Israeli-owned Carnival Cruises for $3,200,000 in December 1975.

Holland-America Line

IV MAASDAM

Builder: N. V., Wilton, Fijenoord, Schidam, Netherlands
Completed: July 1952
Gross tonnage: 15,024
Dimensions: 503' x 69' Depth: 42' Draft: 29'
Engines: Two steam turbines, double-reduction geared
Screws: Single
Watertight bulkheads: Eight
Decks: Four
Normal speed: 16.50 knots
Passenger accommodations: 40 first and 890 tourist
Registry: Holland
Maiden voyage: Rotterdam-New York on August 11, 1952

Originally laid down as the *Diemerdyk,* a passenger-cargo freighter, but changed to *Maasdam* before building. Since the passenger traffic on the North Atlantic was generating high revenues in the early fifties, she was built as a passenger liner. Engaged in the Rotterdam-Le Havre-Southampton-Cobh (Galway and Cobh alternately)-New York run with a call at Halifax on occasion. Later diverted in April 1963 to work out of Bremerhaven for the immigrant trade making Rotterdam her first port of call westbound. During the off season she was employed in a cruise service from New York to Bermuda and the Dutch West Indies as well as other Caribbean ports of call. Following the Second World War many class changes came about and the *Maasdam* like many other liners were fitted with few first class accommodations and for the most part became tourist orientated liners. Painted in a soft dove-grey hull the ship had some shortcomings. Inferiorly designed because of her original intention to be built as a freighter, the *Maasdam's* contracted length and high superstructure caused the ship to pitch at sea. In 1958-59 she made two trips to Montreal and thereafter on occasion. While maneuvering in Bremerhaven on February 15, 1963, she struck a sunken vessel. Her 500 passengers were transferred to the British ship *Harborough* and the Russian *Kholmogory* and the ship taken to drydock. Her hull severely damaged, she did not return to service until April 16th. On October 18, 1965, her voyage out of Bremerhaven was routed through the Suez Canal after calling at Southampton and on to Fremantle, Melbourne, Sydney and Wellington. She made her first call at Boston on May 5, 1961, calling there on occasion eastbound thereafter. In 1966 she was placed in the St. Lawrence trade to Quebec and Montreal in place of New York. Made her last voyage for the Holland-America Line on September 20, 1968, Montreal-Halifax-Rotterdam. Sold to Polish Ocean Lines in December 1968 and renamed *Stefan Batory*. Resold in 1988 to Greek owners and rebuilt as a hotel ship in Shanghai.

Sister ship: *Ryndam*.

I NIEUW AMSTERDAM

Builder: Harland & Wolff, Ltd., Belfast, Ireland
Completed: February 1906
Gross tonnage: 17,149
Dimensions: 616' x 69' Depth: 47' Draft: 35'
Engines: Two 4-cylinder, quadruple expansion
Screws: Twin
Watertight bulkheads: Ten
Decks: Four
Passenger accommodations: 417 first, 391 second and 860 tourist class*
Registry: Holland
Maiden voyage: Rotterdam-New York on April 7, 1906

*Originally carried: 756 first, 684 second, 2,300 steerage

Engaged in the Rotterdam-New York service maintaining regular service throughout World War I. She was the largest Dutch liner built to date when she entered service. Laid up at New York between July 13–November 23, 1917, when she made an eastbound voyage — one of two that year. The following year she was the only liner operated by the Holland-America Line on the Atlantic run. Made her first call at Halifax on December 21, 1923, westbound and incorporated this port on her itinerary westbound on most voyages. In June 1926 she became a three-class ship (first, second, tourist-cabin, and third class). By 1927 her regular route was Rotterdam-Southampton-Cherbourg-New York in both directions. Made her last voyage for the Line on March 11, 1932, Rotterdam-Boulogne-Southampton-New York. Sold to Japanese shipbreakers at Osaka in April 1932.

Note: Most Holland-America Line liners called at Brest and Falmouth until 1919 when changed to Boulogne and Plymouth. By 1923 it was Boulogne and Southampton.

II NIEUW AMSTERDAM

Builder: Rotterdamsche Droogdok Mid. Co., Rotterdam, Netherlands
Completed: May 1938
Gross tonnage: 36,982
Dimensions: 759' x 88' Depth: 55' Draft: 32'
Engines: Eight steam turbines, single-reduction geared
Screws: Twin
Collision bulkhead: One
Watertight bulkheads: Ten
Decks: Seven
Normal speed: 21.50 knots
Passenger accommodations: 302 first and 972 tourist class*
Registry: Holland
Maiden voyage: Rotterdam-Boulogne-Southampton-New York on May 10, 1938

*Originally carried: 568 cabin, 452 tourist and 209 third class. Her new figures were flexible according to demand. Either 691 first and 583 tourist or 302 first and 972 tourist class.

Laid down as the *Prinsendam* but changed to *Nieuw Amsterdam* before major construction began. Engaged in the Rotterdam-Southampton-Cobh-New York service. She was sent pleasure cruising in 1938 out of New York to the Dutch West Indies and other Caribbean ports of call. Laid up in 1939 at the outbreak of the Second World War and taken over by the British Ministry of Transport for troop work. After drydocking at Hoboken, New Jersey, she was refitted at Halifax in September 1940 with accommodations for 8,000 troops and placed under Cunard Line management. She was armed with 36 guns. Returned to Rotterdam on April 10, 1946, after having steamed 530,452 miles and carrying some 378,361 war personnel. Following her total 44 voyages during the war she was reconditioned over a period of eighteen months. She took part in the evacuation of Dutch Nationals fleeing Java in 1945. Re-entered service on October 29, 1947, from Rotterdam to New York. At the time of her construction she was the largest twin-screw ship and the largest in the Dutch merchant marine. She had a promenade deck that stretched 608 feet in length. Built at an estimated cost of £5,000,000 sterling, her postwar refit had cost twelve million Dutch Guilders. Fondly known as the "Darling of the Dutch," she was one of the last truly luxury liners on the North Atlantic; with her chic Art Deco interiors she was a hotel afloat. A most handsome hull, she did not share the almost clumsy look that the two Queens evoked with their enormous size. A cabin class ship in 1956-57 her accommodations were upgraded and full air-conditioning installed throughout the ship. Her traditional black hull was repainted in a soft grey tone for cruising. Converted to a two-class ship between October 1961-early 1962 with the elimination of cabin class, she re-entered service on January 18, 1962. That summer season the lovely liner suffered a serious mechanical breakdown which precluded her trans-atlantic schedule for a time. Following the installation of new boilers which had caused the trouble she was back in service. In the mid-fifties a call at Le Havre had been incorporated into her itinerary and an occasional call at Halifax westbound later on. Built at a time when war was not foreseen, the *Nieuw Amsterdam* was one of the last liners whose design truly mirrored the comfort of its passengers. For example, to lessen noise during mealtime her kitchens were built one deck below and waiters would use an escalator to and from. The *Nieuw Amsterdam* made her last transatlantic crossing from Rotterdam to Port Everglades via Le Havre-Southampton-Cobh, and New York on November 8, 1971, and was based at this port for extensive cruising to the Caribbean and South American ports. Destined to become a statistic because of the oil crisis, she made her last voyage for the Holland-America Line on December 7, 1973, Port Everglades-Curacao-La Guaira-Grenada-Guadeloupe-St. Thomas, returning to Port Everglades, on the 17th. Laid up at Port Everglades she was finally sold to the Nan Feng Steel Company in Taiwan. Arrived at Kaoshiung on February 26. Breaking up commenced on March 5, 1974.

III NIEUW AMSTERDAM

Builder: Chantiers de L'Atlantique, St. Nazaire, France
Completed: 1983
Gross tonnage: 33,930
Dimensions: 702' x 89' Depth: 50' Draft: 25'
Engines: Two 7-cylinder single acting Sulzer 2-stroke diesels with two
  controllable pitch propellers plus a bow thruster forward with a
  controllable propeller
Screws: Twin
Decks: Nine
Normal speed: 21 knots
Passenger accommodations: 1,214 in a single class
Officers and crew: 559
Registry: Netherlands Antilles
Maiden voyage: July 9, 1983, Le Havre-New York arriving on the 18th

Built expressly for Holland-America Cruise Line. The *Nieuw Amsterdam* unlike most of her predecessors was built in France. And unlike her forerunners lacks the gracious lines in marine architecture. Through a pair of binoculars one might think they are gazing at a containership from afar or her flush back stern that of a Naval ship. Inwardly, however, the ship offers a warm atmosphere of old world luxury with her wood panelings of teak, rosewood and other polished veneers. Her 600 cabins can accommodate as many as 1,374 — 413 outside, 194 inside with 20 deluxe cabins with king-size beds and sofa. Built at an astronomical cost of $150,000,000, the company has endeavored to incorporate those more costly amenities of the bygone era with larger than normal-sized cabins. Her main dining room seats 722 persons, and the Lido restaurant 335. Her theatre seats 230 and the main lounge 423. The deluxe cabins have bathtubs but the regular cabin facilities are on the small size. There are two outdoor swimming pools and a heated whirlpool. There is a very nice exercise and sports spa. There are seven elevators situated throughout the ship, a sauna, beauty and barber shops plus a number of boutiques. Shipboard activities extend through to the late hours to keep passengers busy. Technology for keeping in touch with the outside world is the most contemporary. There are several bars and a casino. Engaged in a cruise service out of Vancouver-Ketchikan-Juneau-Sitka— on weekly cruises to Juneau and 4-day cruises to Alaska until late September when she operates on longer 17- and 21-day cruises from West Coast ports to Tampa via the Panama Canal. From mid-October until mid-December she works out of Tampa on weekly cruises to the Caribbean calling at Playa del Carmen-Cozumel-Montego Bay-Grand Cayman. Minimum fares on the Caribbean cruises begin at $1,049. Fully air-conditioned and equipped with motion stabilizers.

Sister ship: *Noordam.*

Note: Her original maiden voyage, which was set for June 26, 1983, had to be cancelled due to mechanical problems.

I NOORDAM

Builder: Harland & Wolff, Ltd., Belfast, Ireland
Completed: March 1902
Gross tonnage: 12,528
Dimensions: 565' x 62' Depth: 45' Draft: 32'
Engines: Two 3-cylinder, triple expansion
Screws: Twin
Watertight bulkheads: Ten
Decks: Four
Normal speed: 15 knots
Passenger accommodations: 470 first, 502 second and 1,983 third
Registry: Holland
Maiden voyage: Rotterdam-New York on May 1, 1902

Engaged in the Rotterdam-New York service year-round. The *Noordam* maintained sailings during World War I but made only two crossings in 1917. Laid up after being damaged twice by mines in the North Sea in November 1914 and in August 1917. Returned to normal service in March 1919, sailing from Rotterdam to Brest, Falmouth and then on to New York. Her promenade deck was 193 feet long and her bulkheads were constructed of cement. She was chartered to the Swedish-American Line in March, 1923. The *Noordam* had been carrying less than 20 percent of her regular complement at the time. The newly-formed Swedish-American Line renamed the ship *Kungsholm* and returned the ship to Holland-America Line in December 1924. Acquiring her original name, she re-entered the Rotterdam-Boulogne-Southampton-New York route with a call at Plymouth homeward. The following year she was mostly inactive, making only two trips in December. Commenced her last voyage for the Line on May 4, 1927, New York-Cherbourg-Southampton-Rotterdam. Sold to F. Rijsdijk's Ind. Onderne Mingen at Hendrik Ido Ambacht in May 1927 and scrapped in the Netherlands in 1928.

Sister ships: *Potsdam* and *Rijndam*.

II NOORDAM

Builder: Machinefabriek en Scheepswerf van P. Smit Jr., Rotterdam, Netherlands
Completed: September 1938
Gross tonnage: 10,726
Dimensions: 502' x 64' Depth: 40' Draft: 31'
Engines: Two 12-cylinder, 2-stroke, single-acting diesels
Screws: Twin
Watertight bulkheads: Eight
Decks: Three
Normal speed: 17 knots
Passenger accommodations: 168 first-class passengers (she is classified as a cargo-passenger liner)
Registry: Holland
Maiden voyage: Rotterdam-New York on September 28, 1938

Engaged in the Rotterdam-New York run until transferred to the Rotterdam-Java-Dutch East Indies trade on August 1, 1940, until October 19. This route had been abandoned by the Holland-America Line during the shipping slump of 1931 until re-opened during the Second World War. Fitted-out as a transport in early 1942, she did not resume regular service until July 1946, when she returned to the Rotterdam-Le Havre-Southampton-Cobh-New York service with an occasional call at Newport News, Virginia on occasion eastbound. Passage on the understated *Noordam* which was considered a cargo-passenger liner was anything but modest. Contrary to what most people think, fares on freighters and cargo-passenger liners are usually higher than on regular passenger liners. The *Noordam's* fares during the high season of 1960 began at $308...Such fares were available in 1970 on many Atlantic liners in tourist class. Though labeled first class there was only one class on such vessels and higher costs to serve such passengers were often reflected in the fares. Made her last voyage for the Holland-America Line on August 27, 1963, from New York to Rotterdam. Sold to the Panamanian Cielomar, a subsidiary of the Italian Costa Line, and renamed *Oceanien*. Chartered to the French Messageries Maritimes for a time. Sold for scrap to Cantieri Navali del Golfo at La Spezia, Italy and arrived there on February 14, 1967.

Sister ship: *Zaandam.*

III NOORDAM

Builder: Chantiers de L'Atlantique, St. Nazaire, France
Completed: 1984
Gross tonnage: 33,930
Dimensions: 702′ x 89′ Depth: 59′ Draft: 24′
Engines: Two 7-cylinder, single acting Sulzer diesels with controllable pitch propellers plus a bow thruster athwartship forward with controllable pitch propeller
Screws: Twin
Decks: Seven
Normal speed: 21 knots
Passenger accommodations: 1,210 in a single class
Officers and crew: 559
Registry: Netherlands Antilles
Maiden voyage: Le Havre-New York on April 8, 1984

Built for Holland-America Line Cruises at a cost of $160,000,000, it seems like the *Noordam* should have emerged from the shipyard as an "Obo" as they say in marine jargon. That is, she has all the appearances of being a bulk carrier or a tanker from afar. When the ship came into service she had some vibration problems and one could watch an ashtray dance across the table. Her insulation between cabins was also a problem with noise. These were later corrected by a change of propellers to resolve the vibration and more insulation between walls. The company should have spent a few hundred thousand more in giving her flat stern a curvature so as to appear like an ocean liner. Holland-America has a "no tipping" policy. If you ask me, tipping is as Victorian as stiff collars or hoop rings in ladies' fashion dresses. Of course it is a step in the right direction since the cruise line can afford to pay their help quite well if they please instead of putting the touch on passengers constantly. For that matter, most waiters I've come across don't deserve to get paid at all until they start fighting with the kitchen to serve their passengers a meal that is prepared properly and served properly. The *Noordam* was built with a bulbous bow which reduces dragging at sea and she is fully air-conditioned and stabilized. Public rooms consist of the Amsterdam Dining Room which accommodates 722 persons, and the Lido Restaurant which seats 335. A theatre seats 230. There are 20 suites amongst her 411 outside cabins and 194 situated inside. Telephone, multi-channel music systems and closed circuit television are fitted into all cabins. There are 7 elevators on this long liner to help passengers get about more easily. Two outdoor swimming pools, gymnasium, dual saunas, masseuse, and whirlpools are available for the agile and the torpid traveller. A nice feature about this ship is that she has both 110 and 220 current, and for those who do not wish to do their own tidying there is laundry and dry cleaning available like most new ships. Between December and mid-May the *Noordam* sails on 7-day cruises from Fort Lauderdale to San Juan-St. Maarten-St. Thomas-Nassau and return with minimum fares beginning at $1,355. Between the end of May until late September she runs from Vancouver-Ketchikan-Juneau on 3-night cruises, and 4-night cruises from Juneau-Glacier Bay-Sitka-Vancouver. The *Noordam* and her sister ship were not built in the traditional manner of keel laying but by the welding of 350 separate steel sections which varied from her lower stern that measured 680 tons on down to a small section of deck which measured 12 tons. Computers were used to guide plasma cutters in the cutting of the steel plates used in the sections and assembled in drydock.

Sister ship: *Nieuw Amsterdam.*

POTSDAM

Builder: Blohm & Voss, Hamburg, Germany
Completed: May 1900
Gross tonnage: 12,522
Dimensions: 571' x 62' Depth: 38' Draft: 32'
Engines: Two 3-cylinder, triple expansion
Screws: Twin
Watertight bulkheads: Ten
Decks: Four
Normal speed: 15 knots
Passenger accommodations: 234 first, 481 second and 2,107 third class
Officers and crew: 248
Registry: Holland
Maiden voyage: Rotterdam-Amsterdam-New York on May 17, 1900

Engaged in the Rotterdam-Amsterdam-New York service, the call at Amsterdam was dropped in 1901. The *Potsdam's* single funnel was heightened considerably because of poor exhaust performance due to her boilers which did not steam very well. This earned her the nickname of "Funneldam." The work performed in July 1908, she was withdrawn from service until March of 1909. Her promenade deck was 195 feet in length. Made her last voyage for the Holland-America Line on May 11, 1915, New York-Rotterdam. Sold to the Swedish-American Line for a high price in 1915 and renamed *Stockholm*. Resold to the Norwegian Odd Company A/S and converted to a whale factory ship in 1928 and renamed *Solgimt*. Captured by the German raider *Pinguin* in the Antarctic on January 14, 1941, and taken to Bordeaux, France. Scuttled by the Germans at Cherbourg, France to block entrance into the harbour in June 1944 after she had been used by the Nazis as a tanker. Unable to refloat her at the end of the war she was blown up on August 30, 1946.

Sister ships: *Noordam* and *Rijndam*.

RIJNDAM

Builder: Harland & Wolff Ltd., Belfast, Ireland
Completed: October 1901
Gross tonnage: 12,535
Dimensions: 565′ x 62′ Depth: 45′ Draft: 32′
Engines: Two 3-cylinder, triple expansion
Screws: Twin
Watertight bulkheads: Ten
Decks: Four
Normal speed: 15 knots
Passenger accommodations: 483 first, 695 second and 2,223 third class
Registry: Holland
Maiden voyage: Rotterdam-New York on October 10, 1901

Engaged in the Rotterdam-New York service. In the spring of 1916 she was damaged by a mine in the North Sea where three Dutch seamen were killed at the time of impact. Laid up at New York on June 20, 1917 after only three voyages. Chartered by the United States as a transport on May 1, 1918, after being tied up at New York harbour for nearly a year. Returned to the Holland-America Line in October 1919, she re-entered service in August 1920 after being reconditioned. Converted to a cabin and third class ship in May 1925, she was later altered to a cabin, tourist cabin and third class ship in 1926. In the fall of 1925 she made a seven-month world cruise with hundreds of students. Inaugurated a call at Halifax westbound on May 22, 1925, she often included this port heading outward. In 1925 her itinerary had become Rotterdam-Boulogne-Southampton-New York with a call at Plymouth and Boulogne homeward. Her route changed somewhat in 1927 when she worked the Rotterdam-Southampton-Cherbourg-New York run in both directions. Made her last voyage for the Line on May 6, 1929, New York-Plymouth-Cherbourg-Rotterdam. Sold to Frank Rijsdijk at Henrik Ido Ambacht, Netherlands in April 1929 for scrap.

Sister ships: *I Noordam* and *Potsdam.*

IV ROTTERDAM

Builder: Harland & Wolff Ltd., Belfast, Ireland
Completed: June 1908
Gross tonnage: 24,149
Dimensions: 668' x 77' Depth: 47' Draft: 33'
Engines: Two 4-cylinder, quadruple expansion
Screws: Twin
Watertight bulkheads: Twelve
Decks: Five
Normal speed: 17 knots
Passenger accommodations: 505 first, 456 second, 650 tourist cabin and 87 third class
Registry: Holland
Maiden voyage: Rotterdam-New York on June 13, 1908

Employed in the Rotterdam-Channel ports-New York service, the *Rotterdam* made several cruises as well. Added a call at Plymouth in 1909 when the Netherlands Government awarded a mail contract to the Line. On February 2, 1914, she made a Mediterranean cruise out of New York. Laid up between March 1916 and February 1919, when she re-entered service on her regular schedule out of New York. The *Rotterdam* made a Mediterranean cruise each year between 1923-25. She began to make occasional westbound calls at Halifax beginning April 23, 1924, when she made her first. Converted to oil-firing in March 1925 and was settled in the Rotterdam-Boulogne-Southampton-New York run with a call at Plymouth eastbound in place of Southampton. In June 1926 she was converted to a first, second, tourist cabin and third class ship and rerouted on the Rotterdam-Southampton-Cherbourg-New York in either direction in 1927. Called at Copenhagen first time on June 5, 1933. On September 30, 1935, the *Rotterdam* ran aground on Morant Cays 45 miles southeast of Jamaica during a severe gale while on a cruise with 424 persons aboard. Passengers were taken off the following day by a British steamer and landed where they could make new passage arrangements. The *Rotterdam* was one of the first large Atlantic liners along with the smaller *Nieuw Amsterdam* to be built with a glassed-in promenade deck and was one of the finest luxury liners of her day in terms of both revenues and appearance. She was an exquisite example of an Edwardian class liner and cruise ship with a moderate speed and plush interiors. Also, she was one of the first vessels to be installed with elevators of which the *Rotterdam* had three. Made her last voyage for the Holland-America Line on May 30, 1939, from New York to Rotterdam. Sold for scrap to Frank Rijsdijk at Hendrik Ido Ambacht in the Netherlands in January 1940 and broken up by March.

Note: On more than one occasion heavy immigrant traffic necessitated the *Rotterdam* to carry nearly 4,000 passengers during the early part of her career when she was a three-class ship.

V ROTTERDAM

Builder: Rotterdamsche Droogdok Maats, Rotterdam, Netherlands
Completed: August 1959
Gross tonnage: 38,644
Dimensions: 748' x 92' Depth: 55' Draft: 30'
Engines: Six 35 Parson steam turbines, double-reduction geared
Screws: Twin
Watertight bulkheads: Thirteen
Decks: Nine
Normal speed: 21.50 knots
Passenger accommodations: 1,114 in a single class*
Officers and crew: 560 (formerly 762)
Registry: Holland
Maiden voyage: Rotterdam-Le Havre-Southampton-Cobh-New York on
September 3, 1959

*Originally carried 647 first, 809 tourist and 730 when cruising.

Engaged in the Rotterdam-Le Havre-Southampton-Cobh-New York service and cruising. She was Holland-America Line's flagship when built. In early 1966 the *Rotterdam* began a series of cruises out of the port of New York to the Pacific, Mediterranean and the West Indies. She also was scheduled for a world cruise nearly every year. On January 22, 1970, she left New York on an 85-day world cruise calling at 22 ports and 16 countries. Equipped with motion stabilizers and fully air-conditioned. Built at a cost of £13,000,000, her theatre has a seating capacity of 607 persons and features fifteen public lounges. She has ten deluxe staterooms. Employed on the North Atlantic run between April and October and cruising during the off season. Her first cruising service had begun in December 1959 when she cruised around the South American continent. She was to become well-known amongst the long-term cruise clients over the years. In 1968 she cruised on a short circuit to Bermuda, Nassau, the Bahamas, and West Indies, but by September 1971, when the Holland America Line had abandoned the North Atlantic trade, the ideal *Rotterdam* was ready for her new career in cruising. With a log book full of successful cruises to her credit, in January 1983 she began the Holland-America Line's Silver Jubilee world cruise, the Line's 25th such cruise. Presently engaged in a weekly cruise service out of Port Everglades to the Caribbean between April-May, September-December, and to Alaska out of Vancouver between June-September. A world cruise every January out of New York and some Transcanal voyages from Los Angeles to Port Everglades make up her varied schedule. Employment varies significantly from season to season. Presently in service. Company now markets its ships under the "Holland-America Cruises" logo.

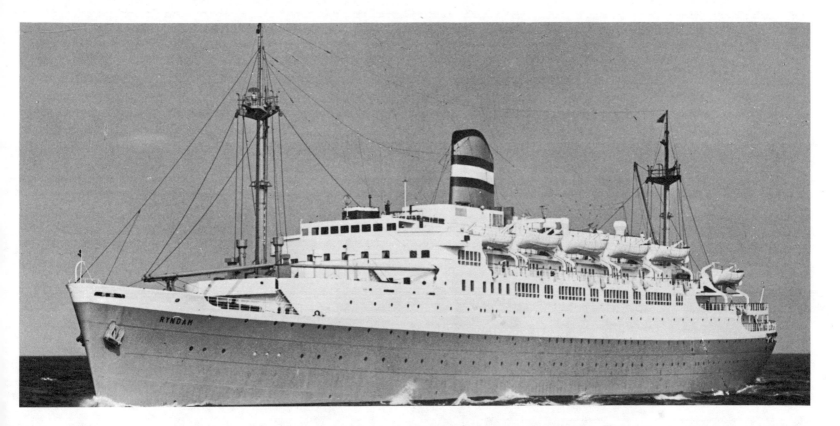

RYNDAM

Builder: Dok-en-Werf Mij. N. V. Wilton, Fijenoord, Schiedam, Netherlands
Completed: July 1951
Gross tonnage: 15,051
Dimensions: 502' x 67' Depth: 42' Draft: 29'
Engines: Two steam turbines, double-reduction geared
Screws: Single
Watertight bulkheads: Eight
Decks: Four
Normal speed: 16.50 knots
Passenger accommodations: 42 first and 888 tourist class
Officers and crew: 297
Registry: Holland
Maiden voyage: Rotterdam-Le Havre-Southampton-New York on July 16, 1951

Originally laid down as the *Dinteldyk*, a freighter, plans were redrawn while still on the stocks for a passenger ship. Christened *Ryndam,* she was employed in the Rotterdam-Le Havre-Southampton-New York service with a westbound call at Halifax, sometimes calling at this port in either direction. On occasion she called at Cobh and Galway, Ireland. In March 1960 she was working the Rotterdam-Channel ports-Montreal-Quebec trade. Fully air-conditioned during the off-seasonal months she was employed in a cruise service from New York to Bermuda and the Caribbean. She was to later become interchangeable working the Rotterdam-Southampton-via Suez Canal-Freemantle-Melbourne-Sydney-Wellington run from November 6, 1964, until February 7, 1966, when she made her last voyage to the South Pacific. Transferred to the Rotterdam-Quebec-Montreal run once again under Holland-America Line's subsidiary company the Europe-Canada Line with transfer to German registry for the ship to take advantage of lower wages paid to German crews. Reverted back to Dutch flag in October 1967. The *Ryndam* had an unusual smoke-stack constructed with a thin profile and narrow lipped at the top to help disperse soot properly without landing on her aft decks. Few of her cabins had private lavatories but one redeeming feature of her time period were her economical tourist class fares of about $200 between New York and Rotterdam. With the North Atlantic trade at a lull the *Ryndam* was chartered out for student summertime cruises at low fares in May 1968 and was renamed *Waterman*. She acquired her original name on October 10, 1968. Re-chartered to the Chapman College of Orange, California, in October 1969 and returned to the line in May 1970. Following another two trips under charter to the Foreign Study League of Salt Lake City, Utah, from Boston to Southampton via Cherbourg, on June 1 and 20, 1970, she was laid up at Rotterdam in February 1971, and later at Schiedam, Holland. Sold to the Greek Epirotiki Lines on August 18, 1972, for $1,500,000 and renamed *Atlas*. Resold to Pride Cruise Lines (American) in 1988 and renamed *Pride of Mississippi*; *Pride of Galveston* in 1991 under Bahamian Registry for conversion to a hotel and casino.

Sister ship: *Maasdam.*

I STATENDAM

Builder: Harland & Wolff, Ltd., Belfast, Ireland
Completed: August 1898
Gross tonnage: 10,491
Dimensions: 530' x 60' Depth: 43'
Engines: Two 3-cylinder, triple expansion
Screws: Twin
Watertight bulkheads: Nine
Decks: Three
Normal speed: 14.50 knots
Passenger accommodations: 204 first, 431 second and 2,015 third class
Registry: Holland
Maiden voyage: Rotterdam-Amsterdam-New York, arriving at New York on October 10, 1898

Engaged in the Rotterdam-Amsterdam-New York run until 1901 when the call at Amsterdam was dropped. The *Statendam* had a promenade deck 190 feet in length and was one of the Holland-America Lines' largest immigrant ships built to date. Inactive between March-November 1909. Experimenting with cruises, she made Holland-America Lines' second cruise to the Holy Land. She made her last voyage for the Line on February 8, 1910, New York-Rotterdam. Sold to the British Allan Line on March 23, 1911, and renamed *Scotian*. In 1914 she was trooping for the Canadian Army. Released on October 1, 1915, she was then managed by the Canadian-Pacific Line from 1916 until 1919 when she was purchased by them. Chartered to the Canadian Government for a time beginning mid-June 1921 and renamed *Marglen* in 1922. Sold for scrap to C. Barterello shipbreakers at Genoa, Italy on December 30, 1926 and broken up.

III STATENDAM

Builder: Harland & Wolff Ltd., Belfast, Ireland
Completed: April 1929
Gross tonnage: 28,291
Dimensions: 698′ x 81′ Depth: 54′ Draft: 33′
Engines: Six steam turbines, single-reduction geared
Screws: Twin
Collision bulkhead: One
Watertight bulkheads: Ten
Decks: Six
Normal speed: 19 knots
Passenger accommodations: 453 first, 793 tourist and 418 third class*
Officers and crew: 600
Registry: Holland
Maiden voyage: Rotterdam-Boulogne-Southampton-New York on April 11, 1929

*Originally carried: 510 first, 344 second, 374 tourist, and 426 third class.

Launched on September 11, 1924, construction was suspended due to newly-enacted American immigration laws restricting incoming immigrants. The hull was later towed to Rotterdam on April 13, 1927, where she was completed by the Wilton Slipway & Engineering Company. Built to replace the second ship with this name which had been taken over by the British during the First World War and converted to a transport under the name of *Justicia*. Engaged in the Rotterdam-Cherbourg-Southampton-Plymouth-New York run. A very economical and popular ship, she was known as the "Queen of the Spotless Fleet." The *Statendam's* aft funnel was a dummy added to give the liner a sleeker symmetry. In 1931 she became a two-class ship. Made her last voyage for the Holland-America Line on November 4, 1939, New York-Boston-Plymouth-Boulogne-Rotterdam and subsequently laid up at Wilhelminakade, Rotterdam. Destroyed by crossfire from both sides of the river while the Dutch resistance fought the Nazi invaders on May 11, 1940. The *Statendam* was ablaze for five days, becoming a total loss. The burned-out hulk was later sold to Frank Rijsdijk at Hendrik Ido Ambacht in August of that year for scrap.

IV STATENDAM

Builder: Dok-en-Werf Mij Wilton Fijenoord N.V. Schiedam, Netherlands
Completed: February 1957
Gross tonnage: 24,413
Dimensions: 640′ x 79′ Depth: 52′ Draft: 26′
Engines: Four Pamatrada steam turbines
Screws: Twin
Collision bulkhead: One
Watertight bulkheads: Ten
Decks: Five
Normal speed: 19 knots
Passenger accommodations: 740 in a single class*
Officers and crew: 437
Registry: Holland (Netherlands Antilles)
Maiden voyage: Rotterdam-Le Havre-Southampton-New York on February 6, 1957

*Originally carried: 91 first, 913 tourist class, 650 in a single class when cruising.

Employed in the Rotterdam-Le Havre-Southampton-New York service year-round. A moderately appointed liner in the context of her times, she was designed with fine paneling in bleached ash and rosewood in several of her public rooms. Fully air-conditioned and equipped with motion stabilizers. The *Statendam* was forced to dock at New York harbour upon her maiden voyage arrival without the assistance of tugs owing to a strike. Crewmen from the ship lowered in life-boats alongside aided in the docking. She was designed with a high flared bow to prevent the sea from coming on the fore-deck during stormy weather. She made a 110-day world cruise on January 7, 1958. Made a first call at Halifax on January 25, 1966, westbound and in the same year was converted to a permanent cruise ship due to a lack of trade on the North Atlantic run. Refitted by the Wilton, Fijenoord, shipyards at a cost of over $5,000,000 between October 1971 and March 3, 1972. The *Statendam* emerged with an additional 87 cabins and all her public rooms were redecorated in a more contemporary fashion to fit the new trends of the cruise market. The following year she and the remainder of the Holland-America liners were transferred to registry in Curacao in an effort to reduce operational costs, customarily higher under Dutch registry. On March 13, 1972, she opened a new service from New York to Bermuda and the West Indies. In the latter part of her career she operated on a more varied schedule with cruises out of Miami and Port Everglades, and some North Cape Cruises and special longer cruises between a wide range of ports. Sold to the French Pacquet Cruise Lines in 1982 and renamed *Rhapsody*. Resold to the Greek-owned Regency Cruises in May 1985 for $10,000,000 and renamed *Regent Star*. Presently in their service.

V STATENDAM

Builder: Fincantieri, Cantiere Navale, Italiani S.p.A, Monfalcone, Italy
Completed: 1992
Gross tonnage: 50,000
Dimensions: 750' x 95' Depth: 35' Draft: 25'
Engines: Diesels
Screws: Twin
Decks: Eight
Normal speed: 20 knots
Passenger accommodations: 1,250 in a single class
Officers and crew: 600
Registry: Netherlands Antilles
Maiden voyage: late 1992

Ordered by the Holland-America Line as a trio of sister ships, the fifth *Statendam* promises to be as luxurious as her predecessors in their day. In addition to the traditional features of cruise ships, she has an expansive lido restaurant and pool area. The *Statendam* promises to have large staterooms and spacious public areas as well as small intimate lounges. A large, two-deck show lounge will be constructed as the competition has been doing over the last few years to give passengers the feeling of having gone to the theatre. Also, a three-deck high atrium; a two-deck, 761-seat dining room with a curved grand entry staircase, also the norm in today's genre of super ships. Above decks will feature a domed lido pool area, with jacuzzis. The lido pool area will adjoin the 395-foot lido restaurant. The movie theatre will seat 249 and there will be two meeting rooms for business groups. The regular amenities of sauna, steam rooms, massage rooms, fitness center, and beauty salon will all be a part of the ship's profile in making each cruise an exercise in leisure itself. Last but not least are where passengers are most concerned when it is time to retire. The staterooms: 120 deluxe and 28 suites will have private balconies and mini-bars. The suites will also have a small private dining area. The *Statendam* will be furnished with art and antiques throughout the public rooms in tradition with HAL practice that began over a half-century ago with the *Nieuw Amsterdam* in 1938. The staff and crew of Indonesian and Filipino add a flavour of their own to the ship's operation. And because the cruise industry is entering another successful decade, two more sister ships will be coming into service in 1993 and 1994.

Note: Photo from an original oil painting by Stephen J. Card.

II VEENDAM

Builder: Harland & Wolff Ltd., Govan, Northern Ireland
Completed: March 1923
Gross tonnage: 15,652
Dimensions: 576' x 67' Depth: 45' Draft: 32'
Engines: Four steam turbines, single-reduction geared
Screws: Twin
Watertight bulkheads: Nine
Decks: Five
Normal speed: 15 knots
Passenger accommodations: 223 first and 363 tourist class*
Officers and crew: 350
Registry: Holland
Maiden voyage: Rotterdam-Boulogne-Plymouth-New York on April 8,
 1923

*Originally carried 270 first, 398 second, 426 tourist-cabin, 339 third class

Laid down for the British Allan Line but purchased while still on the stocks by the Holland-America Line. Engaged in the Rotterdam-Boulogne-Southampton-New York service with a call at Plymouth in place of Southampton eastbound. She inaugurated a westbound call at Halifax on January 19, 1924, and called at that port on many of her westbound voyages. By 1927 she was working on the Rotterdam-Southampton-Cherbourg-New York route and in 1928 she made three cruises to the West Indies out of New York. In the years that followed she made occasional winter cruises. On September 17, 1939, she rescued survivors from the sinking British aircraft carrier *Courageous* which had been torpedoed by U-29. Seized by the Germans on May 11, 1940, at Rotterdam and used as a submarine depotship in the Baltic Sea first at Gdynia, Poland then at Hamburg. Sunk at Hamburg on August 2, 1945, she was refloated on October 25 and taken in tow to Ymuiden, Holland where she arrived on the 16th of January, 1946. After temporary repairs she left Ymuiden on the 31st steaming for Rotterdam. Rebuilt, she returned to service in early 1947. In December she began two-week cruises to the West Indies in the winter of 1950-51. She made her last voyage for the Line on October 30, 1953, from Rotterdam to New York. The *Veendam* consumed 120 tons of fuel per day, which given her size was quite costly even in the fifties. One of the last vintage ships to work after the war, she was somewhat of an anachronism in her post-war career. When she cruised to warmer climates a canvas swimming pool was set up on one of the aft decks, and like many liners of her gendre, a white sheet was often set up in the main lounge for viewing the latest out of Hollywood. Sold for scrap to the Bethlehem Steel Company at Baltimore, Maryland, in November 1953.

Sister ship: *Volendam.*

III VEENDAM

Builder: Ingalls Shipbuilding Corp., Pascagoula, Mississippi
Completed: 1958
Gross tonnage: 15,257
Dimensions: 617′ x 86′ Depth: 43′ Draft: 27′
Engines: Four steam turbines, double reduction geared, plus a bow thruster forward
Screws: Twin
Watertight bulkheads: Twelve (8 to upper deck, 4 to 2nd deck)
Decks: Five
Normal speed: 21 knots
Passenger accommodations: 500 in a single class
Officers and crew: 366
Registry: Netherlands Antilles
Maiden voyage: Rotterdam-Southampton-Cobh-New York on June 17, 1973

Built for the American Moore-McCormack Lines and christened *Argentina*. Sold to the Holland-America Line in July 1972 for $10,000,000 and renamed *Veendam*. She was rebuilt as a cruise ship at Bremerhaven, Germany at the Hapag-Lloyd shipyards and her interior furnishings at Rotterdam. Ninety percent of her cabins are situated outside. Her promenade deck was totally rebuilt and public areas enlarged with new dance floors; the addition of a new lido restaurant; three bars, gift shop and a boutique, library and writing room. Withdrawn from service on May 14, 1974, and laid up at Norfolk, Virginia. She was then chartered out to the Arosa Line and briefly renamed *Brasil*; between December 15, 1974, and April 1975. She reverted back to her owners and was again renamed *Veendam*. Employed mostly on the New York-Freeport-Nassau weekly service, she also made some cruises to the Mediterranean and South America as well. Chartered out once again to the Swiss-owned Arosa Line in 1975, she was renamed *Monarch Star* until January 8, 1978, when she returned to HAL service based out of Miami to Port-au-Prince-Montego Bay-Cartagena-Curacao-Aruba-La Guaira-Grenada-Martinique-St. Thomas under her original name. On May 20, 1978, she was placed on 7-day cruises to Alaska. Equipped with motion stabilizers and fully air-conditioned, the *Veendam* was one of the first ships to make the transition from liner to cruise ship. Sold to the Chinese shipping group of C. Y. Tung in mid-1983 and subsequently leased and later purchased by the Bahamas Cruise (Bermuda Star Line). Renamed *Bermuda Star*. Resold to the Finnish-owned Commodore Cruises in August 1990 and renamed *Enchanted Isle*. Presently in their service.

Sister ship: *Volendam*.

Note: For a very short time in 1976 she was renamed *Edam* (Panama).

I VOLENDAM

Builder: Harland & Wolff, Ltd., Belfast, Northern Ireland
Completed: October 1922
Gross tonnage: 15,434
Dimensions: 576′ x 67′ Depth: 45′ Draft: 32′
Engines: Four steam turbines, single reduction geared
Screws: Twin
Watertight bulkheads: Nine
Decks: Five
Normal speed: 15 knots
Passenger accommodations: 250 first and 335 tourist class*
Officers and crew: 350
Registry: Holland
Maiden voyage: Rotterdam-Boulogne-Plymouth-New York on
  November 4, 1922

*Originally carried: 245 first, 435 second, 370 tourist-cabin and 637 third class.

Engaged in the Rotterdam-Boulogne-Southampton-New York run with a call at Plymouth eastbound in place of Southampton. In 1927 her route became Rotterdam-Southampton-Cherbourg-New York. The *Volendam* chanced to be at sea when the Germans invaded the Netherlands on May 10, 1940. From this date onward she began working out of British ports on her westbound voyages. Torpedoed by a submarine 300 miles northwest of Bloody Foreland, Ireland on August 30, 1940, at 11 p.m. while in a westbound convoy. The torpedo which hit her number one cargo hold caused both holds one and two to fill with water. Beached on the island of Bute, Scotland. Her 900 passengers including 335 British children abandoned the ship to awaiting vessels. In the transfer one life was lost. Towed back to the Clyde in Scotland for repairs; an unexploded torpedo was found lodged in her hull. She emerged as a transport ten months later under the control of the British Ministry of Transport with management under the Cunard Line. Reconditioned after the war, in mid-1946 she was chartered by the Dutch Government for a period carrying Dutch troops to Indonesia and evacuees homebound. She also made a number of transatlantic crossings, though in a rather spartan mode with 1,682 passengers in a single class. A few trips were also made down under to Australia with Dutch immigrants. It was almost like a revival of the turn of the century with the *Volendam's* interiors a drab reflection of her wartime service and her speed a slow 13.50 knots. She made her last transatlantic crossing on November 3, 1951, from New York to Rotterdam. Sold for scrap to Frank Rijsdijk at Hendrik Ido Ambacht in the Netherlands in January 1952 and broken up by March.

Sister ship: *Veendam.*

II VOLENDAM

Builder: Ingalls Shipbuilding Corp., Pascagoula, Mississippi, U.S.A.
Completed: 1958
Gross tonnage: 15,631
Dimensions: 617' x 86' Depth: 43' Draft: 27'
Engines: Four steam turbines, double-reduction geared
Screws: Twin
Watertight bulkheads: Twelve (8 to upper deck, 4 to 2nd deck)
Decks: Five
Normal speed: 23 knots
Passenger accommodations: 500 in a single class
Officers and crew: 366
Registry: Netherlands Antilles
Maiden voyage: Rotterdam-Southampton-Cobh-New York on April 16, 1973

Built for the American-owned Moore-McCormack Lines and christened *Brasil*. Sold to the Holland-America Line on July 19, 1971, for $10,000,000 and renamed *Volendam*. Rebuilt at the Hapag-Lloyd shipyards in Bremerhaven, Germany and at Rotterdam as a cruise ship. The new amenities included rebuilding of the promenade deck; enlargement of the public areas and a new lido restaurant, swimming pool, three bars, a gift and boutique shop, newsstand, library and writing room. Carpeted throughout the ship's interior thoroughfares and staterooms. Placed in a weekly service out of New York to the Bahamas with calls at Freeport and Nassau. The *Volendam* made several North Cape and Mediterranean cruises and the Caribbean as well, working mostly out of New York. She was laid up on January 6, 1974, at Hampton Roads, Virginia temporarily and later at Norfolk in late October 1974 because of a lack of revenues during the transitional years of liners to cruise ships. On August 31, 1974, she made a Mediterranean cruise out of New York and then called at Fort Lauderdale, helping to establish the latter port as a new port of call in the beginnings of what would later help to usher in the cruise ship era of today. Chartered out to the Arosa Line in August 1975, she was renamed *Monarch Sun*. Holland America Line would later purchase the Swiss-owned Arosa Line in 1976 for $2.2 million. Equipped with motion stabilizers and fully air-conditioned. Resold to C. Y. Tung in 1983 and leased out to their subsidiary American Hawaiian Cruises with renaming to *Island Sun* in February 1984. Renamed *Liberté* in 1985. Sold to the Bermuda Star Line on March 11, 1987, and renamed *Canada Star*; *Queen of Bermuda* in May 1988. Sold once again to the Swedish-Finnish partnership of Commodore Cruises in August 1990 and renamed *Enchanted Odyssey* in September; *Enchanted Seas* in November 1990. Presently in their service.

Sister ship: *Veendam*.

I WESTERDAM

Builder: N. V. Wilton–Fijenoord, Schiedam, Netherlands
Completed: June 1946
Gross tonnage: 12,149
Dimensions: 518′ x 66′ Depth: 41′ Draft: 31′
Engines: Two 5-cylinder, 2-stroke, double-acting diesel
Screws: Twin
Decks: Three
Normal speed: 16 knots
Passenger accommodations: 152 one class passengers
Registry: Holland
Maiden voyage: Rotterdam-New York on June 30, 1946

Floated out of drydock on July 27, 1940, a month later on the 27th of August, she was hit by an Allied attack on Schiedam, Holland. Raised by the Nazis who had planned to sink her at the entrance of the harbour and thus block entrance, they were pre-empted by the Dutch Resistance who sank the ship at a location convenient to their future use. Raised for a second time she was sunk a third time by the Dutch. Following the war she was refloated on September 13, 1945, and taken back to her original builders and completed in June 1946. Employed in the Rotterdam-Le Havre-Southampton-Cobh-New York service. Classified as a cargo-passenger liner, she was the first liner to re-establish service to America for the Holland-America Line when she arrived in New York on July 8, 1946. Being of pre-war design she was unable to compete with new vessels of her class built in the fifties and when both cargo and passenger revenues fell in the mid-sixties she was withdrawn from service in December 1964 after making her last voyage for Holland-America Line from New York-Cobh-Southampton-Rotterdam-Amsterdam on October 30, 1964. Sold to Spanish shipbreakers at Alicante in February 1965 and broken up by March of that year.

Sister ship: *Zuiderdam*.

II WESTERDAM

Builder: Joseph L. Meyer GmbH & Co., Papenburg, West Germany
Completed: May 1986
Gross tonnage: 52,000
Dimensions: 798' x 95' Depth: 36' Draft: 24'
Engines: Two Burmeister & Wain 2-stroke, single-acting 10-cylinder diesels plus two bow thrusters forward
Screws: Twin (controllable pitch)
Decks: Eight
Normal speed: 19 knots
Passenger accommodations: 1,476 in a single class
Officers and crew: 590
Registry: Netherlands Antilles
Maiden voyage: Port Everglades-San Juan-St. Maarten-St. Thomas-Little Stirrup Cay-Port Everglades on November 27, 1988

Built for the Greek-owned Home Lines and christened *Homeric*. Sold to the Holland-America Line in April 1988 and delivered on November 2nd. The Dutch decided to jumboize the *Westerdam* in 1989 and she was sent to the Meyer Werft shipyards in Emden, Germany in October. The ship was cut in half and a 132-foot centre section inserted thus increasing her overall length from 666' to the present figure. Her gross tonnage was also increased dramatically from 42,092 to 52,000 gross tons. Among the new fixtures and fittings is a two-tier sun lounge. The ship is furnished with a fine Dutch collection of seventeenth and eighteenth century Dutch exploration art and antiques to keep in line with the company's tradition of style over the years. A most welcome feature about HAL ships is the no-tipping policy for dining room personnel, bartenders, and cabin stewards. The Dutch have always been a step ahead in many areas besides gracious living and travel...The *Westerdam* returned to service on March 25, 1990, on a series of 10-day cruises out of New York to Bermuda. In the summer of 1991 she was cruising on a weekly basis out of Vancouver along the Inside Passage to Glacier Bay and return. Her winter route was based out of Port Everglades to Ocho Rios-Grand Cayman-Progresso, Mexico. Equipped with motion stabilizers and fully air-conditioned. Her theatre holds 237 people. The main lounge seats 453 and a smaller one an additional 290. There are a number of ultra suites and suites. All staterooms have radio and telephone and some with remote control television. In all there are a total of thirteen public rooms, five elevators, two swimming pools, sauna, gymnasium, etc.... Presently in service.

II ZAANDAM

Builder: N. V. Wilton-Fijenoord, Schiedam, Netherlands
Completed: January 1939
Gross tonnage: 10,909
Dimensions: 502' x 64' Depth: 40' Draft: 31'
Engines: Two 6-cylinder, 2-stroke, double-acting diesels
Screws: Twin
Watertight bulkheads: Eight
Decks: Three
Normal speed: 16.50 knots
Passenger accommodations: 140 first-class passengers
Registry: Holland
Maiden voyage: Rotterdam-New York on January 7, 1939

Engaged in the Rotterdam-New York service. Transferred to the New York-Java-East Indies trade in the spring of 1940 — a service which the company had abandoned during the shipping slump in 1931. Fitted-out as a transport in early 1942, she was hit by two torpedoes from a German U-boat 400 miles off Cape Recife, Brazil on November 2, 1942, in position 1°16' north, 36°51' west. The *Zaandam* sank within 10 minutes, taking 128 down with her. Aboard there were 169 passengers. A group of five men, three American and two Dutch, made their way to immediate safety on a raft. Following perhaps the longest recorded survival at sea 83 days later, three of the men survived. Picked up by a United States Navy patrol ship on January 24, 1943, the three men — one American and the two Dutchmen were living skeletons. One of the deceased was an American passenger who survived 66 days, the other an ensign in the U.S. Navy who survived 77 days. When their raft had set out there had been water and food for only 16 days. A true testament to the will to survive in the exposure of the open sea.

Sister ship: *Noordam*.

Home Lines

ARGENTINA

Builder: Cammell, Laird & Co. Ltd., Birkenhead, England
Completed: September 1913
Gross tonnage: 11,015
Dimensions: 530′ x 61′ Depth 33′ Draft 26′
Engines: Two 4-cylinder, quadruple-expansion engines and two low-pressure turbines, double-reduction geared
Screws: Twin
Watertight bulkheads: Eight
Decks: Three
Normal speed: 15 knots
Passenger accommodations: 32 first and 969 tourist class
Maiden voyage: Genoa-Rio de Janeiro-Buenos Aires on January 13, 1947

Built for the Norwegian-American Line and christened *Bergensfjord*. Sold to the Home Lines in November 1946 and renamed *Argentina*. Engaged in the Genoa-Naples-Rio de Janeiro-Santos-Montevideo-Buenos Aires run until September 1949 when her route was limited to the Genoa-Naples-Caribbean-La Guaira trade. Reallocated once again to the Genoa-Naples-Lisbon-New York trade in 1951-52 with a call at Halifax outward. She finished out her career on the northern run to Germany making her last voyage for Home Lines on December 20, 1952, New York-Plymouth-Le Havre-Southampton-Bremerhaven-Cuxhaven-Hamburg. Sold to the Israeli Zim Lines in the spring of 1953 and renamed *Jerusalem*; *Aliya* in 1957. The *Argentina* was the first liner of Home Lines as well as Zim-Israel Lines. Sold for scrap to the Terreste Marittima at La Spezia, Italy in October 1959.

I ATLANTIC

Builder: William Cramp Sons Shipbuilding Engineering Co., Philadelphia, Pennsylvania, USA
Completed: October 1927
Gross tonnage: 21,239
Dimensions: 582' x 83' Depth: 45' Draft: 29'
Engines: Eight steam turbines, single-reduction geared
Screws: Twin
Watertight bulkheads: Twelve
Decks: Five
Normal speed: 22 knots
Passenger accommodations: 200 first, 1,278 tourist class (Originally carried: 349 first, 203 cabin, and 626 tourist class)
Registry: Greece*
Maiden voyage: Genoa-New York on May 14, 1949.

*Originally registered Panama

Launched on June 26, 1926 as Yard #509. Built for the American Matson Lines and christened *Malolo*; *Matsonia* in 1937. Sold to the Home Lines in 1948 and renamed *Atlantic* in 1949. Refitted at the Ansaldo shipyards at Genoa in 1948-49. Engaged in the Naples-Genoa-New York trade until reallocated to the Southampton-Le Havre-Halifax service on February 29, 1952. On April 21, 1952 she sailed to Quebec City in place of Halifax. Reverting back to her Mediterranean route in December 1954, she was transferred to a subsidiary company operating under the name of the National Hellenic-American Line. Under her new role she was renamed *Queen Frederica* and placed under the Greek flag. She worked out of Piraeus-Naples-Palermo-Gilbraltar-Halifax-New York with an occasional call at Malaga and Kalamata, Greece beginning on January 29, 1955. Refitted between November 1960–January 1961, her accommodations were altered to a two-class ship — first and tourist with 75% of cabins affording private facilities. Between 1958 and 1961 she had been calling on occasion at Barcelona and Cannes and either Messina or Palermo. On many eastbound voyages she called at Boston and did occasional cruising out of New York during off seasonal months. On November 7, 1957 she had made an eastbound voyage from Halifax to Rotterdam. Like many Greek flag ships she was very flexible in her itineraries depending upon the market at the time. Made her last voyage for the Line on November 1, 1965, New York-Gibraltar-Barcelona-Genoa-Naples-Palermo-Messina-Piraeus. Sold to the Greek Chandris Lines in the same month, she made her last transatlantic crossing for Chandris on September 30, 1967, New York-Piraeus. I remember seeing my father off on this particular voyage. Twelve years before the whole family had crossed over on this lovely liner and she was the impetus for my avocation as a chronicler of maritime history. The *Queen Frederica* had 16 deluxe suites and a very spacious upper promenade deck. Her first class dining room rivaled those of her foreign peers with its Ionic pillars, palms, and colorful murals of the sea encircling the spacious room. Above there was a small balcony walk where musicians played at dinnertime. I saw her for the last time in drydock at Southampton on May 18, 1971 while in route to Spain on the Spanish Line *Begoña*. How elated I was to see this splendid ship. Laid up on September 22, 1971 in the River Dart, England and later moved to Piraeus in 1972.

Note: She made her sea trials on May 24, 1927 and maiden voyage on November 16, 1927 for Matson, San Francisco-Honolulu. Sold for scrap in May 1977 to Eleusis Shipbreakers, she caught fire while being dismantled in Greece in February 1978.

II ATLANTIC

Builder: Construction-Naval & Industrie de la Mediterranee, La Seyne, France
Completed: 1982
Gross tonnage: 19,337
Dimensions: 670′ x 89′ Depth: 56′ Draft: 26′
Engines: Two Fiat 2-stroke, single-acting, 10-cylinder diesels
Screws: Twin with controllable pitch propellers & one bow thruster propeller forward
Normal speed: 23.50 knots
Decks: Six
Passenger accommodations: 950 in a single class
Officers and crew: 550
Registry: Liberia
Maiden voyage: New York-Bermuda on April 17, 1982

Built exclusively for the Greek-owned Home Lines. Equipped with motion stabilizers and fully air-conditioned, the new *Atlantic* is far from what her namesake was in both looks and interior. Cabin walls are comparable to sheet rock and the acoustics excellent if you want to know what your neighbour is doing. Engaged in a cruise service out of New York since her debut on weekly cruises to Bermuda. These varied with five to sixteen day cruises out of Port Everglades to the Caribbean until early April when she was on the New York-Bermuda run with occasional cruises to nowhere for two days up until mid October when she was back to the Caribbean route after a couple of longer 10- to 12-day voyages out of New York. Built exclusively for cruises the ship affords 493 cabins of which 188 are deluxe with bedroom, sitting room and television: 8 are suites, 75% located outside. A spacious lounge accommodates 550, theatre 250. Along with the usual shipboard facilities there are two outdoor pools, one with a large sliding glass magrodome roof. There is a full orchestra disco and live variety shows. All cabins are equipped with telephone and individual climate control. In this age of cutting cost the owners or the builders skimped on the ship's hull it seems. Upon her maiden crossing the *Atlantic* suffered some damage to her aft area when New York tugs nudged her into her basin and dented her hull. This area was covered by some heavy plating. Her actual capacity load is for 1,292 passengers and she cruises at 21 knots. Total deck space is 13,800 square feet. Built at a cost of $100,000,000. Sold to Holland-America Line in April 1988 she was delivered in October. Resold to Premier Cruise Lines and renamed *Starship Atlantic*. Presently in their service.

DORIC

Builder: Chantiers de L'Atlantique, St. Nazaire, Penhoet Loire, France
Completed: March 1964
Gross tonnage: 25,320
Dimensions: 628' x 82' Depth 49' Draft: 27'
Engines: Four C.E.M. Parsons-Atlantique double reduction geared steam turbines
Screws: Twin
Collision bulkhead: One
Watertight bulkheads: Eleven
Decks: Six
Normal speed: 20 knots
Passenger accommodations: 725 in a single class
Officers and crew: 420
Registry: Panama
Maiden voyage: Port Everglades-San Juan-St. Thomas-Martinique-Barbados-La Guaira-Curacao-Aruba-Port au Prince on February 16, 1974

Built for the Zim-Israel Line and christened *Shalom*. Sold to the German Atlantic Line in October 1967 and renamed *Hanseatic*. Resold to Home Lines in July 1973 and renamed *Doric*. Refitted by the OARN S.A. in Genoa; some extra cabins were later added at Newport News, Virginia. Her original maiden voyage had been slated for December 22, 1973 but was held up due to a faulty condenser thereby cancelling five scheduled cruises. Employed in the Port Everglades-Caribbean ports trade from December to May annually when she was positioned to work the New York-Bermuda run during the summer and autumn every Saturday beginning on May 10, 1975. By 1977 she was making calls at Nassau as well. The *Doric* is fully air-conditioned and equipped with stabilizers and a designed flare in her hull both fore and aft to reduce pitching. The pair of kingposts on her foredeck were removed when she became a cruise ship and her aft upper deck area extended to provide a lido area. Eighty-two percent of her cabins are outside. Sold to the Greek Royal Cruise Line on January 6, 1981 and renamed *Royal Odyssey*. Resold to the Greek-owned Regency Cruises in 1987 for delivery in November 1988. Renamed *Regent Sun*, she is presently in their service.

HOMELAND

Builder: Alexander Stephen & Sons Ltd., Glasgow, Scotland
Completed: March 1905
Gross tonnage: 10,043
Dimensions: 538' x 60' Depth 41'
Engines: Steam turbines, single-reduction geared
Screws: Triple
Watertight bulkheads: Seven
Decks: Four
Normal speed: 17 knots
Passenger accommodations: 85 first and 866 tourist class
Officers and crew: 250
Registry: Panama
Maiden voyage: Genoa-South America on July 27, 1948

Built for the British Allan Line and christened *Virginian*. Sold to the Canadian-Pacific Line on October 1, 1915, she retained her original name. Resold once again to the Swedish-American Line on February 14, 1920 and renamed *Drottningholm*. Resold once again to the Home Lines in April 1948 and renamed *Brasil*; *Homeland* in June 1951. Engaged in the Genoa-Buenos Aires run primarily, but made five voyages from Naples to New York in the spring of 1950. Later on that year she was refitted in Italy in the winter of 1950-51. Reallocated to the Hamburg-Southampton-Cherbourg-Halifax-New York service on June 16, 1951, but reverted back to the Genoa-Naples-New York service in the spring of 1952. Diverted once again to the northern waters, she was placed in the Hamburg-Cuxhaven-Bremerhaven-Southampton-Cherbourg-Halifax-New York service. She ultimately finished up her career on the southern route, leaving New York for the first time on November 6, 1954 steaming for Ponta Delgada-Gibraltar-Palermo-Naples-Messina-Genoa-Piraeus where she was subsequently laid up. Sold for scrap to the Sidarma S.A. on March 29, 1955 and scrapped at Trieste, Italy.

Note: The *Homeland* when originally built was the first Atlantic liner to be driven with the experimental Parson direct-action steam turbines. These were very powerful turbines that unleashed tremendous thrust and while great at sea were often difficult when maneuvering in port. Despite its shortcomings it was a system which was fitted into many liners at the turn of the century and universally accepted as revolutionary in speed performance.

I HOMERIC

Builder: Bethlehem Shipbuilding Corp., Quincy, Massachusetts, USA
Completed: December 1931
Gross tonnage: 18,563
Dimensions: 638' x 79' Depth 45' Draft: 27'
Engines: Six steam turbines, single-reduction geared
Screws: Twin
Watertight bulkheads: Eleven
Decks: Five
Normal speed: 21 knots (attained a speed of 23.50 knots on her trials)
Passenger accommodations: 96 first and 846 tourist class* (750 in a single class when cruising)
Officers and crew: 500
Registry: Panama
Maiden voyage: Venice-Mediterranean ports-Halifax-New York on January 24, 1955

*Originally carried 338 first and 1096 tourist class

Built for the American Matson Lines and christened *Mariposa*. Sold to the Home Lines in November 1953 and renamed *Homeric* in 1954. Refitted at Trieste, Italy, for over $3,000,000 and began service a year later on the Naples-Mediterranean ports-New York run and some cruising out of New York to the West Indies. She made her first voyage to New York from Southampton on May 3, 1955. Reverted to the Cuxhaven-Southampton-Le Havre-Plymouth-Quebec service on August 12, 1957 and to Montreal by April 1958 with an occasional New York voyage to the Mediterranean after her annual drydock in Genoa. Later on in her career she went on to Naples-Sicily and Piraeus during the mid-sixties. In April 1961 her route was Cuxhaven-Bremerhaven-Zeebrugge-Southampton-Le Havre-Quebec-Montreal. Beginning October 1963 she was working mostly out of New York cruising to Nassau and the West Indies. A very lovely liner with interiors that complemented her beautifully designed hull, she became fondly known as "The Fun Ship" because of the numerous parties held aboard. She began cruising out of Port Everglades on December 23, 1972 to the Caribbean, reverting to New York in the summer. Made her last voyage for the Line on June 19, 1973, New York-San Juan-St. Thomas-Martinique-Barbados-St. Maarten. On her second voyage out of New York after her turn-around, she was gutted by fire which broke out in the galley in the early hours of the morning on July 1, 1973 around 4:00 a.m. while headed south one day out of New York, 90 miles west of Cape May. After returning to New York for emergency repairs she sailed for Genoa on July 7th, arriving there on the 18th. Following insurance settlements the company decided to sell the ship for scrap. She left Genoa for the scrapper's yard on December 11, 1973 via the Panama Canal at a speed of 12.75 knots. Arriving there on January 26, 1974 she was handed over to her buyers, Messrs. Nan Feng Steel Enterprise Co. of Kaoshiung, Taiwan.

Note: This American built liner along with others of her time period were in the author's opinion the perfect embodiment of what a liner should look like. And if the adage that "Americans build the best ships but cannot manage them" holds true.

II HOMERIC

Builder: Joseph L. Meyer GmbH & Co., Papenburg, Germany
Completed: May 1986
Gross tonnage: 42,092
Dimensions: 666′ x 95′ Depth: 36′ Draft: 24′
Engines: Two B & W 2-stroke, single-acting,10-cylinder diesels, plus two
  bow thrusters forward with controllable pitch propellers
Screws: Twin (controllable pitch)
Decks: Eight
Normal speed: 19 knots
Passenger accommodations: 1,030 in a single class
Officers and crew: 590
Registry: Panama
Maiden voyage: New York-Bermuda on May 6, 1986

Built for the Greek-owned Home Lines and christened *Homeric*. Built in drydock at a cost of $150,000,000. Her actual passenger certificate allows for 1,132 passengers. The total number of cabins are 521 of which 5 are suites with full bathtub; 16 deluxe also with full bath; 315 outside and only 173 inside cabins with shower. All staterooms have radio and telephone. Some feature television with remote control. Equipped with motion stabilizers and fully air-conditioned. The *Homeric* was engaged on the New York-Bermuda run and other cruises until the company concluded on getting out of the cruise ship business after nearly 50 years of service. Sold to the Holland-America Line in 1988 and renamed *Westerdam*. Presently in their service.

ITALIA

Builder: Blohm & Voss, Hamburg, Germany
Completed: October 1928
Gross tonnage: 21,532
Dimensions: 609' x 78' Depth: 43' Draft: 29'
Engines: Two 8-cylinder, 4-stroke, double-acting B & W diesels
Screws: Twin
Watertight bulkheads: Ten
Decks: Five
Normal speed: 17 knots
Passenger accommodations: 680 in a single class (Originally carried 192 first and 1,320 tourist)
Officers and crew: 340
Registry: Panama
Maiden voyage: Genoa-Rio de Janeiro-Santos-Montevideo-Buenos Aires on July 27, 1948

Built for the Swedish-American Line and christened *Kungsholm*. Sold to the Home Lines in 1947 and renamed *Italia*. Engaged in the Genoa-Rio de Janeiro-Santos-Montevideo-Buenos Aires trade. When the immigrant trade to South America had petered-out she was placed in the Genoa-Naples-Mediterranean ports-New York service on June 12, 1949. On her second voyage out of New York June 28, 1949, gangster Meyer Lansky sailed for Naples in the ship's grand suite for $2,600 one-way. In March 1952 she was transferred to a new route. This time on the Hamburg-Cuxhaven-Zeebrugge-Southampton-Le Havre-Plymouth-Halifax-New York service. On October 6, 1954 while at Cuxhaven the *Italia* had a collision with the ship *Fairplay* in which two deaths resulted. Her itinerary was later extended to calls at Quebec City and Montreal beginning on March 24, 1959 and she also made an occasional trip to New York from the Mediterranean after her annual drydocking in Genoa. As most Home Lines ships she was registered in Panama and had Greek or Italian officers and Italian and German crews. When the transatlantic trade itself began to decline she was sent to Genoa for a full refit for operation as a cruise ship in the autumn of 1960. Added were an aft lido deck and two swimming pools. Cabins and public lounges were redone. Her passenger accommodations were combined into a single class. In December 1960 she returned to service. Working out of New York to Nassau on 7-day trips every Saturday year round. Fares ran about $172.50 on average and it should be mentioned that Home Lines more than any other operator familiarized the public with the new concept of cruising especially on the Nassau and Bermuda route. Made her last transatlantic crossing from Piraeus-Messina-Palermo-Naples-Genoa-Majorca-Tangiers-Lisbon arriving at New York on the 8th of November 1962. Withdrawn in April 1964 she was sold to the Canaveral International Corporation for $466,000 for conversion to a floating hotel and renamed Imperial Bahama Hotel. Moored at Freeport, Grand Bahama the operation failed and she was put up for auction in June 1965 after being taken over by the Bahamian Government for mismanagement by her former owners. When no bids came in she was sold to Spanish shipbreakers at Bilbao, Spain on September 8, 1965 and broken up by December of that year.

OCEANIC

Builder: Cantieri Riunitie dell' Adriatico, Monfalcone, Italy
Completed: March 1965
Gross tonnage: 27,645
Dimensions: 781' x 95' Depth: 46' Draft: 28'
Engines: Four steam turbines, double-reduction geared
Screws: Twin
Watertight bulkheads: Thirteen
Decks: Eight
Normal speed: 26.50 knots
Passenger accommodations: 1,034 in a single class (originally carried 230 first and 1,370 tourist)
Officers and crew: 560
Registry: Panama
Maiden voyage: Genoa-New York on April 3, 1965

Built at a cost of $35,000,000, she was the largest cruise ship ever built at the time of her construction. Fully air-conditioned and equipped with Denny-Brown motion stabilizers. Engaged in the cruise service out of New York to Nassau and the Bahamas, she later cruised to Bermuda and the Caribbean, mostly for one-week cruises. The *Oceanic* made longer cruises also from Port Everglades in the latter part of her career but for the most part cruised to Bermuda and Nassau between May and November and occasionally to South American ports. The *Oceanic's* lido deck area is over 10,000 square feet. She has two swimming pools covered by a retractable transparent megadome. Her dining room is one of the largest afloat and all cabins are equipped with television. Her theatre accommodates 420. Sold to Premier Cruise Lines in late 1985 and renamed *Starship Oceanic*. Presently in their service.

Italian Line

ANDREA DORIA

Builder: Societa Anonima Ansaldo, Sestri Ponente, Genoa, Italy
Completed: January 1953
Gross tonnage: 29,083
Dimensions: 700' x 90' Depth: 50' Draft: 30'
Engines: Six steam turbines: high-pressure, double-reduction geared; intermediate-pressure and low-pressure, single-reduction geared
Screws: Twin
Watertight bulkheads: Ten
Decks: Five
Normal speed: 23 knots
Passenger accommodations: 228 first, 340 cabin and 942 tourist class
Registry: Italy
Maiden voyage: Genoa-Mediterranean ports-New York on January 14, 1953

Employed in the Genoa-Cannes-Naples-Gibraltar-New York service. Unfortunately, this lovely liner was rammed and sunk by the Swedish-American Liner *Stockholm* in calm waters in a dense fog on the night of July 25, 1956. The *Stockholm,* which hit the *Doria's* starboard bow at 11:22 p.m., tore a large hole on her starboard side allowing the sea to pour into her empty ballast tanks. She took a heavy list to starboard which made it impossible to launch the portside lifeboats. This was caused by the absence of water ballast on the port side which may have righted the ship at the time of the collision. The 18 degree list soon increased to a dangerous 22 degrees. Distress signals were sent out before the gracious liner foundered at 10:09 the following morning by capsizing. This modern day tragedy occurred off the perilous Nantucket shoals where many a ship has been lost prior to this incident. The loss of life reached 54 persons including 5 from the *Stockholm.* Those lost on the Swedish liner were mostly crew whose quarters were located near the bow. Some of those lost on the *Doria* were trapped in their cabins when the collision caused the doors to jam while others were listed as missing. Amongst the first ships to arrive at the scene was the United Fruit liner *Cape Ann* who was shortly accompanied by the U.S. Army transport *William H. Thomas* and the French Line's *Ile de France;* the latter rescued a considerable number of the *Doria's* passengers and crew. Along with the *Stockholm* which despite her mangled bow remained afloat, the three ships rescued 1,565 persons and brought them to New York. Among them was actress Ruth Roman. Captain Calamai of the *Andrea Doria* when interviewed was quoted as saying "All my life I love the sea, now for the first time, I hate it." Many attempts to raise the *Andrea Doria* which lies some 39 fathoms below have all proven extremely difficult. The ship has over the years been nearly covered in silt and sand due to the tremendous underwater activity in the region caused by currents and no doubt the forces of the Gulf Stream and Labrador Current which meet in this area and are responsible for the fog itself.

Note: One attempt was made in August 1973 to no avail and the U.S. Coast Guard later forbade any further diving. In the early 1980s Roger Gimble, a professional diver, made a successful dive on the liner and retrieved her safe.

Sister ship: *Cristoforo Colombo.*

I AUGUSTUS

Builder: Societa Anonima Ansaldo, Cantiere Navale, Sestri Ponente, Genoa, Italy
Completed: November 1927
Gross tonnage: 30,418
Dimensions: 711'x 83' Depth: 52' Draft: 30'
Engines: Four M.A.N. 6-cylinder, 2-stroke, double-acting diesels
Screws: Quadruple
Watertight bulkheads: Eleven
Decks: Six
Normal speed: 19.50 knots
Passenger accommodations: 302 first class, 504 second class and 1,404 third class
Officers and crew: 500
Registry: Italy
Maiden voyage NGI: Genoa-Naples-Palermo-New York arriving on September 8, 1928

Built for the Navigazione Generale Italiana. Transferred to the newly formed Italian Line on January 2, 1932 upon amalgamation of the NGI and the Lloyd Sabaudo which formed the new company. Employed in the Genoa-Mediterranean ports-New York service until October 7, 1933, when she made her last voyage from New York to Genoa. Reverted to the Genoa-South American trade but made some trips to New York shortly before the outbreak of World War II. Laid up in 1939, but made some voyages from Trieste to New York, her first on May 27, 1940. Laid up indefinitely, she was taken over by the Italian Navy and converted to an aircraft carrier in March 1943 with renaming to *Sparviero*. Damaged by bombing at Genoa on June 26, 1944. She had been partly dismantled by the Germans when she was sunk by them on April 25, 1945 at the west entrance. She fell on top of a smaller merchant ship at the entrance to Genoa harbour. Refloated in 1946 and sold for scrap on July 7, 1947, with work commencing on August 12th of that year.

Sister ship: *Roma.*

II AUGUSTUS

Builder: Cantieri Riuniti dell' Adriatico, Trieste, Italy
Completed: February 1952
Gross tonnage: 27,090
Dimensions: 679' x 86' Depth: 49' Draft: 28'
Engines: Two Fiat, 12-cylinder, 2-stroke, double-acting diesel
Screws: Twin
Watertight bulkheads: Eleven
Decks: Five
Normal speed: 21 knots
Passenger accommodations: 325 first and 830 tourist class*
Officers and crew: 493
Registry: Italy
Maiden voyage: Genoa-Mediterranean ports-South American ports-Buenos Aires in March 1952

*Originally carried: 222 first, 344 cabin and 931 tourist class

Placed in the Naples-Genoa-Cannes-Barcelona-Gibraltar-Lisbon-Rio de Janeiro-Santos-Montevideo-Buenos Aires trade until February 7, 1957, when she was diverted to the Naples-Genoa-Cannes-Gibraltar-Lisbon service. The *Augustus* made an inaugural call at Halifax on January 19, 1959 westbound and Boston eastbound on her return voyage on the 23rd calling there on occasion thereafter. Reverted back to her original service in October 1960 and was converted to a two class ship in 1969. The elimination of cabin class afforded more space for the two classes. Her theatre seated 250 and she was fully air-conditioned and equipped with motion stabilizers. The *Augustus* was built with a bulbous bow to help increase her speed. Her regular voyages from Genoa to Buenos Aires took from 17 to 18 days. Laid up on January 16, 1976 and sold the same month to the Ocean King Navigation Company of the Philippines and renamed *Great Sea*; *Ocean King* in 1980; *Philippines* in 1983 and converted to a stationary floating hotel at Songdo, South Korea. Resold to Philippine President Lines and renamed *President* in 1985; *Asian Princess* in 1988. Presently laid up.

Sister ship: *Giulio Cesare.*

Note: Registered port, Manila, Philippines.

COLOMBO

Builder: Palmers Shipbuilding & Iron Co., Ltd., Jarrow, England
Completed: July 1917
Gross tonnage: 12,037
Dimensions: 536′ x 64′ Depth: 35′ Draft: 28′
Engines: Two 4-cylinder, quadruple expansion
Screws: Twin
Watertight bulkheads: Eight
Decks: Four
Normal speed: 17 knots
Passenger accommodations: 84 first, 853 second and 1,725 third class (NGI figures)
Registry: Italy
Maiden voyage: Under NGI Genoa-New York arriving on December 6, 1921

Built for the Sicula-Americana Line and christened *San Gennaro*. Sold to the Navigazione Generale Italiana in 1921 and renamed *Colombo*. Passed on to the Italian Line on January 2, 1932, when the NGI and the Lloyd Sabaudo merged to form the Italian Line. Engaged in the Genoa-South American trade. Many of the early Italian liners offered a dual second and third class which were split into two categories: second class economy and second class ordinary; third class distinctive and third class ordinary. Sold to the Lloyd Triestino in 1937, she was scuttled off Massawa, Ethiopia on April 4, 1941 during an allied invasion. She was raised and scrapped in 1949.

CONTE BIANCAMANO

Builder: William Beardmore & Co. Ltd., Glasgow, Scotland
Completed: November 1925
Gross tonnage: 23,562
Dimensions: 665' x 76' Depth: 48' Draft: 26'
Engines: Four steam turbines, double-reduction geared
Screws: Twin
Collision bulkhead: One
Watertight bulkheads: Nine
Decks: Five
Normal speed: 20 knots
Passenger accommodations: 215 first, 339 cabin and 1,310 tourist class
Registry: Italy
Maiden voyage: Under Lloyd Sabaudo, Genoa-Naples-New York arriving at New York on November 20, 1925

Built for the Italian Lloyd Sabaudo. She came under Italian Line ownership upon the merger of the Lloyd Sabaudo and the Navigazione Generale Italiana on January 2, 1932 which came to form the Italian Line. Employed in the Genoa-Mediterranean ports-South American trade in the off seasonal months and to New York during the summer months. In 1935 she did some troop work to Ethiopia carrying Italian troops during the invasion of East Africa. Two years later she was sold to the Lloyd Triestino. Seized by the United States at Colon, Panama in March 1941, she was renamed *Hermitage* and commissioned for use as a transport in April 1942 until August 1946. Returned to Italy in 1947 and reconditioned with two new funnels to replace the old ring-topped type and her raked stem curved. She was now placed under the ownership of the Societa Marittima Nazionale. Chartered by the Italian Line and later sold to the company for a nominal sum, the Italian Line itself being nearly state-owned. She resumed services on November 10, 1949 from Genoa to Buenos Aires. The *Conte Biancamano* worked in the North and South American trades and sailed from Genoa to New York via Naples-Barcelona-Lisbon and Halifax. In 1957 she worked the South American route year-round but returned to the New York service the following year until September 1959 with an occasional call at Boston eastbound. Commenced her last voyage for the Line on April 7, 1960, New York-Boston-Lisbon-Naples. Sold for scrap in Italy in October 1960 and broken up by December of that year. She and her sister ship were two of the most lavishly appointed liners of their day with their Rococo designed interiors.

Sister ship: *Conte Grande.*

CONTE DI SAVOIA

Builder: Cantieri Riuniti dell' Adriatico, Trieste, Italy
Completed: November 1932
Gross tonnage: 48,502
Dimensions: 860′ x 96′ Depth: 53′ Draft: 31′
Engines: Twelve steam turbines, single-reduction geared
Screws: Quadruple
Watertight bulkheads: Twelve
Decks: Six
Normal speed: 27.50 knots (attained a speed of 30 knots on her trials)
Passenger accommodations: 360 first, 778 tourist and 922 third class
Officers and crew: 786
Registry: Italy
Maiden voyage: Genoa-New York on November 30, 1932

The keel was laid down for the Lloyd Sabaudo and was to be named *Conte Azzuro*. Passed on to Italian Line ownership when the Lloyd Sabaudo and the Navigazione Generale Italiana consolidated to form the Italian Line on January 2, 1932. A second name was considered once again, *Dux* as a running mate to the *Rex*. Employed in the Genoa-Mediterranean ports-New York run year-round. The *Conte Di Savoia* was one of the first liners to be equipped with Sperry gyro stabilizers which reduced the ship's roll to less than two and a half degrees under the worst weather conditions. On her maiden voyage she was held up 88 miles outside of New York when a broken exhaust valve blew a hole in her hull plating. The damage was repaired and she lost only a day's time. Her upper deck was 460′ long. Her bulkheads were partially constructed out of steel and cement. Made her last voyage for the Italian Line from New York on December 27, 1939. Laid up in early 1940 until 1943 when she did some troop work. Laid up once again at Malamocco, Venice, where she was disguised as an island. Attacked by U.S. fighter bombers who scored six direct hits on the liner on September 11, 1943. Refloated on October 16, 1945 with the intention of reconstructing her. However, it was later decided to scrap her as rebuilding was too costly. Sold for scrap at Monfalcone, Italy in 1950 and broken up.

CONTE GRANDE

Builder: Stabilimento Tecnico, Trieste, Italy
Completed: February 1928
Gross tonnage: 23,842
Dimensions: 667′ x 78′ Depth: 48′ Draft: 27′
Engines: Four steam turbines, double-reduction geared
Screws: Twin
Collision bulkhead: One
Watertight bulkheads: Nine
Decks: Five
Normal speed: 20 knots
Passenger accommodations: 215 first, 379 cabin and 950 tourist class
Officers and crew: 532
Registry: Italy
Maiden voyage: Under Lloyd Sabaudo Genoa-Naples-New York arriving on
  April 14, 1928

Built for the Lloyd Sabaudo. Transferred to the Italian Line on January 2, 1932 upon amalgamation of the Lloyd Sabaudo and the Navigazione Generale Italiana which formed the new company name. Engaged in the Genoa-South American trade with occasional voyages to New York between the wars. Requisitioned for troop work to East Africa in October 1935, she later resumed regular sailings. Seized by the Brazilian government on August 22, 1941 and sold to the United States who converted her to a troopship under the name of *Monticello* in April 1942. Decommissioned in May 1946 and returned to the Italian Government on July 23, 1947. She was placed under the auspices of the Societa Marittima Nazionale. Chartered to the Italian Line and later purchased by them. Reconditioned extensively with her two old style funnels replaced with broader modern looking ones and redesigned completely inside. Resumed sailings on July 14, 1949 from Genoa to Buenos Aires. The *Conte Grande* was now placed in the Naples-Genoa-Cannes-Rio de Janeiro-River Plate service. Diverted to the Naples-Genoa-Cannes-New York service in July 1956 to maintain the service because of the loss of the *Andrea Doria*. She made her last such voyage on September 25, 1956. Withdrawn from this service on her return voyage out of New York on October 9, 1956 to Cannes-Genoa-Naples. Withdrawn from service to South America in late 1960, she made one voyage to Australia for the Lloyd Triestino in December of that year. Sold for scrap at Spezia, Italy in September 1961 after being laid up. She was broken up by June 1962.

Sister ship: *Conte Biancamano.*

CRISTOFORO COLOMBO

Builder: Societa Anonima Ansaldo, Sestri Ponente, Genoa, Italy
Completed: July 1954
Gross tonnage: 29,429
Dimensions: 701' x 90' Depth: 50' Draft: 30'
Engines: Six steam turbines: high-pressure, double-reduction geared; intermediate-pressure and low-pressure, single-reduction geared
Screws: Twin
Watertight bulkheads: Ten
Decks: Five
Normal speed: 23 knots
Passenger accommodations: 257 first class, 358 cabin and 969 tourist class
Officers and crew: 563
Registry: Italy
Maiden voyage: Genoa-Mediterranean ports-New York on July 15, 1954

The name *Caio Duilio* originally contemplated but changed. The *Cristoforo Colombo* was employed in the Naples-Genoa-Cannes-Gibraltar-New York run with an occasional call at Halifax westbound and Palermo eastbound until June 1960 when she was diverted to the Trieste-Venice-Piraeus-Messina-Palermo-Naples-Malaga-Lisbon-Halifax-New York run with a call at Boston and Ponta Delgadea, Azores on her eastbound voyages. Equipped with motion stabilizers and fully air-conditioned, the *Colombo* was a most elegant liner with three swimming pools and three separate dining rooms for her three classes. She was one of the few liners with a truly extensive and interesting itinerary. In fact, many voyagers made the trip in the form of a Mediterranean cruise and simply took the round-trip. The *Colombo*, which originally entered service with the traditional black hull, was painted white in mid-1967. Her itinerary varied later on to include such ports as Corfu, Dubrovnik and Barcelona. She made her last voyage from New York on January 20, 1973 and was diverted to the South American trade on February 1st. Her new ports of call included Naples-Genoa-Cannes-Barcelona-Lisbon-Rio de Janeiro-Santos-Montevideo-Buenos Aires with occasional calls at Messina and Corfu while on this route. She also included Palermo homebound. Withdrawn from service permanently in 1976 and sold to the C.V.G. Siderugica del Orinoco C.A. for $6,800,000 and registered at Ciudad Bolivar, Venezuela as an accommodation ship for steel workers at a plant in Puerto Ordaz. On March 12, 1983 she broke adrift six miles from the River Orinoco Sea Buoy. Taken in tow to Kaohsiung where she arrived on July 24, 1983. Sold to Yi Shen Steel Enterprises Co. with demolition beginning on August 8th of that year.

Sister ship: *Andrea Doria.*

DONIZETTI

Builder: Cantieri Riuniti dell' Adriatico, Trieste, Italy
Completed: April 1951
Gross tonnage: 13,226
Dimensions: 528' x 69' Depth: 42' Draft: 27'
Engines: Two 10-cylinder, 2-stroke, single-acting Sulzer diesels
Screws: Twin
Watertight bulkheads: Nine
Decks: Four
Normal speed: 17.50 knots
Passenger accommodations: 103 first and 446 tourist class
Officers and crew: 236
Registry: Italy

Built for the Lloyd Triestino and christened *Australia*. Bartered to the Italian Line for another ship in the spring of 1963 and renamed *Donizetti*. Employed in the Genoa-Naples-Cannes-Barcelona-Funchal or Tenerife-La Guaira-Curacao-Cartegena-Buena Ventura-Guayaquil-Callao-Arica-Antofagasta-Valparaiso service. A very interesting and colourful itinerary. The *Donizetti* and her sister ships were known as "the musicians" since they were named after famous Italian composers. Equipped with motion stabilizers and fully air-conditioned, she worked the South American route almost without interruption until laid up on October 15, 1976. Sold to the Cantieri del Golfo at La Spezia in June 1977 for scrap at a price of 300,000,000 Italian Lire.

Sister ships: *Rossini* and *Verdi*.

DUILIO

Builder: Societa Anonima Ansaldo, Sestri Ponente, Genoa, Italy
Completed: October 1923
Gross tonnage: 23,635
Dimensions: 636' x 76' Depth: 50' Draft: 30'
Engines: Four direct-action steam turbines
Screws: Quadruple
Watertight bulkheads: Fifteen
Decks: Five
Normal speed: 21 knots
Passenger accommodations: 284 first, 702 second and 1,072 third class
Officers and crew: 480
Registry: Italy
Maiden voyage: Under the NGI Genoa-New York arriving on November 9, 1923

Built for the Navigazione Generale Italiana. Transferred to the Italian Line on January 2, 1932 upon amalgamation of the NGI and the Lloyd Sabaudo to form the Italian Line. Employed in the Genoa-South American trade until she was diverted to the Genoa-Capetown service after being overhauled in September 1933. After a refit in 1934 passenger accommodations were reduced to 757 in 3 classes. Sold to the Lloyd Triestino in 1936. She was utilized by the Italians as a hospital ship during World War II and her cabin fittings were partly removed by the Germans in June 1944. Sunk by allied aircraft at San Sabba, Trieste on July 10, 1944. Found capsized by the allies in May 1945 and sold for scrap in 1948 with work commencing on February 14th. The *Duilio's* second class accommodations were split into two categories called regular second and intermediate second.

Sister ship: *Giulio Cesare.*

I GIULIO CESARE

Builder: Swan, Hunter & Wigham Richardson Ltd., Wallsend-on-Tyne, England
Completed: November 1921
Gross tonnage: 21,900
Dimensions: 636′ x 76′ Depth: 50′ Draft: 30′
Engines: Four steam turbines, single-reduction geared
Screws: Quadruple
Watertight bulkheads: Fifteen
Decks: Five
Normal speed: 19 knots
Passenger accommodations: 259 first, 328 second and 1,700 third class
Officers and crew: 542
Registry: Italy
Maiden voyage: Under NGI Genoa-New York arriving on August 22, 1922

Built for the Navigazione Generale Italiana. Transferred to the Italian Line on January 2, 1932 when the NGI and the Lloyd Sabaudo amalgamated to form the Italian Line. Engaged in the Genoa-South American trade until reconditioned in November 1933 and placed in the Genoa-Marseilles-Capetown, South Africa service. Sold to the Lloyd Triestino in 1936. Her cabin fittings were partly removed by the Germans in June 1944 and she was sunk by allied aircraft at Trieste on September 11, 1944. Found capsized by the allies in May 1945 and sold for scrap in 1948 with work commencing on February 11th. She was scrapped under the name of *Achille Lauro* and it appears that she was sold to the Lauro Line at some time though the information is obscure as to when this took place.

Sister ship: *Duilio.*

Il GIULIO CESARE

Builder: Cantieri dell' Adriatico, Monfalcone, Italy
Completed: September 1951
Gross tonnage: 27,078
Dimensions: 681' x 88' Depth: 49' Draft: 28'
Engines: Two Fiat 12-cylinder, 2-stroke double-acting diesels
Screws: Twin
Watertight bulkheads: Eleven
Decks: Five
Normal speed: 21 knots
Passenger accommodations: 325 first and 780 tourist class
Officers and crew: 493
Registry: Italy
Maiden voyage: Venice-Mediterranean ports-South American ports-
  Buenos Aires on October 27, 1951

*Originally she had accommodated 218 first class, 340 cabin and 1,062 tourist class.

Engaged in the Naples-Genoa-Lisbon-Rio de Janeiro-Santos-Montevideo-Buenos Aires trade until transferred to the North Atlantic service on June 29, 1956, working the Genoa-Cannes-Naples-Gibraltar-Halifax-New York route with an occasional call at Boston and Ponta Delgada, Azores eastbound. Reverted back to her original service on July 1, 1960, with an occasional new call at Barcelona or Funchal in the Canary Islands. In 1969 she was converted to a two-class ship by the elimination of cabin class. The changeover afforded more space for tourist class passengers with an additional dining room area, ballroom and bar. The *Giulio Cesare's* career was shortened by a serious problem with her rudder during a voyage in December 1972. Due to the slackening of trade at the time, she was laid up on the 27th after finishing her last voyage from Buenos Aires. Laid up at Naples on January 14, 1973, she was soon sold for scrap to the Terrestre Marittima for 400,000,000 Italian lire. Left Naples for the breaker's yard at La Spezia on May 10, 1973, arriving the following day in tow. Demolition was delayed pending government authorization. The breaking up commenced April 4, 1974. She and her sister were large motor ships with special engines designed by Fiat. The developers of the ship's engines inspected them after each voyage for performance. Equipped with motion stabilizers, fully air-conditioned, with a 250 seat theatre, the liner was built with a bulbous bow.

Sister ship: *Augustus.*

LEONARDO DA VINCI

Builder: Ansaldo SpA. Cantiere Navale, Sestri, Genoa, Italy
Completed: June 1960
Gross tonnage: 33,340
Dimensions: 767' x 92' Depth: 51' Draft: 31'
Engines: Four steam turbines, double-reduction geared
Screws: Twin
Watertight bulkheads: Fourteen
Decks: Five
Normal speed: 23 knots (attained a speed of 25.50 knots on her sea trials)
Passenger accommodations: 381 first, 373 cabin and 927 tourist class
(accommodations limited to 550 when cruising)
Officers and crew: 580
Registry: Italy
Maiden voyage: Genoa-Cannes-Naples-New York on June 30, 1960

Employed in the Naples-Genoa-Barcelona-Algeciras-Lisbon-Halifax-New York service with a call at Palma, Majorca in place of Barcelona eastbound; Halifax only westbound. On June 8, 1966 she made a first time call at the port of Boston eastbound. Calls at Palermo and Messina as well as North Africa were included in her itinerary from time to time. Cruising during the off season became a part of her scheduled program during the seventies, stretching even into the summer months of June and July. Built to replace the loss of the *Andrea Doria,* she was designed so as to be able to be converted to nuclear propulsion at a later date. Equipped with motion stabilizers and fully air-conditioned. The *Leonardo* was built with a bulbous bow and she was known to be exceptionally smooth at sea. However, in her early years she had some difficulty with rolling until 3,000 tons of iron scrap were inserted between her double bottom hull.

She was one of the first liners to replace the traditional teak deck with a new brick coloured rubberized flooring in her enclosed promenade deck area. In 1966 her black hull was changed to a gleaming white livery. The largest single-funnelled ship at the time of her construction. A victim of the oil crisis of the mid-seventies, she made her last transatlantic crossing in June 1976 and later began cruising in the Mediterranean, Genoa-Naples-Rhodes-Beirut-Alexandria on September 19th. Passed on to the newly formed Italian Line Cruises with the demise of the Italian Line and managed by Costa Line in July 1977 after being laid up for a time. Due to her excessive fuel consumption, however, she was laid up on September 23rd at La Spezia after having done a sprint on the Miami-Nassau service. Following much speculation for reactivating the ship all of which failed to materialize, she became the victim of a suspicious fire which totally destroyed the liner. On July 3, 1980 at approximately 4:00 p.m. a fire broke out in her chapel and raged for four days. Towed outside the harbor she burned so fiercely that she had to be scuttled. Just when it was feared the flames would reach her fuel tanks she listed heavily to starboard and settled on the bottom. Declared a total loss in December and on the 26th of March 1981 she was refloated. Towed to La Spezia where she arrived in tow at noon of the 31st and subsequently sold to a syndicate of scrapyards. Demolition began by Cantieri Navale Lotti on May 6, 1982. Suspicion had surrounded the vessel since she had been insured for $7,700,000 yet worth little more than $1,000,000 at the time. A beautiful ship she was. The *Da Vinci* was furnished with separate dining rooms and lounge areas for her three classes and had six swimming pools; one indoor and one outdoor for each class.

Note: Made her first voyage in the form of a cruise in the Mediterranean on June 17, 1960.

MICHELANGELO

Builder: Cantieri Riuniti dell' Adriatico, Trieste, Italy
Completed: April 1965
Gross tonnage: 45,911
Dimensions: 905′ x 102′ Depth: 52′ Draft: 31′
Engines: Four steam turbines, double-reduction geared
Screws: Twin
Watertight bulkheads: Sixteen
Decks: Six
Normal speed: 26.50 knots (attained a speed of 29.15 knots during her trials)
Passenger accommodations: 438 first, 569 cabin and 1085 tourist class
Officers and crew: 720
Registry: Italy
Maiden voyage: Genoa-Cannes-Naples-New York on May 12, 1965

Employed in the Genoa-Cannes-Naples-Algeciras-New York run with cruises to the West Indies by the late sixties becoming intermediate between transatlantic voyages. On April 12, 1966 the liner encountered 35 foot waves while enroute from Genoa to New York. The ship hove for hours with her engines shut down and sustained heavy damages when part of her bow was nearly crumbled by a huge 50 foot wave which smashed some 40 feet of bulwark and railing from the bridge. The incident caused the loss of three lives of the 768 passengers aboard at the time. The *Michelangelo*'s unusual funnels were constructed of fiber-glass. She was built with a bulbous bow to help reduce drag and increase her speed. In 1966 new propellers were fitted to the ship and she attained a new speed of 31.69 knots on her trial runs. Fully air-conditioned and equipped with motion stabilizers, she was the Italian Line's flagship at the time of construction. Due to the oil crisis in the mid-seventies the *Michelangelo* made only five transatlantic crossings in 1975, her last on June 26, 1975 from New York to Algeciras-Naples-Cannes-Genoa. Part of the reason for her demise was the financial position of the nearly bankrupt Italian Government which could not continue to subsidize the liners of the fleet. Operational costs for such a superliner were in the vicinity of $40,000 per day which was offset by a subsidy of around $750 per passenger carried. Tied up at the Calata Zingari, Stazione Marittima, Genoa where she arrived on July 5, 1975. On September 15th, she was moved to La Spezia pending her sale. Sold to the Iranian Navy in December 1976 to be used as an accommodation ship for naval officers and their families for the sum of $18,000,000. Delivered to Iran in July 1977, renamed *Fujaira* and tied up at Chahbar, Iran. Reported fallen into disuse following 1979 Revolution and partially dismantled in Iranian waters. Broken up at Gadani Beach, Pakistan in June 1991. Arriving on the 6th, work commenced on the 8th of June. She was sold for $155 per long ton.

Sister ship: *Raffaello*.

NEPTUNIA

Builder: Cantieri Riuniti dell' Adriatico, Monfalcone, Italy
Completed: September 1932
Gross tonnage: 19,475
Dimensions: 590' x 76' Depth: 46'
Engines: Two 8-cylinder and two 9-cylinder, 2-stroke, single-acting Sulzer diesels
Screws: Quadruple
Watertight bulkheads: Ten
Decks: Four
Normal speed: 19 knots (attained a speed of 21.08 knots on her trial runs)
Passenger accommodations: 175 cabin and 709 third class
Registry: Italy
Maiden voyage: Under Cosulich Line, Naples-Buenos Aires on October 7, 1932

Built for the Italian Cosulich Line. Transferred to the Italian Line in January 1935 upon absorption of the Cosulich Line. Engaged in the Genoa-Bombay-Shanghai service via the Suez Canal beginning February 1935 onwards. Sunk by the British submarine H.M.S. *Upholder* in the Mediterranean while enroute from Taranto, Italy to Tripoli, Libya while transporting Italian troops on September 18, 1941.

Sister ship: *Oceania*.

Note: The *Neptunia* commenced her maiden voyage following a promotional voyage from Naples to Venice on the 5th of October 1932.

OCEANIA

Builder: Cantieri Riuniti dell' Adriatico, Monfalcone, Italy
Completed: July 1933
Gross tonnage: 19,507
Dimensions: 590' x 77' Depth: 46'
Engines: Four Fiat 8-cylinder, 2-stroke, single-acting diesels
Screws: Quadruple
Watertight bulkheads: Ten
Decks: Four
Normal speed: 19 knots (attained a speed of 22.12 knots during her trials)
Passenger accommodations: 200 cabin, 400 third and 650 steerage
Officers and crew: 250
Registry: Italy
Maiden voyage: Under Cosulich Line, Trieste-Buenos Aires on
  April 6, 1933

Built for the Italian-owned Cosulich Line. Transferred to the Italian Line in January 1935 upon absorption of the Cosulich Line. Engaged in the Genoa-Bombay-Shanghai service via the Suez Canal from February 1935 onwards. Fitted-out as a troop transport by the Italian Government in the Second World War, she was transporting troops from Taranto to Tripoli when she was attacked by the British submarine H.M.S. *Upholder* on September 18, 1941. The *Oceania* was in a convoy with other Italian merchant ships and was escorted by five Italian destroyers. Following a direct hit, she was taken in tow by one of the destroyers sixty miles off the coast of North Africa. The *Upholder* returned four hours later and after two more torpedoes were fired sank the ship. Her sister ship, the *Neptunia*, which was a part of the convoy, was also sunk the same day and between the estimated 5,500 onboard both ships 384 people died.

Sister ship: *Neptunia.*

ORAZIO

Builder: Cantieri ed Officine, Meridionale, Baia, Italy
Completed: October 1927
Gross tonnage: 11,669
Dimensions: 506′ x 62′ Depth: 36′ Draft: 27′
Engines: Two 8-cylinder, 4-stroke, single-acting diesels
Screws: Twin
Watertight bulkheads: Nine
Decks: Four
Normal speed: 14 knots
Passenger accommodations: 110 first, 190 second and 340 third class
Officers and crew: 200
Registry: Italy

Built for the Navigazione Generale Italiana. Transferred to the Italian Line on January 2, 1932 upon amalgamation of the NGI and the Lloyd Sabaudo. Engaged in the Genoa-Mediterranean ports-Central and South American ports-Valparaiso service. The *Orazio* burned just outside of Marseilles, France while enroute from Genoa to Valparaiso after an explosion. Abandoned on January 21, 1940 by her officers, crew and the passengers most of whom were Jewish refugees fleeing Europe. It was believed that the explosion was the work of the German Gestapo or Italian Fascists. Broken up by March 1940.

Sister ship: *Virgilio.*

RAFFAELLO

Builder: Cantieri Riuniti dell' Adriatico, Monfalcone, Italy
Completed: July 1965
Gross tonnage: 45,933
Dimensions: 905' x 102' Depth: 52' Draft: 31'
Engines: Four steam turbines, double-reduction geared
Screws: Twin
Watertight bulkheads: Sixteen
Decks: Six
Normal speed: 26.50 knots (attained a speed of 30.15 knots on her trials)
Passenger accommodations: 452 first, 538 cabin and 1,111 tourist class
Officers and crew: 720
Registry: Italy
Maiden voyage: Genoa-Cannes-Naples-New York on July 5, 1965

Employed in the Genoa-Cannes-Naples-Barcelona-Algeciras-Madeira-New York service with occasional calls later at Port Everglades when making a triangular crossing: Halifax westbound on occasion; Tenerife-Casablanca-Palma de Majorca and Palermo on occasion. Fully air-conditioned and equipped with motion stabilizers. The *Raffaello* was constructed with a bulbous bow to eliminate drag and increase her speed. Her smokestacks were constructed of a fiber glass casing enclosing the conventional funnel. The innovativeness of the new style caught one's attention but seemed a bit ostentatious for a liner. Employed in the cruise market to the West Indies, by the late sixties she was working the transatlantic run intermittently. Both the *Raffaello* and her sister ship, the *Michelangelo*, were fitted with an evaporating plant to convert sea water to fresh water. On October 31, 1965 a fire broke out in her engine room and she returned to Genoa while being propelled by one engine driving a single screw. When the oil crisis hit she was sent mostly cruising in 1974 and the following year made only two transatlantic crossings. Financial difficulties forced the nearly bankrupt Italian Government to stop making subsidies to the Italian Line and the ship was forced into an early retirement. Made her last voyage for the Italian Line on April 21, 1975 from New York to Algeciras-Naples-Cannes-Genoa arriving on the 30th. Later laid up at anchor off Portovenere near La Spezia on June 6, 1975 pending her sale. Sold to the Iranian Government in December 1976 for $18,000,000 to be used as an accommodation ship for naval officers and their families at Bandar Abbas, Iran. Reportedly sold for scrap though details sketchy.

Sister ship: *Michelangelo.*

REX

Builder: Societa Anonima Ansaldo, Sestri Ponente, Genoa, Italy
Completed: September 1932
Gross tonnage: 51,062
Dimensions: 880' x 97' Depth: 61' Draft: 33'
Engines: Twelve steam turbines, single-reduction geared
Screws: Quadruple
Watertight bulkheads: Fourteen
Decks: Six
Normal speed: 28 knots (attained a speed of 28.90 knots on her trials)
Passenger accommodations: 378 first, 378 second, 410 tourist and 866 third class
Officers and crew: 810
Registry: Italy
Maiden voyage: Genoa-New York on September 27, 1932

The keel was originally laid down for the Navigazione Generale Italiana and was to be named *Guglielmo Marconi*. Passed on to the Italian Line ownership when the NGI and the Lloyd Sabaudo merged on January 2, 1932 to form the Italian Line. Employed in the Genoa-New York run year-round. The *Rex's* maiden voyage was marred by technical problems with her turbo dynamos causing her to put in at Gibraltar for repairs. After three days she resumed her transatlantic crossing but many of her passengers had left the ship to make other means of transportation. The embarrassment fell more on her owners but the liner still received the tumultuous welcome all liners receive when entering New York harbour for the first time. On August 16, 1933 she more than made up for the mishap when she made the run from Tarifa Point to Ambrose Lighthouse in 4 days, 13 hours, and 58 minutes at a speed of 28.92 knots, thereby winning the coveted Blue Riband from the North German Lloyd's *Bremen*. In March 1937 she experienced one of her worst passages when she was caught in a gale between the Azores and Cape Vincent. One crew member was killed when an immense wave struck the ship, causing a list of 20 degrees. Several passengers were also injured at the time o occurrence. The *Rex's* upper promenade deck was 619' long. Laid up temporarily at Bari, Italy in October 1939, she made her last voyage for the Italian Line leaving New York for the last time on December 14, 1939 On September 8, 1944 she was attacked by British Beaufighters who scored 123 hits on the lovely *Rex* and sank her in low water just outside o Capo d'Istria, Trieste, Italy where she lay on her port side. All movable property had been stripped by the Germans prior to her destruction Refloated in 1947 with the hope of salvaging the remaining hulk, the *Rex* now lay in a section of the harbour belonging to Yugoslavia, and to the discretion of the Slavs, it was concluded to sell her for scrap. The Italian had to settle for the ship's brass bell as a token of her memory. Broken up at Trieste in July 1947 where demolition began on July 30th. The *Rex* was the only Italian liner to ever win the Blue Riband and to the testament o my father who travelled on her, one of the best looking liners to ever wear the colours of the Italian Line. The *Rex's* half-ton bronze bell stood in the foyer of the Italian Line's head office in Genoa until the company was dissolved in 1977.

ROMA

Builder: Societa Anonima Ansaldo, Sestri Ponente, Genoa, Italy

Completed: September 1926

Gross tonnage: 30,816

Dimensions: 710' x 83' Depth: 52' Draft: 30'

Engines: Eight steam turbines, single-reduction geared

Screws: Quadruple

Watertight bulkheads: Twelve

Decks: Six

Normal speed: 19 knots

Passenger accommodations: Under N.G.I.-281 first, 672 second and 757 third class

Officers and crew: 510

Registry: Italy

Maiden voyage: Under N.G.I., Genoa-New York arriving at New York on October 1, 1926

Built for the Navigazione Generale Italiana. Transferred to the Italian Line on January 2, 1932 when the N.G.I. and the Lloyd Sabaudo consolidated to form the Italian Line. Engaged in the Genoa-New York service until 1933 when she was reallocated to the Genoa-Capetown route. Roma's second class was divided into a regular and intermediate category. Made only two voyages to New York in 1939, her last leaving from New York on September 12, 1939. Acquired by the Italian Navy in October 1940 and renamed *Aquila* in 1943. Her cabin fittings were being removed by the Germans when she was damaged by five direct hits from allied aircraft at Genoa on June 20, 1944. At the time she was being converted to an aircraft carrier and nearly completed. Bombed and sunk at Genoa on July 14, 1945. She was refloated and sold for scrap at La Spezia, Italy in 1950.

Sister ship: *Augustus*.

ROSSINI

Builder: Cantieri Riuniti dell' Adriatico, Trieste, Italy
Completed: September 1951
Gross tonnage: 13,225
Dimensions: 528' x 69' Depth: 42' Draft: 27'
Engines: Two 10-cylinder, 2-stroke, single-acting Sulzer diesels
Screws: Twin
Watertight bulkheads: Nine
Decks: Four
Normal speed: 19.5 knots
Passenger accommodations: 103 first and 446 tourist class
Officers and crew: 236
Registry: Italy

Built for the Lloyd Triestino and christened *Neptunia*. Bartered to the Italian Line in the spring of 1963 and renamed *Rossini*. Engaged in the Genoa-Naples-Cannes-Barcelona-Lisbon-Tenerife-La Guaira-Curacao-Cartagena-Cristobal-Buena Ventura-Guayaquil-Callao-Arica-Antofagasta-Valparaiso service. Equipped with motion stabilizers and fully air conditioned. The *Rossini* and her sister ships *Donizetti* and *Verdi* were often referred to as "the musicians." Withdrawn from service and sold for scrap to the C.N.S. Maria at La Spezia, Italy. Dismantling began on November 14, 1977.

Sister ships: *Donizetti* and *Verdi*.

SARDEGNA

Builder: Bremer Vulkan, Vegesack, Germany
Completed: August 1923
Gross tonnage: 11,452
Dimensions: 512' x 66' Depth: 34'
Engines: Two 3-cylinder, triple expansion
Screws: Twin
Watertight bulkheads: Nine
Decks: Four
Normal speed: 14 knots
Officers and crew: 250
Registry: Italy

Built for the North German Lloyd Line and christened *Sierra Ventana*. Sold to the Italian Line in 1935 and renamed *Sardegna*. Sold to the Lloyd Triestino in 1937. Engaged in the Genoa-South American trade; later used mostly as a troop ship to transport Italian soldiers to Abyssinia (Ethiopia). Sunk by the Greek submarine *Papa Nicolaou*, a former American submarine from World War I, on December 29, 1940 while on a troop-carrying mission from Brindisi to Albania.

SATURNIA

Builder: Cantiere Navale Triestino, Monfalcone, Italy
Completed: September 1927
Gross tonnage: 24,346
Dimensions: 651' x 80' Depth: 47' Draft: 29'
Engines: Two 10-cylinder, 2-stroke, double-acting Sulzer diesels
Screws: Twin
Collision bulkhead: One
Watertight bulkheads: Nine
Decks: Five
Normal speed: 21 knots
Passenger accommodations: 272 first, 332 cabin and 1,322 tourist class
Registry: Italy
Maiden voyage: Under Cosulich Line, Trieste-Patras-Palermo-Naples-New York, arriving at New York on February 16, 1928

Built for the Cosulich Line, the *Saturnia* was transferred to the Italian Line in January 1937 when it absorbed the Cosulich Line and was employed in the Trieste-Mediterranean ports-New York run. In 1935 her Burmeister and Wain eight-cylinder, four-stroke diesel engines were replaced by the type listed. Requisitioned for troop service to East Africa on August 24, 1935 to transport Italian troops. One of the first mot ships in the Italian merchant marine, the *Saturnia* and her sister carri thousands of Italians to the United States before and after the War. La up for much of the Second World War, the *Saturnia* was requisitioned the United States for use as a hospital ship in 1943 and renamed *Franc Y. Slanger*. Returned to the Italian Line in November 1946, she revert to her original name after being laid up at New York for a time. Resum transatlantic service (Naples-Genoa-New York) after being recondition on January 20, 1947. She later reverted to her home port of Trieste a worked the Venice-Patras-Naples-Palermo-Gibraltar-Lisbon-Halifax-N York route, beginning on November 8, 1955. The *Saturnia* made occasional eastbound call at Boston and Ponta Delgada. With the debut the new *Michelangelo* in the offing, the *Saturnia* was withdrawn fro service, making her last crossing for the line on March 25, 1965, N York-Boston-Lisbon-Gibraltar-Palermo-Naples-Patras-Venice-Tries Upon arrival on April 4th, the ship was laid up and sold for scrap to t Terrestre Marittima S.p.A. She arrived at La Spezia on October 7t Dismantling began on December 1, 1965.

Sister ship: *Vulcania.*

VERDI

Builder: Cantieri Riuniti dell' Adriatico, Trieste, Italy
Completed: August 1951
Gross tonnage: 13,226
Dimensions: 529' x 69' Depth: 42' Draft: 27'
Engines: Two 10-cylinder, 2-stroke, single-acting Sulzer diesels
Screws: Twin
Watertight bulkheads: Nine
Decks: Four
Normal speed: 17.50 knots
Passenger accommodations: 103 first and 446 tourist class
Officers and crew: 236
Registry: Italy

Built for the Lloyd Triestino and christened *Oceania*. Bartered to the Italian Line in the spring of 1963 for another vessel and renamed *Verdi*. Employed in the Genoa-Naples-Cannes-Barcelona-Lisbon-Tenerife-La Guaira-Curacao-Cartagena-Cristobal-Buena Ventura-Guayaquil-Callao-Arica-Antofagasta-Valparaiso service. Equipped with motion stabilizers and fully air-conditioned. Withdrawn from service in the spring of 1977 and sold for scrap to the Terrestre Marittima at La Spezia, Italy where breaking up commenced on June 23rd.

Sister ships: *Donizetti* and *Rossini*.

VIRGILIO

Builder: Cantieri ed Officine, Meridionali, Baia, Italy
Completed: April 1928
Gross tonnage: 11,718
Dimensions: 506' x 62' Depth: 36' Draft: 27'
Engines: Two 8-cylinder, 4-stroke, single-acting diesels
Screws: Twin
Normal speed: 14 knots
Passenger accommodations: 110 first, 190 second and 340 third class
Officers and crew: 200
Registry: Italy

Built for the Navigazione Generale Italiana. Transferred to the Italian Line on January 2, 1932 upon amalgamation of the NGI and the Lloyd Sabaudo. Employed in the Genoa-Mediterranean ports-Central and South American ports-Valparaiso service. Converted to a hospital ship in June 1940. Seized by the Germans at Toulon, France after Italy's surrender to the allies in September 1943. She was damaged by a torpedo attack in December 1943. Obstructing the entrance into Toulon harbour, she was scuttled by the Germans in June 1944.

Sister ship: *Orazio.*

VULCANIA

Builder: Cantiere Navale Triestino, Monfalcone, Italy
Completed: December 1928
Gross tonnage: 24,496
Dimensions: 652′ x 80′ Depth: 47′ Draft: 29′
Engines: Two Fiat 10-cylinder, 2-stroke, double-acting diesels
Screws: Twin
Collision bulkhead: One
Watertight bulkheads: Nine
Decks: Five
Normal speed: 21 knots (attained a speed of 23.33 knots on her trials)
Passenger accommodations: 199 first, 269 cabin and 1,275 tourist class
Registry: Italy
Maiden voyage: Under Cosulich Line, Trieste-Patras-Palermo-Naples
   arriving at New York on December 31, 1928

Built for the Cosulich Line. Transferred to the Italian Line in January 1937 after absorption of the Cosulich Line. Employed in the Trieste-Mediterranean ports-New York service. In 1935 her former Burmeister & Wain eight-cylinder, four-stroke diesel engines were replaced by the presently stated type of propulsion. Commandeered by the United States in 1943 for troop work. In the early hours of February 15, 1946 she collided with an iceberg but sustained little damage to her hull. Returned back to the Italian Line after having been decommissioned on December 14, 1946. She resumed scheduled sailings from Genoa to Naples-New York on August 29, 1947. The *Vulcania* made an occasional call at the port of Boston eastbound. Differing somewhat from her sister ship, the *Vulcania* was the first luxury liner to offer privately partitioned promenade deck space for first class passengers. She reverted back to working out of her home port of Trieste on October 28, 1955 and worked to Venice-Patras-Naples-Palermo-Gibraltar-Lisbon-Halifax-New York. In her later years, calls at Dubrovnik and Barcelona were also made. She commenced her last voyage for the Italian Line on April 21, 1965, New York-Lisbon-Gibraltar-Palermo-Naples-Patras-Venice-Trieste. Sold to the Italian Grimaldi-Siosa Line in May 1965 and renamed *Caribia* in late 1965. Sold to Italian scrappers in January 1973. Resold to Spanish scrappers in September. Resold in February to breakers in Taiwan, she left Barcelona in tow on March 15, 1974. After her arrival at Kaohsiung she sank in the harbour due to leakages in her hull on July 20, 1974. She was eventually raised and dismantled. One of Italy's most luxurious liners ever built. I often found it a lark to look over a ticket my father had purchased for a transatlantic crossing on this lovely liner back in 1934.

Sister ship: *Saturnia.*

North German Lloyd

BARBAROSA

Builder: Blohm & Voss, Hamburg, Germany
Completed: January 1897
Gross tonnage: 10,984
Dimensions: 526' x 60' Depth: 35'
Engines: Two 4-cylinder, quadruple expansion
Screws: Twin
Decks: Four
Normal speed: 13.50 knots
Passenger accommodations: 221 first, 554 second and 1,984 third class
Officers and crew: 226
Registry: Germany
Maiden voyage: Bremen-Australia, January 8, 1897*

*Maiden voyage to the United States, Bremen-New York, arriving on June 7, 1897

Employed in the Bremen-New York run during the summer season and from Bremen-Southampton to Adelaide-Melbourne-Sydney in the winter months via the Suez Canal. While working the North Atlantic run she also made occasional calls at Philadelphia, Baltimore, and Galveston. The *Barbarosa* also made a few trips from the Mediterranean to New York between 1906-1910. Made her last voyage to Australia from Bremen-Southampton-Suez Canal-Adelaide-Melbourne-Sydney on December 25, 1910. Reverted to the New York run in May 1911, with voyages to the Mediterranean by 1913. Interned at the port of New York upon arrival on July 29, 1914, and seized by the United States Government upon America's entry into World War I on April 6, 1917. Commissioned as a troop ship on August 3, 1917, and renamed *Mercury*. She was released from transport work in September 1919 but retained by the United States Government. Laid up and sold for scrap in 1924.

Sister ship: *Bremen.*

II BERLIN

Builder: A. G. Weser, Bremen, Germany
Completed: April 1909
Gross tonnage: 17,324
Dimensions: 613' x 70' Depth: 42' Draft: 31'
Engines: Two 4-cylinder quadruple expansion
Screws: Twin
Watertight bulkheads: Ten
Decks: Four
Normal speed: 17 knots
Passenger accommodations: 263 first, 464 second and 2,618 third class
Officers and crew: 410
Registry: Germany
Maiden voyage: Bremen-New York on May 1, 1909

Employed in the Genoa-New York service interchangeable with the Bremen-New York run. In 1910 she worked the Mediterranean route year-round making only one voyage on the Bremen-New York route in 1911. The following year she was again interchangeable between Bremen-New York and the Mediterranean service. She made her last voyage from New York to Bremen on July 18, 1914, and was converted to a minelayer on September 18, 1914. The *Bremen* is alleged to have laid the mine that sunk the British battleship *Audacious* off the Ulster coast of Ireland on October 26th of that year. Interned at Trondheim, Norway on November 17, 1914, she was allocated to Britain on December 13, 1919, and managed by the P & O Line until sold by the British Shipping Controller to the White Star Line in November 1920. Renamed *Arabic*, she also ran under the services of the closely-affiliated Red Star Line. Both companies were at one time controlled by the American-owned International Mercantile Marine of J. P. Morgan, the American financier. Reverted back to the White Star Line in 1930 and sold for scrap in Genoa, Italy in December, 1931.

Sister Ship: *Prinz Friedrich Wilhelm.*

III BERLIN

Builder: Bremer Vulkan, Vegesack, Germany
Completed: September 1925
Gross tonnage: 15,286
Dimensions: 572' x 69' Depth: 39'
Engines: Two 4-cylinder triple expansion
Screws: Twin
Decks: Four
Normal speed: 16.50 knots
Passenger accommodations: 257 cabin, 294 tourist and 361 third class*
Officers and crew: 326
Registry: Germany
Maiden voyage: Bremen-Southampton-New York on September 26, 1925

*Originally carried: 263 first, 294 second and 546 third class.

Employed in the Bremen-Southampton-Cherbourg-New York service. On November 12, 1928, the Berlin rescued 23 people from the sinking British Lamport & Holt liner *Vestris* which was enroute from New York to Barbados. She later picked up 202 survivors from 8 lifeboats. Made two West Indies cruises out of New York in 1931. In 1932 she was converted to a cabin class ship. The *Berlin* made her last transatlantic crossing from Bremen-Southampton-Galway-Halifax-New York on October 11, 1938, and was subsequently laid up upon her return to Germany. Chartered by the Nazis in May, 1939, as a workers' cruising ship and was later used as a hospital ship during the war. At one time she was used to repatriate Germans from European ports to the fatherland following the German invasion of Poland, Austria, and the Sudetenland. Sunk by a mine off Swinemunde Bay, Poland on February 1, 1945, she was refloated and salvaged by the Russians in 1948 and renamed *Admiral Nakhimov*. Re-entered their service in May 1957. Placed under their Black Sea S. S. Company, she was rammed and sunk by the Soviet freighter *Pyotr Vasyev* nine miles from the port of Novorossiysk, Russia on August 31, 1986 with a heavy loss of life.

IV BERLIN

Builder: W. G. Armstrong, Whitworth & Co., Ltd., Newcastle-on-Tyne, England
Completed: November 1925
Gross tonnage: 18,600
Dimensions: 590' x 74' Depth: 43' Draft: 29'
Engines: Two 6-cylinder, 4-stroke, double-acting Burmeister & Wain diesels
Screws: Twin
Watertight bulkheads: Ten
Decks: Five
Normal speed: 15.50 knots
Passenger accommodations: 206 first and 987 tourist class
Officers and crew: 354
Registry: Germany
Maiden voyage: Bremerhaven-Halifax-New York on January 8, 1955

Built for the Swedish-American Line and christened *Gripsholm*. Sold to the Bremen-Amerika Line on January 30, 1954, a partnership firm between the Swedish-American Line and the North German Lloyd. Sailing with the colours of both lines, a white hull and buff stacks, she later passed on to full ownership under the North German Lloyd in January 1955 and was renamed *Berlin*. Engaged in the Bremerhaven-New York service with a call at Halifax westbound and sometimes eastbound. She added Cherbourg to her itinerary in January 1959, and Halifax became only a westbound call. The *Berlin* was the first liner to inaugurate service between Germany and the United States since 1939. The port of Southampton was incorporated into her route in June 1960. During her latter years she began making an annual crossing to Montreal and several experimental cruises from New York to Bermuda, the Caribbean. Cruises from Bremerhaven to Scandinavia and the Canaries and the Mediterranean made up her schedule during the summer months. Made her last voyage for the North German Lloyd on September 3, 1966, New York-Cherbourg-Southampton-Bremerhaven. Sold to Italian shipbreakers on October 15, 1966, and was broken up at La Spezia beginning November 26th.

Note: Made her first voyage under the Bremen-Amerika Line on January 12, 1954, New York-Bremen-Gothenburg-Copenhagen-New York, as *Gripsholm*.

II BREMEN

Builder: F. Schichau, Danzig, Germany
Completed: May 1897
Gross tonnage: 11,540
Dimensions: 569′ x 60′ Depth: 35′
Engines: Two 4-cylinder, quadruple expansion
Screws: Twin
Decks: Four
Normal speed: 18.50 knots
Passenger accommodations: 297 first, 427 second and 1,725 third class
Officers and crew: 250
Registry: Germany
Maiden voyage: Bremen-New York on June 5, 1897

Engaged in the Bremen-Southampton-Adelaide-Melbourne-Sydney trade via the Suez Canal. The *Bremen* worked this route interchangeable with the Bremen-Southampton-New York service in the summer months, reverting to the Australian run the first four and last four months of the year. In 1898 she did not make any trips to New York. The *Bremen* was present at the great dock fire at Hoboken, New Jersey on June 30, 1900, and was seriously damaged in her above deck area. The fireboat *New Yorker* managed to rescue 28 persons off the *Bremen* during the blaze but 12 persons lost their lives. The liner was later towed and beached in shallow water off Weehawken, New Jersey. Repaired and her length increased from 525 feet to 550 feet registered length. She re-entered service on October 11, 1901, after rebuilding at the Vulkan Shipyards in Stettin, Germany. Reallocated to the Bremen-New York run on a permanent basis after making her last trip to Australia on October 1, 1911. The *Bremen* remained on this route until July 4, 1914, when she made her last New York-Bremen voyage. Allotted to the British in 1919 as a World War I reparation. Transferred to the British P & O Line for management on April 4 until she was sold to the National Greek Line and renamed *Byron* in December, 1921; *Constantinople* in 1923. Resold to the Steam Navigation Company, Ltd., of Greece in 1923 and renamed *King Alexander*; *Moreas* in May 1925. Sold for scrap in Italy in 1929.

Sister ship: *Barbarosa.*

IV BREMEN

Builder: A. G. Weser, Bremen, Germany
Completed: June 1929
Gross tonnage: 51,731
Dimensions: 938' x 102' Depth: 48'
Engines: Twelve steam turbines, single-reduction geared
Screws: Quadruple
Watertight bulkheads: Fourteen
Decks: Seven
Normal speed: 27.50 knots (she attained a speed of 28.50 knots on her trial runs)
Passenger accommodations: 723 first, 600 second, 908 third class
Officers and crew: 944
Registry: Germany
Maiden voyage: Bremen-Southampton-Cherbourg-New York on July 16, 1929

Engaged in the Bremen-Southampton-Cherbourg-New York service. The *Bremen* won the Blue Riband from the Cunard Line's *Mauretania* on her maiden voyage by making the run from Cherbourg to Ambrose Lighthouse in 4 days, 17 hours and 42 minutes at a speed of 27.83 knots. She was the first liner to be built with a bulbous bow, intended by her German designers to increase her speed by displacing the water in front of the ship's track. Her hull featured a new method of construction, overlapping the plating from the bow to the stern, thereby increasing her

speed another half knot or so. The largest liner ever built to date for the German merchant fleet she consumed 830 tons of oil every 24 hours. She was fitted with anti-rolling tanks to stabilize her in bad weather. Her funnels were later raised 15 feet because of lingering exhaust residue on her aft decks. In February 1939 the *Bremen* passed through the Panama Canal while on a pleasure cruise around South America. At the time she was the largest ship to ever pass through the canal. Anticipating war between Great Britain and Germany, the *Bremen* slipped out of New York harbour on the night of August 30, 1939, just two days after her arrival there for the last time. She made her clandestine voyage without passengers and headed for the port of Murmansk, Russia by way of Scotland and Norway, thus avoiding the English Channel. Enroute her crew members were slung alongside in the vessel's lifeboats and painted the ship battle grey to camouflage her. During the voyage she had been spotted by the British submarine *Salmon* but was fortunate to escape being sunk. Arriving at Murmansk on December 10th, she later crossed to Germany and was secretly berthed in Bremerhaven. On March 16, 1941, the majestic *Bremen* was badly damaged by fire. The Germans claimed to have extinguished the flames the following day but a Berlin correspondent of a Gothenburg newspaper stated that the liner was totally destroyed. She remained at Bremerhaven, burnt-out amidships; by May 1945 the ship was considered a total loss. It is possible, according to Lloyd's of London, that she suffered additional damage by "war causes." She was slowly being broken up in February 1949, and by 1953 had become a part of history.

Sister ship: *Europa.*

V BREMEN

Builder: Chantiers & Ateliers de Penhoet, St. Nazaire, France
Completed: August 1939
Gross tonnage: 32,360
Dimensions: 697' x 90' Depth: 48' Draft: 31'
Engines: Four Parson steam turbines, single-reduction geared
Screws: Quadruple
Decks: Five
Normal speed: 23.50 knots
Passenger accommodations: 216 first and 1,034 tourist class
Officers and crew: 544
Registry: Germany
Maiden voyage: Bremerhaven-Southampton-Cherbourg-New York on
  July 9, 1959

Built for the French Compagnie Sud-Atlantique and christened *Pasteur*. Sold to the North German Lloyd on September 18, 1957. Rebuilt by the Bremen Vulkan Shipyards between 1958-July 1959. Following a nearly complete rebuilding she was renamed *Bremen* in 1959. Employed in the Bremerhaven-Southampton-Cherbourg-New York run with some cruising during the off seasonal months to the West Indies. The Bremen was purchased for a cost of £2,000,000 sterling and refitted at a cost of an additional £6,000,000. On September 1, 1970, she passed on to a joint ownership between the North German Lloyd and the line's arch rival, the German Hamburg-American Line. The new line that was formed became known as Hapag-Lloyd. With each holding a 50 percent interest the merger arose more out of economic necessity amidst the competitiveness of the blooming cruise market. In 1971 the *Bremen* was sent cruising when transatlantic travel began to taper off. Unfortunately, the *Bremen* developed serious engine problems and she was soon retired. Made her last transatlantic crossing on December 14, 1971, New York-Cherbourg-Southampton-Bremerhaven. Thereafter she made one last cruise for the Line from Bremerhaven-Southampton-Funchal-Dakar-Sao Vicente, Cape Verde Islands-Las Palmas-Lisbon-Southampton-Bremerhaven. In the interim she had already been sold to the Greek Chandris Lines for $3,000,000. Delivered to them in January 1972, she was renamed *Regina Magna*. Resold to the Philippine Singapore Port Corporation in 1977 for use as a floating hotel and renamed *Saudi Phil I*. Renamed *Filipinas Saudi I* in March 1978. Sold for scrap in April 1980 to Taiwanese breakers, she capsized and sunk while being towed from Jeddah, India to Kaohsiung, Taiwan on June 9, 1980. A sad ending for a beautifully rebuilt ship. The *Bremen* had a world map which adorned her first class area with each country inlaid in fancy walnut burls. Their geographical lines as exacting and precise as the nation under which she was registered. She was the last flagship of the famed North German Lloyd.

II COLUMBUS

Builder: F. Schichau, Danzig, Germany
Completed: November 1923
Gross tonnage: 32,581
Dimensions: 775' x 83' Depth 49'
Engines: Two single-reduction geared turbines
Screws: Twin
Decks: Five
Normal speed: 23 knots
Passenger accommodations: 482 first, 757 second, and 705 third class
Officers and crew: 576
Registry: Germany
Maiden voyage: Bremen-New York on April 22, 1924

Laid down as the *Hindenburg* in 1914. It was later decided to give her the name of the former surrendered vessel *Columbus*, turned over to the allies after World War I. Christened *Columbus* upon launching in August 1922, she engaged in the Bremen-Southampton-New York service with a call at Plymouth eastbound in place of Southampton. In December 1929 she was re-engined and refitted. Her funnels were replaced by two shorter ones of greater diameter, making her appear somewhat like the sister ships *Bremen* and *Europa*. At the time of her overhaul she was converted from coal-firing to oil and her reciprocating engines replaced by the turbine engines listed. Re-entering service in May 1930, she made a world cruise that year. During the early '30s she cruised to the Canary Islands. Between February 8 and April 14, 1935, she cruised to Africa and India and made her last transatlantic voyage for the North German Lloyd from Bremen-Southampton-Cherbourg, arriving at New York on June 28, 1939. Placed in a cruise service out of New York, she made her last voyage to the West Indies on August 19, 1939, New York-Curacao-San Juan-Havana. Following the outbreak of war the *Columbus* avoided American ports because of prowling British warships in the area. On December 14, 1939, she was spotted by the U.S. cruiser *Tuscaloosa*, which radioed her approximate position to the British cruiser *Hyperion*, which intercepted her as she was attempting to sail for Germany. Since all of her passengers had been forced to disembark at her last port of call, Havana, the *Columbus* was on her own. In order to prevent the British from capturing her as a war prize Captain Daehne ordered the ship to be scuttled and set on fire 320 miles off Cape Hatteras. Two crew members were lost in the course of the ordeal. As the *Columbus* went down, the British, steaming abreast of the foundering liner to pick up survivors, ceremoniously lowered their ensign in a last salute.

II DRESDEN

Builder: Bremer Vulkan, Vegesack, Germany
Completed: January 1915
Gross tonnage: 14,690
Dimensions: 550' x 67' Depth: 39' Draft: 29'
Engines: Two 4-cylinder, quadruple expansion
Screws: Twin
Watertight bulkheads: Thirteen
Decks: Four
Normal speed: 15 knots
Passenger accommodations: 319 first, 156 second, 342 third, and 1,348 steerage class
Officers and crew: 320
Registry: Germany
Maiden voyage: Bremen-Southampton-Cherbourg-New York on August 5, 1927

Launched as the *Zeppelin* on June 9, 1914, but completion was suspended. Surrendered to the United States on March 28, 1919, for five trips to repatriate American troops from Europe. Allotted to the British Shipping Controller in November 1919 and managed by the White Star Line. Sold to the Orient Line in 1920 and renamed *Ormuz*. Resold to the North German Lloyd in April 1927 and renamed *Dresden*. She had originally been built for the Australian trade but was used in the Bremen-Cherbourg-New York service. With the drop in revenues brought about by the Great Depression she was sent cruising. Made her last voyage for the Line on September 21, 1933, New York-Bremen. Struck a submerged rock ripping her bottom in the Bokn Fjord near Kopervik, Norway on June 20, 1934, while on a North Sea cruise with about one thousand passengers aboard. The *Dresden* was beached on the island of Karmoy but became a total loss and sank the following day. Her mostly Nazi society passengers were rescued by the Danish ship *Kon Haakon* but four women lost their lives when a lifeboat capsized.

II EUROPA

Builder: Blohm & Voss, Hamburg, Germany
Completed: March 1929
Gross tonnage: 49,746
Dimensions: 936' x 102' Depth: 48'
Engines: Twelve steam turbines, single reduction geared
Screws: Quadruple
Watertight bulkheads: Fourteen
Decks: Seven
Normal speed: 27.50 knots
Passenger accommodations: 723 first, 616 tourist and 905 third class
Officers and crew: 970
Registry: Germany
Maiden voyage: Bremen-Southampton-Cherbourg-New York on
  March 19, 1930

Launched on August 15, 1928, her maiden voyage was held up due to a fire onboard on March 26, 1929, while being fitted out. Employed in the Bremen-Channel ports-New York service, the *Europa* won the Blue Riband from her sister the *Bremen* in 1930 by making the run from Cherbourg to Ambrose Lighthouse in 4 days, 17 hours, and 6 minutes at a speed of 27.91 knots. A fast liner but not as swift as her sister ship, she soon lost the position. *Europa* also carried a catapult as did the Bremen for launching a seaplane to expedite the mail as she approached land. Maintaining service for over a decade on the North Atlantic run, she made her last voyage for the North German Lloyd on August 23, 1939, from New York to Bremen via Cherbourg and Southampton. In September 1939 she was moved to Hamburg and later used as a naval accommodation ship at Kiel, Germany for a time. Sold to the German-American Line in 1945 and made three voyages as an American transport beginning in May. Allotted to France in May 1946 as a World War II reparation and transferred to the French Line in July 1946 and renamed *Liberté*. Sold to Italian shipbreakers on December 30, 1961, at La Spezia and broken up by June 1962.

Sister ship: *Bremen.*

III EUROPA

Builder: De Schelde N.V., Flushing, Netherlands
Completed: October 1953
Gross tonnage: 21,514
Dimensions: 600' x 77' Depth: 49' Draft: 26'
Engines: Two Burmeister & Wain 8-cylinder, 2-stroke, single-acting diesel
Screws: Twin
Collision bulkhead: One
Watertight Bulkheads: Eight
Decks: Five
Normal speed: 17.50 knots
Passenger accommodations: 122 first and 721 tourist class (accommodations are reduced to 400 in a single class when cruising)
Officers and Crew: 308
Registry: Germany
Maiden voyage: Bremerhaven-Southampton-Cherbourg-Halifax-New York on January 9, 1966

Built for the Swedish-American Line and christened *Kungsholm*. Sold to the North German Lloyd on October 16, 1965, and renamed *Europa*. Engaged in the Bremerhaven-Southampton-Cherbourg-New York run with cruises during the off-season months to the West Indies and with special longer cruises to the South American continent. A most beautifully designed liner with many old world concepts and comforts. All cabins were located outside; she was fully air-conditioned and equipped with Denny Brown stabilizers. The *Europa's* fore-funnel was a dummy. She had a fuel capacity of some 1,712 metric tons and a daily consumption of 55 metric tons. She began a series of cruises from Bremerhaven and Genoa between April 25 and August 25, 1971. The drop in transatlantic trade assured her position in European waters and she began making 7-day cruises to the Baltic and up to 17-day cruises to West Africa thereafter, with an occasional 100-day cruise to the Middle East and the South Pacific via the Suez Canal. In September 1978 she called at New York while on a long cruise to the Caribbean. Sold to the Italian Costa Line in October 1981 and renamed *Columbus C.* in 1982; subsequently renamed *Costa Columbus* in early 1984. The *Europa* had come under Hapag-Lloyd ownership on September 1, 1970, when the two venerable lines of the Hamburg-American Line and the North German Lloyd merged. She rammed the breakwater at Cadiz, Spain on September 29, 1984, and was taken in tow after a heavy list developed following engine room flooding. Sunk at the passenger pier, she was refloated on November 2nd. Towed to Barcelona and sold for scrap to the Demoliciones Espanolas S.A., with work commencing on June 1, 1985. I had the pleasure of making the last transatlantic crossing of this lovely ship on March 31, 1971. I remember vividly the lovely dining room and afternoon tea in the main lounge accompanied by Viennese music; the midnight sailing out of New York harbour; a warm note sent to my cabin from the Captain George H. Will which I quote, "I am always pleased to meet people who are willing to keep alive the memories of fine and splendid ships whose times will never come back." Now the *Europa* is also one of those ships.

IV EUROPA

Builder: Bremer Vulkan, A.G. Bremen, Vegesack, Germany
Completed: 1981
Gross tonnage: 33,819
Dimensions: 653' x 98' Depth: 59' Draft: 28'
Engines: Two MAN 2-stroke single-acting, 7-cylinder diesel plus an athwartship propeller forward
Screws: Twin
Decks: Seven
Normal speed: 21 knots
Passenger accommodations: 758 in a single class
Officers and crew: 280
Registry: Germany
Maiden voyage: Genoa-Mediterranean on January 8, 1982

Built exclusively for Hapag-Lloyd. This fourth *Europa** is the first to be built on German soil since the North German Lloyd had relied on older foreign-owned tonnage that made up its postwar liner fleet. When international shipping was suffering the former rivals Hamburg-American Line and North German Lloyd merged on September 1, 1970, to form the new company. This vessel though thoroughly modern lacks the ultra-conservatism that was an intricate part of the former liners. Some of her public rooms are finished with contemporary tones. Though one redeeming feature is that her cabins, most of which are situated forward and in the central part of the ship, are devoid of any engine vibrations emanating from below. Cabins are spacious considering she is a newly-built liner. But like many new liners which seem to be designed after high skyscrapers she is top-heavy looking, and her somewhat shallow draft could make any true mariner think twice before cruising in rougher seas. Since many new ships are being built with considerably shallower drafts and flatter bottoms in order to cruise in such heretofore inaccessible waterways as the Amazon River, there is no need to worry since weather and routing are programmed as accurately as humanly possible when making itineraries. The *Europa* caters mostly to a European market but has made an occasional call at New York in the past. The *Europa* also offers a number of beautiful suites and her itineraries are worldwide and her timetable changes considerably from year to year as well as ports of call. At the time of this writing the *Europa* was rammed on her starboard side aft on April 29, 1992 while on a cruise in the South China Sea by the Greek containership *Instant Glory* just 207 miles outside of Hong Kong. The containership's bow penetrating the *Europa's* side nearly twenty feet inward around the main deck level. Neither ship was in danger of sinking.

Note: The ship is actually owned by the German Government's Bundesminister fur Forschung und Technologie.

*The Hamburg-American Line built the first *Europa* in 1891. The following ships to bear the name were ships of the North German Lloyd. These were built in 1905, 1930, 1953.

FRIEDRICH DER GROSSE

Builder: A.G. Vulkan, Stettin, Germany
Completed: November 1896
Gross tonnage: 10,771
Dimensions: 546' x 60' Depth: 35'
Engines: Two 4-cylinder, quadruple expansion
Screws: Twin
Watertight bulkheads: Twelve
Decks: Four
Normal speed: 15 knots
Passenger accommodations: 220 first, 350 second and 1,956 third class
Officers and crew: 222
Registry: Germany
Maiden voyage to the U.S.: Bremen-New York arriving at New York on April 17, 1897

Employed in the Bremen-Southampton-New York run during the summer months and in the Bremen-Southampton-Adelaide-Melbourne-Sydney trade via the Suez Canal during the winter season. She began her first voyage to Australia in November 1896. On January 27, 1908, she began running from New York to the Mediterranean and also became interchangeable between New York and Bremen. The following year she worked mostly on the North Atlantic run and Bremen-Sydney but again made a number of voyages from New York to the Mediterranean in 1910. Three years later she reverted back to the Bremen-New York and Bremen-Sydney route once again and in November of 1913 became a second class ship. Made her last voyage to Australia on January 18, 1914, and was then re-routed to work the Bremen-Philadelphia-Baltimore route in June. When World War I broke out she was interned at Baltimore on July 22, 1914. Seized by the United States Government on April 6, 1917, and commissioned as a troopship on July 25, 1917, with renaming to *Huron*. Decommissioned in September 1919, she was sold to the Munson Line in 1921 and subsequently to the Los Angeles Steamship Company in 1922 and renamed *City of Honolulu*. Caught fire on her return maiden voyage from Honolulu to San Pedro just 200 miles outside of Los Angeles on October 12, 1922. She was sunk by gunfire from the U.S. Army transport *Thomas* after evacuating her passengers and crew on the 17th.

GEORGE WASHINGTON

Builder: A. G. Vulkan, Stettin, Germany
Completed: June 1909
Gross tonnage: 25,570
Dimensions: 723' x 78' Depth: 50'
Engines: Two 4-cylinder, quadruple expansion
Screws: Twin
Watertight bulkheads: Twelve
Decks: Six
Normal speed: 19 knots
Passenger accommodations: 525 first, 534 second and 2,115 third class
Officers and crew: 585
Registry: Germany
Maiden voyage: Bremen-Southampton-Cherbourg-New York on
  June 12, 1909

Employed in the Bremen-Southampton-Cherbourg-New York run with a call at Plymouth eastbound in place of Southampton. In 1913 Mr. Ferencz Vaszily purchased the ten millionth ticket from the North German Lloyd by booking on the *George Washington* and was given a special accommodation by the Line. The *George Washington* had a promenade deck that extended 328 feet. Made her last transatlantic voyage for the North German Lloyd on July 25, 1914, from Bremen and was laid up upon arrival at New York on August 4th. Seized by the United States on April 4, 1917, and converted to a transport without a change in name on September 6th. The liner was used to carry President Wilson and his staff to the Versailles Peace Conferences and was not released until November 1919. Turned over to the newly-established United States Shipping Board the same year, she was later managed by the United States Mail Line from August 1920 until August 31, 1921, when the company went into bankruptcy. Ownership then passed to the United States Lines, a newly-formed company established by the U. S. Shipping Board. Returned to the U. S. Government in September 1931 and laid up in the Patuxent River. Taken over by the British in 1940 and renamed *Catlin* in 1941 and became a transport. Returned to the United States Government in February 1942 and recovered her own name. Decommissioned in March 1947, she was laid up at Baltimore. Sold for scrap after having been destroyed by fire on January 16, 1951.

II GNEISENAU

Builder: Deutsche Schiff-und-Mashinenbau, A.G. Weser, Bremen, Germany

Completed: December, 1935

Gross tonnage: 18,160

Dimensions: 652' x 74' Depth: 45' Draft: 27'

Engines: Two sets of steam turbines

Screws: Twin

Decks: Four

Passenger accommodations: 186 first and 150 second class

Officers and Crew: 281

Registry: Germany

Maiden voyage: Bremerhaven-East Asia on January 3, 1936

Employed in the Bremen-Southampton-Genoa-Shanghai service via the Suez Canal. She and her sister ship the *Scharnhorst* were the largest ships to date built with a maierform bow and were classified as cargo-passenger liners. Cargo capacity is for 10,800 tons. The *Gneisenau* became an accommodation ship for Nazi marines in 1940 and was later converted to an aircraft carrier by the Kriegsmarinewerft at Wilhelmshaven in 1942. Sunk by a mine in the Baltic Sea while enroute to Russia with troops on May 2, 1943. The *Geneisenau* was beached on the island of Lloland, Denmark where she lay on her side half submerged. She was later broken up by Danish shipbreakers after the war.

Sister ship: *Scharnhorst*.

GROSSER KURFURST

Builder: F. Schichau, Danzig, Germany
Completed: April 1900
Gross tonnage: 13,102
Dimensions: 580′ x 62′ Depth: 36′
Engines: Two 4-cylinder quadruple expansion
Screws: Twin
Watertight bulkheads: Twelve
Decks: Four
Normal speed: 16 knots
Passenger accommodations: 434 first, 524 second and 2,215 third class
Officers and crew: 273
Registry: Germany
Maiden voyage: Bremen-New York on May 5, 1900

Engaged in the alternate services from Bremen to New York and Central American ports during the summer and from Bremen to Southampton-Albany-Adelaide-Melbourne-Sydney via the Suez Canal during the winter months. On November 7, 1900, she made her first voyage to Australia; on March 8, 1904, her first New York-Mediterranean cruise. She made two more such cruises in 1909 with her last on February 3, 1910, out of New York. Her last voyage to Australian waters was made on January 21, 1912. Thereafter, she worked mostly on the North Atlantic run to New York and inaugurated an eastbound call at Baltimore on December 19, 1912. On October 9, 1913 she rescued 105 persons from the British Royal Line's emigrant ship *Volturno* ablaze in the Atlantic while on a westbound voyage. The *Grosser Kurfurst* played a major role in the life-saving operations. The first to arrive on the scene, she rescued 521 persons along with the assistance of eight other vessels. Interned at New York on July 22, 1914, and seized by the United States Government on April 6, 1917. Converted to a transport she was commissioned on July 28, 1917 and renamed *Aeolus*. Reverting back to the United States Shipping Board in September 1919 and laid up at Baltimore. Chartered over to the American Munson Line in 1920 and subsequently sold to the Los Angeles Steamship Company in June 1922, with renaming to *City of Los Angeles*. Transferred to the American Matson Lines in 1933 when they purchased the Los Angeles Steamship Company. Sold for scrap in Japan in February 1937.

KAISER FRIEDRICH

Builder: F. Schichau, Danzig, Germany
Completed: May 1898
Gross tonnage: 12,480
Dimensions: 582′ x 64′ Depth: 44′
Engines: Two sets of 10-cylinder, quadruple expansion engines
Screws: Twin
Decks: Four
Normal speed: 19 knots
Passenger accommodations: 400 first, 250 second and 700 third class
Officers and crew: 420
Registry: Germany
Maiden voyage: Bremen-Southampton-New York on June 7, 1898

Built expressly for the line, she was a disappointment for her owners when she made the transatlantic crossing at a poor speed of 19.12 knots, arriving in New York in seven and a half days. She made her last voyage for the line on June 2, 1899, from New York to Bremen and was returned to the builder as unsatisfactory since she was unable to meet the contract speed. F. Schichau in turn offered her for sale. Chartered by the Hamburg-American Line in March 1900, she made a total of seven round-trip voyages for them, her last in October. Laid up at Hamburg, she was offered to the newly formed Norwegian-America Line around 1907, but they declined. Finally sold to the French Compagnie Sud-Atlantique on May 1, 1912, after having been tied up at Danzig for nearly a decade. Sold for nearly one-third of her original cost and renamed *Burdigala*. Laid up at Bordeaux in November 1913, she became a French troop-ship in March 1915, and was sunk by the German U-73 between the Greek Islands of Mykonos and Tinos in the Aegean Sea on November 14, 1916.

KAISER WILHELM II

Builder: A. G. Vulkan, Stettin, Germany

Completed: March, 1903

Gross tonnage: 19,361

Dimensions: 707' x 72' Depth: 52'

Engines: Four 4-cylinder, quadruple expansion

Screws: Twin

Watertight bulkheads: Sixteen

Decks: Six

Normal speed: 22.75 knots

Passenger accommodations: 646 first, 499 second and 960 third class

Officers and crew: 600

Registry: Germany

Maiden voyage: Bremen-Southampton-Cherbourg-New York on April 14, 1903

Employed in the express service Bremen-Southampton-Cherbourg-New York with a call at Plymouth eastbound. The *Kaiser Wilhelm II* won the Blue Riband from the Kronprinz Wilhelm in September 1904, when she made the run from Sandy Hook to Plymouth in 5 days, 8 hours, and 20 minutes at a speed of 23.30 knots. Her coal bunkers held 5,625 tons of coal and she consumed 700 tons each 24 hours. At the time of construction she was the largest merchant ship under the German flag. Made her last transatlantic voyage for the Line on July 15, 1914, Bremen-New York and was interned at New York upon arrival on August 5. Seized by the United States Government on April 6, 1917, and commissioned as a transport on August 21st with renaming to *Agamemnon*. Transferred to the United States Mail Line by the United States Shipping Board in 1920 but never sailed again. Laid up in the reserve fleet along Chesapeake Bay and renamed *Monticello* in 1929. Offered to Britain in 1940 but was declined. Sold for scrap for the sum of $183,500 to the Boston Iron Works of Baltimore in July 1940 and broken up by September.

Sister ship: *Kronprinzessin Cecilie.*

KAISER WILHELM DER GROSSE

Builder: A.G. Vulkan, Stettin, Germany
Completed: September 1897
Gross tonnage: 14,349
Dimensions: 649' x 66' Depth: 43'
Engines: Two 4-cylinder, quadruple expansion
Screws: Twin
Watertight bulkheads: Fourteen
Decks: Four
Normal speed: 22.50 knots
Passenger accommodations: 436 first, 443 second, and 1,074 third class
Officers and crew: 492
Registry: Germany
Maiden voyage: Bremen-Southampton-New York on September 19, 1897

Engaged in the Line's express service from Bremen to New York via Southampton and Cherbourg with an eastbound call at Plymouth. She won the Blue Riband from the Cunard Line's *Lucania* on her maiden crossing by making the run from the Needles to Sandy Hook in 5 days, 22 hours, and 45 minutes at a speed of 21.39 knots, She was the first liner to win the title for the North German Lloyd and for Germany. She also held the place of being the first liner ever to have four smoke-stacks. Her promenade deck extended 400 feet in length. In February 1900 she was the first German liner to be fitted with a wireless radio with a power radius of 25 miles. Another of her first-to-carry innovations were remote control watertight doors. On June 30, 1900 she was present at the great dock fire at Hoboken, New Jersey but was towed away from the blazing wharves without being damaged. On August 9, 1910 Mayor William J. Gaynor of New York City was seriously wounded by a gunshot when about to go aboard the ship by a recently discharged dock-worker. To maintain her high speeds she consumed 528 tons of coal every 24 hours. At the beginning of 1914 she was converted to carry only third class passengers with a capacity for 2,246. Commenced her last transatlantic voyage for the line on July 21, 1914. New York-Bremen and was fitted-out as an armed merchant raider on August 2nd, upon her arrival. On the 28th of August she was, after her brief career as a commerce raider, damaged by gunfire from the British cruiser *Highflyer* at Rio de Oro, Africa while taking on bunkers. The crew, anticipating inevitable capture, scuttled the ship and escaped to the Hamburg-American Line's store-ship *Bethania* which chanced to be alongside of her. Before her demise there was an exchange of gunfire which killed a sailor of the *H.M.S. Highflyer*. During her brief career as a commerce raider the *Kaiser Wilhelm Der Grosse* sank the British steamers *Hyodes*, *Arfanza*, and the *Galacian*.

Sister ship: *Kronprinz Wilhelm.*

KÖNIG ALBERT

Builder: A. G. Vulkan, Stettin, Germany
Completed: September 1899
Gross tonnage: 10,484
Dimensions: 499' x 60' Depth: 35'
Engines: Two 4-cylinder quadruple expansions
Screws: Twin
Decks: Four
Normal speed: 15 knots
Passenger accommodations: 237 first, 269 second, and 1,799 third class
Officers and crew: 230
Registry: Germany
Maiden voyage: Bremen-Yokohama on October 4, 1899*

*Maiden voyage to New York from Bremen, March 13, 1903

Engaged in the Bremen-Eastern Asia service until diverted to the Bremen-Cherbourg-New York run on March 13, 1903. Reallocated once again to the Mediterranean service out of New York to Naples in April 1903. From April 1904 until October 1910 she worked only the Mediterranean route and thereafter made some interchangeable voyages on the New York-Bremen route. In July 1913 she became a second and third class ship and made two westbound calls at Baltimore. Commenced her last voyage for the North German Lloyd on July 4, 1914, New York-Naples where she remained for the early part of the First World War. Interned at Genoa in August 1914 and later seized by the Italian Government on May 25, 1915. Converted to a hospital ship and renamed Ferdinando Palasciano. On June 15, 1920 she was transferred to the Navigazione Generale Italiana and worked the Genoa-New York route for a time. In May 1921, she reverted back to the Italian Government and was later renamed in 1923. Laid up in 1925 she was scrapped the following year.

KÖNIGIN LUISE

Builder: A.G. Vulkan, Stettin, Germany
Completed: March 1897
Gross tonnage: 10,785
Dimensions: 544' x 60' Depth: 42'
Engines: Two 4-cylinder, quadruple expansion
Screws: Twin
Watertight bulkheads: Twelve
Decks: Four
Normal speed: 15 knots
Passenger accommodations: 227 first, 310 second, and 1,564 steerage
Officers and crew: 231
Registry: Germany
Maiden voyage: Bremen-New York on March 22, 1897

Engaged in the Bremen-New York service during the summer months and from Bremen to Adelaide, Melbourne and Sydney, Australia via Southampton and the Suez Canal in the off seasonal months. Reallocated to the Naples-New York run in February 1903 until June 1909 when she reverted back to the Australian service becoming interchangeable with the Mediterranean service. She made her last voyage on the Australian run on October 29, 1911 from Bremen via Southampton-Suez Canal-Adelaide-Melbourne-Sydney and was reallocated to the Breman-New York run in March 1912. Passage on the *Königin Luise* was £66 for the first and £3 sterling for second class, from Bremen to New York. In April 1914 she was converted to a two class ship accommodating second and third class passengers only and reverted once again to the Bremen-Philadelphia-Baltimore trade. Made her last transatlantic voyage for the North German Lloyd on July 15, 1914 from Baltimore to Bremen. The *Königin Luise* was one of the first liners to be fitted with Doerr's hydraulic system for the closing of her watertight doors by remote control located on the bridge. Her coal bunkers held 1,780 tons with a reserve load of 1,115 tons for those long voyages down under. There were 5 double-ended boilers and single-ended cylindrical boilers within her two boiler rooms. Laid up for much of the first World War she was allotted to Britain on April 10, 191 as a reparation of war and sold by the British Shipping Controller to the British Orient Line in 1921. Renamed *Omar,* she was again resold to the Greek Byron Steamship Company in July 1924 and renamed *Edison* in October. Resold to the Greek Embiricos Bros of Andros for their Nation. Steam Navigation Company in 1927 and retained her name. Sold for scrap to Italian shipbreakers in July 1935.

KRONPRINZESSIN CECILLE

Builder: A. G. Vulkan, Stettin, Germany
Completed: July 1907
Gross tonnage: 19,503
Dimensions: 706'x 72' Depth: 52'
Engines: Four 4-cylinder quadruple expansion
Screws: Twin
Watertight bulkheads: Sixteen
Decks: Six
Normal speed: 22.75 knots
Passenger accommodations: 617 first, 345 second, and 834 third class
Officers and crew: 602
Registry: Germany
Maiden voyage: Bremen-Southampton-Cherbourg-New York on
  August 6, 1907

Engaged in the Bremen-Southampton-Cherbourg-New York service with a call at Plymouth eastbound. Made her last voyage for the North German Lloyd on July 14, 1914, Bremen-Cherbourg-New York and was laid up at New York upon her arrival on the 22nd. The flagship of the Line, she was ordered to make a run for the homeland when the First World War broke out in August. She headed eastbound with an elite passenger clientage and gold bullion worth an estimated 40,000,000 German Marks. In consideration for her passengers and their safety from British raiders prowling the North Atlantic waters, her Captain Pollack ordered the crew to paint the funnels black at their tops so as to appear to be the White Star liner *Olympic*. Orders were then given to steam back to American waters and on the morning of August 4, 1914 she anchored at Bar Harbor, Maine. As predicted, word had spread that the White Star liner *Olympic* was anchored off shore. The incident gave rise to her being known thereafter as "The Kaiser's Treasure Ship." Seized by the United States Government on April 6, 1917 at Boston where she had been interned since the outbreak of the First World War. Commissioned as a troopship on July 28, 1917, and renamed *Mount Vernon*. Torpedoed on September 8, 1918, off Brest, France, she managed to make port with a list of 15 degrees and a drop in speed of six knots. Thirty-six lives were lost when the bulkheads of her engine room were closed after she was hit. Released from service in September 1919, she then reverted to the United States Shipping Board but was destined never to sail again. She was vainly offered to Britain in 1940 and refused after having laid in Chesapeake Bay for nearly 20 years. Sold for scrap to the Boston Iron & Metal Company of Baltimore for $178,300 in July 1940, and was broken up by September.

Sister ship: *Kaiser Wilhelm II.*

KRONPRINZ WILHELM

Builder: A. G. Vulkan, Stettin, Germany
Completed: August 1901
Gross tonnage: 14,908
Dimensions: 663' x 66' Depth: 43'
Engines: Two 6-cylinder, quadruple expansion
Screws: Twin
Watertight bulkheads: Ten
Decks: Four
Normal speed: 22.75 knots (attained a speed of 23.34 knots on her trials)
Passenger accommodations: 593 first, 378 second and 1,021 third class
Officers and crew: 527
Registry: Germany
Maiden voyage: Bremen-Southampton-Cherbourg-New York on
  September 17, 1901

Engaged in the Bremen-Southampton-Cherbourg-New York run with a call at Plymouth in place of Southampton eastbound. The *Kronprinz Wilhelm* won the Blue Riband for the Hamburg-American Line's *Deutschland* in September 1902, when she made the run from Cherbourg to Sandy Hook in 5 days, 11 hours, and 57 minutes at a speed of 23.09 knots. She made her last voyage for the North German Lloyd on July 21, 1914, from Bremen to New York via Cherbourg. Leaving New York harbour on the night of August 2, 1914, she headed for the West Indies escorted by the German cruiser *Karlsruhe* because of the pending hostilities between Britain and Germany. When World War I finally broke out she was fitted-out as an armed merchant raider. On April 10, 1915, she appeared back in American waters just outside Chesapeake Bay where she was greeted by a blockade of British cruisers. Awaiting for night to fall, the *Kronprinz Wilhelm* made a last desperate run to break through with all her lights out. The stokers fed the burning coals incessantly to produce the needed steam. The *Kronprinz* with all her throttle open fully began to tremble as she moved ahead, her pressure gauges were steady at their highest level. The *Kronprinz* moved so swiftly that she broke through the array of British cruisers before they had a chance to set their guns on her, but had burst her lungs in the process. Seized by the United States at Norfolk, Virginia on April 6, 1917, for use as a troop ship with renaming to *von Steuben*. Returned to the U.S. Shipping Board in 1919 and laid up in the reserve fleet. Sold for scrap in 1923 to the Boston Iron and Steel Company in Baltimore, after having been completely worn out by her war service and laying in reserve. During her career as a German commerce raider, the *Kronprinz Wilhelm* sank 26 vessels totalling over 58,000 gross tons and steamed over 37,000 nautical miles mostly in the South Atlantic. One of the *Kronprinz's* redeeming features was whenever she encountered and captured a merchant ship she always sent on a boarding crew; disembarked the officers and crew as prisoners of war; removed her food stores and coal then scuttled the ship all without taking a human life. One of my most cherished possessions is a hand-wrought pewter cup depicting the *Kronprinz Wilhelm*.

Sister ship: *Kaiser Wilhelm der Grosse.*

II MAIN

Builder: Blohm & Voss, Hamburg, Germany
Completed: April 1900
Gross tonnage: 10,058
Dimensions: 520' x 58' Depth: 37'
Engines: Two 4-cylinder, quadruple expansion
Screws: Twin
Decks: Four
Normal speed: 13.50 knots
Passenger accommodations: 511 first and 2,887 third class*
Officers and crew: 174
Registry: Germany
Maiden voyage: Bremen-New York-Baltimore on April 28, 1900

*Originally carried: 369 first, 217 second, and 2,865 third class

Employed in the Bremen-New York and Baltimore service. The *Main* was present at the great dock fire at Hoboken, New Jersey on June 30, 1900 and capsized partially. The fire, which had broken out at 4:00 p.m. on Pier 3 amidst some unprotected bales of cotton and turpentine, had spread to a number of ships when a strong breeze blew flames toward the tied-up liners. Aboard the *Main* 15 of the 150 were to survive. Originally, 16 of them had taken refuge behind a coal bunker where they waited in desperation for help to come. At 11:30 p.m. their cries were heard and they were hauled out through a coal port. One person later died. Refloated on July 27th, she was refitted at the Newport News shipyards by October. Returning to service she began making calls at Philadelphia between 1910-1912 and 1914, her first on May 4, 1910. Commenced her last voyage for the Line on July 8, 1914, Baltimore-Bremen. Laid up at Antwerp, Belgium following the German invasion between 1914-1918 and allocated to Britain on May 21, 1919, as a World War I reparation. Transferred to the British Holt Line for a time and later to France under the same circumstances on January 30, 1920. Sold for scrap in October 1925 in France.

Sister ships: *Neckar* and *Rhein*.

III MÜNCHEN

Builder: Vulkan Werkes, Stettin, Germany
Completed: May 1923
Gross tonnage: 14,660
Dimensions: 551' x 65' Depth: 35'
Engines: Two 4-cylinder, triple expansion engines and one low-pressure turbine
Screws: Twin
Watertight bulkheads: Twelve
Decks: Four
Normal speed: 16 knots
Passenger accommodations: 214 cabin, 358 tourist, and 221 third class*
Officers and Crew: 356
Registry: Germany
Maiden voyage: Bremen-New York on June 21, 1923

*Originally carried: 171 first, 350 second and 573 third class

Built for the North German Lloyd she was engaged in the Bremen-Southampton-Cherbourg-New York service with a call at Plymouth eastbound in place of Southampton. She also made an occasional call at Halifax when headed eastbound. Converted to a cabin, tourist and third class ship in 1926. Damaged severely by fire on February 11, 1930, just inside New York harbour. The fire had begun in her cargo hold, which held potassium nitrate. This in turn ignited large volumes of shellac, which comprised the bulk of her cargo. Following a number of violent explosions she sank at her pier side. When it was learned that the hull rested above the Hudson Tunnel between Manhattan and Hoboken, the underground area was evacuated for fear she would rupture the ceiling thereby flooding the passageway and trapping drivers. Refloated on April 3rd, she was taken to the Brooklyn shipyards where she was given temporary repairs. She sailed back to Germany under her own power on May 12th and arrived at Bremerhaven on the 25th. Rebuilt by A. G. Weser she was given a pair of low-pressure turbines and her tonnage was increased from 13,325 to the present figure. Her two funnels were replaced by a single stack and a new maierform bow making her highly indistinguishable from her former profile. Converted to oil fuel and renamed *General von Steuben*, she re-entered service on January 20, 1931. In 1933 she was used almost exclusively for cruising but made some voyages to New York the following year, her last for the Line on November 25, 1934, New York-Bremen. Her name was later contracted to *Steuben* in 1938, when it was rumored that the Prussian General after whom the ship had been named had left the Prussian Army for allegiance to another country. Taken over by the Nazis in September 1939, she was used as an accommodation ship at Kiel. In August 1944 she was used as a transport for Germans wounded between Baltic ports and Germany. On February 4, 1945 while in convoy from Pillau, East Prussia to Kiel with about 4,000 people including East Prussian immigrants, crew and around 2,000 wounded soldiers, she was hit by two torpedoes from the Russian submarine S-13 off Stolpmunde and sank on the 10th. There were only about 300 survivors but the death toll climbed above 3,000. The S-13 was the same submarine which had sunk the German passenger liner *Wilhelm Gustloff* only 10 days earlier with a loss of 5,196 lives.

Sister ship: *Stuttgart.*

POTSDAM

Builder: Blohm & Voss, KaA Hamburg, Germany
Completed: June 1935
Gross tonnage: 17,528
Dimensions: 634' x 74' Depth: 45' Draft: 27'
Engines: Steam turbines connected to electric motors
Screws: Twin
Watertight bulkheads: Eleven
Decks: Four
Normal speed: 20 knots
Passenger accommodations: 227 first and 166 tourist class
Officers and crew: 275
Registry: Germany
Maiden voyage: Bremerhaven-Southampton-East Asia via the Suez Canal on July 5, 1935

Engaged in the Bremen-Southampton-Genoa-Shanghai trade via the Suez Canal. Originally laid down for the Hamburg-American Line, she was purchased by the North German Lloyd while still on the stocks. Launched on January 16, 1935 and delivered on June 28th. On March 11, 1936 fire broke out in her engine room while she was sailing through the English Channel. She was forced to land her passengers by tender at Southampton and return home. Converted for war services in 1940 at Hamburg. In December 1942 she was converted to an aircraft carrier by the shipyards of Blohm & Voss. Captured by the allies in 1945, she was allotted to the British Ministry of Transport and renamed *Empire Jewel*; *Empire Fowey* in 1946. Laid up in the Firth of Forth, Scotland in November 1946. Refitted in 1947 by Alexander Stephen & Sons, Glasgow and resumed services in 1950 for the P&O Line. Sold to the Pan-Islamic Steamship Company in May 1960 and renamed *Safina-E-Hujjaj*. Sold for scrap in Karachi, Pakistan in May 1976 and broken up by October that year.

PRINZESS ALICE

Builder: AG Vulkan, Stettin, Germany
Completed: December 1900
Gross tonnage: 10,981
Dimensions: 523' x 60' Depth: 38'
Engines: Two 4-cylinder quadruple expansion
Screws: Twin
Watertight bulkheads: Thirteen
Decks: Four
Normal speed: 15.50 knots
Passenger accommodations: 255 first, 300 second, and 1,863 third class
Officers and crew: 230
Registry: Germany
Maiden voyage: Bremen-East Asia in February 1904*

*Maiden voyage to New York, Bremen-New York, arriving on April 2, 1904

Built for the Hamburg-American Line and christened *Kiautschou*. Sold to the North German Lloyd in 1903 and renamed *Prinzess Alice*. Engaged in the Bremen-Far Eastern trade but made some voyages to New York between March 1904 and July 1907, mostly during the summer months. She made only one voyage to New York in the years 1908, 1909, and 1910, her last on June 2, 1910, when she left New York for Bremen. Returning to the Far Eastern trade, she was interned at Manila in August 1914 and seized by the United States Government on August 6, 1917. Commissioned as a troop ship on April 27, 1918 and renamed *Princess Matoika*. Released in September 1919. Transferred to the United States Mail Line in 1921 and made four voyages until taken over by the newly-formed United States Lines in August 1922, and renamed *President Arthur*. Laid up on November 1, 1923 and chartered to the American-Palestine Line in April 1924 for two voyages. Sold to the Palace Line in the same year and renamed *White Palace*. Resold once again to the Los Angeles Steamship Company in 1926 and renamed *City of Honolulu* in June 1927. Damaged by fire on May 25, 1930 at Honolulu. She was able to make the trip back to Los Angeles and was subsequently withdrawn. Sold to Japanese shipbreakers at Osaka in August 1933.

Sister ship: *Prinzess Irene.*

PRINZESS IRENE

Builder: AG Vulkan, Stettin, Germany
Completed: September 1900
Gross tonnage: 10,893
Dimensions: 523' x 60' Depth: 38'
Engines: Two 4-cylinder, quadruple expansion
Screws: Twin
Watertight bulkheads: Thirteen
Decks: Four
Normal speed: 15.50 knots
Passenger accommodations: 240 first, 350 second and 1,954 third class
Officers and crew: 230
Registry: Germany
Maiden voyage: Bremen-Southampton-Suez Canal-China-Japan on November 3, 1900*

*Maiden voyage to New York from Mediterranean in March 1903

Engaged in the Bremen-Southampton-Far Eastern trade. Reallocated to the Mediterranean-New York run on March 27, 1903 year-round but made an annual transatlantic voyage to Bremen for drydocking. Laid up at New York on July 24, 1914 and was seized by the United States on April 6, 1917. Fitted-out for troop work and renamed *Pocahontas*. Commissioned on July 25, 1917 and released in November 1919. Transferred to the United States Shipping Board and subsequently to the United States Mail Line in 1921 but made only three trips. Returned to the U. S. Shipping Board and offered for sale. Repurchased by the North German Lloyd in September 1922. Renamed *Bremen* in 1923 she resumed successful service for them returning to New York under the German flag on April 7, 1923 as a cabin and third class ship. In 1924 she began calling at Halifax westbound on occasion. In 1926 she offered accommodations for cabin, cabin-tourist, and third class passengers. The following year she was working on the Bremen-Southampton-Cherbourg-New York route. Renamed *Karlsruhe* in 1928, she made her last documented arrival at New York on October 27, 1930. Sold for scrap in Germany in July 1933.

Sister ship: *Prinzess Alice.*

PRINZ FRIEDRICH WILHELM

Builder: J. C. Tecklenborg, A.G. Gaestmunde, Germany
Completed: May 1908
Gross tonnage: 17,082
Dimensions: 613' x 68' Depth: 39'
Engines: Two 4-cylinder, quadruple expansion
Screws: Twin
Watertight bulkheads: Ten
Decks: Four
Normal speed: 17 knots
Passenger accommodations: 416 first, 372 second, and 1,741 third class
Officers and crew: 401
Registry: Germany
Maiden voyage: Bremen-New York on June 6, 1908

Engaged in the Bremen-Southampton-Cherbourg-New York run beginning on April 2, 1910, with an eastbound call at Plymouth instead of Southampton. The *Prinz Friedrich Wilhelm* had been built as an extra service liner for the company, being moved from one service to another depending on the traffic demands. She made her last voyage for the Line on June 27, 1914, from New York to Plymouth-Cherbourg-Bremen. Laid up at Kiel, Germany in 1916, after some voyages for the United States Navy, she was allotted to the British Shipping Controller on March 30, 1919. Chartered to the Canadian-Pacific Line in February 1920 and purchased by them on May 13, 1921. Renamed *Empress of China* on May 30, 1921 and made two voyages as such. Renamed Empress of India on August 13, 1921 under Cunard Line management; *Montlaurier* in October 1922 and again to *Montnairn* on June 19, 1925. Sold for scrap to the Ligure Demolitori Navale S.A. in Genoa, Italy on December 23, 1929 and broken up by March 1930.

Sister ship: *Berlin.*

II RHEIN

Builder: Blohm & Voss, Hamburg, Germany
Completed: December 1899
Gross tonnage: 10,058
Dimensions: 520' x 58' Depth: 37'
Engines: Two 4-cylinder quadruple expansion
Screws: Twin
Watertight bulkheads: Eleven
Decks: Four
Normal speed: 13.50 knots
Passenger accommodations: 486 second and 2,865 third
Officers and crew: 174
Registry: Germany
Maiden voyage: Bremen-New York on December 9, 1899

Engaged in the Bremen-New York-Baltimore service during the summer months and Bremen-Southampton-Albany-Adelaide-Melbourne-Sydney trade via the Suez Canal during the winter. Completed her last Australian voyage on November 27, 1904 and was diverted to the North Atlantic service. She also made a number of direct voyages between Bremen and Baltimore. In November 1912 she made a direct trip from Bremen to Galveston, Texas, and made her first call at Philadelphia on February 1, 1913, westbound. Laid up at Baltimore on July 29, 1914, due to impending hostilities between Germany and Great Britain. She was eventually seized by the United States Government on April 6, 1917 upon U.S. entry into World War I. Commissioned as a troopship on September 5, 1917, and renamed *Susquehanna*. Laid up in 1919 and handed over to the United States Shipping Board. The U.S. Shipping Board, which was created by an Act of Congress in 1916 to manage excess merchant tonnage and those produced during the War, transferred the ship to the newly formed United States Mail Line in August 1920. Passed on to the United States Lines the following August 31st. Her tonnage now stood at 9,959 gross. Made her last voyage on August 31, 1922 and was laid up on October 6, 1922. Sold to Japanese shipbreakers in November 1928 for scrap: unknowingly at the time to implement weapons for another war.

Sister ships: *Main* and *Neckar*.

II SCHARNHORST

Builder: Deutsche Schiff-und-Maschinenbau, AG Weser, Flensburg, Germany
Completed: April 1935
Gross tonnage: 18,184
Dimensions: 652' x 74' Depth: 45' Draft: 27'
Engines: Two steam turbines connected to two electric motors
Screws: Twin
Decks: Four
Normal speed: 20 knots (attained a speed of 21 knots during her trials)
Passenger accommodations: 186 first and 150 tourist class
Officers and crew: 281
Registry: Germany
Maiden voyage: Bremerhaven-Far East on May 3, 1935

Launched on December 14, 1934. Engaged in the Bremen-Southampton-Genoa-Shanghai trade via the Suez Canal. She and her sister ship, the *Gneisenau* were the largest ships built to date with a maierform bow and were classified as cargo-passenger liners with a cargo capacity for 10,800 tons. Sold to the Japanese on February 7, 1942, she was laid up in Japan on July 2, 1942 and later renamed *Jinyo* in December 1943, when she was converted to an escort aircraft carrier. Sunk by the American submarine U.S.S. Spadefish 140 miles northeast of Shanghai on November 17, 1944, in position 33° 02' north –123° 33' east.

Sister ship: *Gneisenau*.

II SIERRA CORDOBA

Builder: Bremer Vulkan, Vegesack, Germany
Completed: January 1924
Gross tonnage: 11,492
Dimensions: 511' x 66' Depth: 34' Draft:
Engines: Two 3-cylinder triple expansion
Screws: Twin
Watertight bulkheads: Nine
Decks: Four
Normal speed: 14.50 knots
Passenger accommodations: 150 first, 270 second, and 890 third class
Officers and crew: 300
Registry: Germany
Maiden voyage: Bremerhaven-La Plate, South America on January 26, 1924

Engaged in the Bremen-South American trade. She made her first voyage from Bremen to New York arriving at New York on September 6, 1927 and made two similar voyages in June and August, 1928. Appropriated by the Nazi Labour Ministry in 1935 and carried 1,000 passengers in a single class. At the time of this tenure she was painted with an all white hull but remained under North German Lloyd management. In 1940 she was converted at Kiel, Germany for war purposes. Taken over by the British in May 1945 at Hamburg. Burned out at Hamburg on January 13, 1946, with the loss of three lives, she was idle for a time thereafter. On January 18, 1948, two years after the incident, she was being taken to the Clyde for scrapping but misfortune once again befell the ship when she struck an iceberg at 55° 50' north, 70° 33' east and sank.

Sister ships: *Sierra Morena* and *Sierra Ventana*.

SIERRA MORENA

Builder: Bremer Vulkan, Vegasack, Germany
Completed: October 1924
Gross tonnage: 11,430
Dimensions: 511' x 66' Depth: 34'
Engines: Two 3-cylinder triple expansion
Screws: Twin
Watertight bulkheads: Nine
Normal speed: 14.50 knots
Passenger accommodations: 150 first, 270 second and 890 third class
Officers and crew: 298
Registry: Germany
Maiden voyage: Bremerhaven-La Plate, South America on October 25, 1924

Employed in the Bremen-South American trade. Renamed *Der Deutsche* on July 2, 1934 and had her hull repainted in a white livery. Appropriated by the Nazi Germany Labour Ministry in 1935 but remained under North German Lloyd management. She now carried her complement of 1,000 passengers in a single cabin class capacity. In 1940 she became a German transport ship. Later converted to an accommodation ship between Konigsberg*, Gotenhafen, and Gdynia. Bombed out on May 3, 1945, she was ceded to the Russians on March 18, 1946, as a World War II reparation and renamed *Aziya*. Reconditioned, she re-entered service for them in June 1950, after being refitted by the Warnow Werft shipyard in East Germany. Scrapped in Russia in 1966.

Sister ship: *Sierra Cordoba* and *Sierra Ventana*.

*Kaliningrad

II SIERRA VENTANA

Builder: Bremer Vulkan, Vegesack, Germany
Completed: August 1923
Gross tonnage: 11,392
Dimensions: 511' x 66' Depth: 34'
Engines: Two 3-cylinder triple expansion
Screws: Twin
Watertight bulkheads: Nine
Decks: Four
Normal speed: 14.50 knots
Passenger accommodations: 692 cabin and 540 third class*
Officers and crew: 264
Registry: Germany
Maiden voyage: Bremerhaven-New York on September 8, 1924

*Originally carried: 149 first, 240 second and 890 third class

Built expressly for the North German Lloyd, the *Sierra Ventana* was launched on May 16, 1923. Employed primarily in the Bremen-South American Trade, she did make a number of voyages to New York via Southampton-Cherbourg. In 1925 she made a couple of westbound calls at Halifax, her first on June 2nd. The following year she became a cabin, tourist-cabin and third class passenger ship. Between 1923-27 she made about four voyages to New York each year, her last in September 1927, westbound, and left New York for the last time on October 4, 1927. Sold to the Italian Line in 1935 and renamed *Sardegna*. Resold to the Lloyd Triestino in 1937 without a change in name. Sunk by a Greek submarine at 40° 31' north, 19° 02' east, while carrying Italian troops to Valona, Albania on December 29, 1940.

Sister ships: *Sierra Cordoba* and *Sierra Morena*.

II STUTTGART

Builder: Vulkan Werkes, Stettin, Germany
Completed: January 1924
Gross tonnage: 13,387
Dimensions: 551' x 65' Depth: 35'
Engines: Two 3-cylinder triple expansion
Screws: Twin
Watertight bulkheads: Twelve
Decks: Four
Normal speed: 16 knots
Passenger accommodations: 163 first, 421 second and 555 third class
Officers and crew: 356
Registry: Germany
Maiden voyage: Bremerhaven-New York on January 15, 1924

Built for the North German Lloyd and christened *Stuttgart,* she was employed in the Bremen-New York service with a call at Halifax westbound, her first on April 8, 1924. The *Stuttgart* made regular calls at Southampton and Cherbourg until placed in the Far Eastern trade sometime after 1927. She made her last trip to America in 1936 arriving at New York for the last time on September 12th. Appropriated by the Nazi German Labour Ministry and converted to carry 990 passengers in a single class in 1937 but remained under North German Lloyd management. Later she was converted to a hospital ship in September 1939. On October 9, 1943 while lying in Gotenhafen (Gdynia, Poland) she was hit by a force of 127 B-24 and B-17 bombers of the U.S. Air Force while on an air-raid. The *Stuttgart* was engulfed by flames and was deliberately towed out of the harbour and sunk with hundreds of bodies of victims still aboard.

Sister ship: *München.*

Norwegian–America Line

I BERGENSFJORD

Builder: Cammell, Laird & Co., Ltd., Birkenhead, England
Completed: September 1913
Gross Tonnage: 11,015
Dimensions: 530' x 61' Depth: 33' Draft: 26'
Engines: Two 4-cylinder, quadruple expansion engines with two low-pressure turbines, double-reduction, geared
Screws: Twin
Watertight bulkheads: Eight
Decks: Three
Normal speed: 15 knots
Passenger accommodations: 156 first, 310 second, and 887 third class
Registry: Norway
Maiden voyage: Kristiania*-Bergen-New York on September 25, 1913, arriving on October 7

*Now Oslo

Built at a cost of 4.1 million Norwegian kroner. Engaged in the Kristiania-Bergen-New York service year-round. She maintained regular sailings between Bergen and New York throughout World War I. On October 29, 1914 the *Bergensfjord* was stopped while on an eastbound voyage from New York just thirty kilometers outside of Norwegian waters by a British war ship. Her cargo and German passengers were taken off the ship and she was then allowed to continue her voyage. She inaugurated a westbound call at Halifax on February 26, 1914 and called there on occasion. In 1923 she ran from Oslo-Kristiansand-Stavenger-Bergen-New York and Halifax became a regular port of call by 1924 westbound. From 1927 she operated on a regular port of call by 1924 westbound. From 1927 she operated on the Oslo-Bergen-Halifax-New York run calling at Copenhagen periodically. Originally driven by reciprocating engines until 1932 when two Bauer-Woch low-pressure turbines were added at the Deutsche-Schiff-und-Maschinnenbau A.G. in Bremen, Germany. The *Bergensfjord* had since 1926 become a cabin class ship. Arriving at New York on April 15, 1940, she was subsequently laid up until taken over for troop work. Sent to Halifax to be converted to a transport she was placed under the management of the British Furness-Withy Line around November 1941, and sailed some 301,419 nautical miles. Working in the Mediterranean and North African theatres of war, she carried 164,746 persons during the war. Decommissioned on June 24, 1945, she was laid up. Sold to the Greek-owned Home Lines in November 1946 for approximately 7 million kroner and renamed *Argentina* after having served Norwegian-America Line for three long decades. Resold to the Zim-Israel Lines in 1952 and renamed *Jerusalem; Aliya* in 1957. Sold to the Terrestse Marittima for scrapping at Spezia, Italy in October 1959.

Sister ship: *Kristianiafjord.*

II BERGENSFJORD

Builder: Swan, Hunter & Wigham Richardson, Ltd., Wallsend-on-Tyne, England
Completed: May 1956
Gross Tonnage: 18,739
Dimensions: 578' x 72' Depth: 47' Draft: 28'
Engines: Two 8-cylinder, 2-stroke, double-acting diesel
Screws: Twin
Watertight bulkheads: Ten
Decks: Five
Normal speed: 20 knots
Passenger accommodations: 136 first and 774 tourist class (450 when cruising)
Officers and crew: 335
Registry: Norway
Maiden voyage: Oslo-Copenhagen-Stavanger-Bergen-New York on May 30, 1956

Christened by Her Royal Highness Princess Astrid, *Bergensfjord* was the line's flagship and was employed on the Oslo-Copenhagen-Kristiansand-New York run, calling at Stavanger instead of Kristiansand during the summer months. She called at Halifax on occasion when westbound but eliminated this port by 1958. The *Bergensfjord* cruised out of Port Everglades to the West Indies during the off-season months. She made a world cruise each year from 1959 to 1968 and a North Cape cruise each year from 1957 to 1966. On October 20, 1970 she commenced a 59-day cruise from New York, calling at 16 ports in the Pacific. The superstructure of the *Bergensfjord* was made of aluminum. Equipped with motion stabilizers and fully air-conditioned, she was a stately looking ship. She made her last voyage for the line on September 19, 1971, a 22-day cruise Oslo-London-La Coruna-Cadiz-Malaga-La Goulette-Messina-Naples-Cagliari-Tangier-Lisbon-London-Oslo. She was sold to the French Line and, handed over on November 5, 1971, was renamed *De Grasse*. Resold to Thorensen Co. of Singapore in November 1973 and renamed *Rasa Sayang*. Sold to a Greek firm in 1978 and renamed *Golden Moon* for Sunlit Cruises Limited. Resold to another Greek firm, Aphrodite Maritime Co., in July 1980 and reverted to her former name of *Rasa Sayang*. On August 27, 1980, while undergoing a refit, she caught fire and was gutted out at Perama. Towed to Kynoscoura, she was beached at latitude 37.56, longitude 54 north. The vessel was almost submerged but her port side remained above the waterline. The ship was later scrapped.

KRISTIANIAFJORD

Builder: Cammell, Laird & Co., Ltd., Birkenhead, England
Completed: May 1913
Gross Tonnage: 10,669
Dimensions: 530' x 61' Depth: 33' Draft: 26'
Engines: Two 4-cylinder, quadruple expansion engines and two low-
   pressure turbines, double-reduction geared.
Screws: Twin
Watertight bulkheads: Eight
Decks: Three
Normal speed: 15 knots
Passenger accommodations: 165 first, 235 second, and 907 third class
Registry: Norway
Maiden voyage: Kristiania-Bergen-New York on June 7, 1913

Engaged in the Kristiania-Bergen-New York service with an occasional call at Halifax during the off season. Built at a cost of 4.1 million Norwegian kroner, she made two trips to New York after American entry into World War I in April 1917. She was the line's first ship and was launched on November 23, 1912. When celebrating her first anniversary as a NAL liner, tickets were so difficult to obtain that one American was said to have offered $1,000 to anyone able to secure him a cabin on the ship. She made her last commercial voyage for the line on July 7, 1917, from New York. On July 15 she was wrecked seven miles off Cape Race, Newfoundland. The 868 passengers aboard were rescued by the Swedish-American liner *Stockholm*, which brought them to Norway. For a time it seemed that the ship could be salvaged but a severe storm on July 28 destroyed all hopes of saving the ship.

Sister ship: *Bergensfjord.*

II OSLOFJORD

Builder: Deutsche Schiff-und-Maschinenbau, A.G. Weser, Bremen, Germany
Completed: June 1938
Gross Tonnage: 18,673
Dimensions: 588' x 73' Depth: 43'
Engines: Four 7-cylinder, 2-stroke, double-acting diesel
Screws: Twin
Normal speed: 18 knots
Passenger accommodations: 152 first, 307 tourist, and 401 third class
Officers and crew: 240
Registry: Norway
Maiden voyage: Oslo-Bergen-New York on June 4, 1938

Built at a cost of 19.5 million Norwegian kroner, she was employed in the Oslo-Scandinavian ports-New York service and cruised out of New York to the West Indies during the winter of 1938-39, completing six such voyages with an average complement of 370 passengers. She called at Copenhagen for the first time on July 29, 1939 while enroute from Bremen-Oslo. Laid up at the Bayonne terminal at New York in the spring of 1940. On October 26, 1940 she was taken to Halifax and by November had been fitted-out as a transport. The *Oslofjord* was sunk by an acoustic mine at South Shields near the mouth of the Tyne River, England on December 13, 1940, while enroute to join the British Ministry of Transport Fleet. All of her 240 crew and officers were saved except one. The liner was beached but became totally submerged by February 1941 with only her two masts visible and was declared a total loss. It was an extremely short life for a good-looking ship with nice contoured lines and a great financial setback for the Norwegian-America Line.

III OSLOFJORD

Builder: Netherland Dock & Engineering Co., Amsterdam, Netherlands
Completed: November 1949
Gross Tonnage: 16,923
Dimensions: 577' x 72' Depth: 38' Draft: 27'
Engines: Two 7-cylinder, 2-stroke, double-acting Stork diesels
Screws: Twin
Decks: Five
Normal speed: 20 knots (attained a speed of 21.74 knots on her trials)
Passenger accommodations: 188 first and 542 tourist class (375 in a single first class capacity when cruising)
Registry: Norway
Maiden voyage: Oslo-Copenhagen-Kristiansand-Stavanger-Bergen-New York on November 26, 1949

Built for the Norwegian-America Line at a cost of 44 million Norwegian Kroner. She was christened by Her Royal Highness Crown Princess Martha on her day of launching, April 2. Employed for eight months of the year on the Oslo-Copenhagen-Kristiansand-Stavanger-Bergen-New York run with an occasional call at Halifax westbound until dropped in 1958. Between January and April of each year she would cruise to the Caribbean and make longer cruises to the Mediterranean out of New York. Between 1954-58 she made a series of cruises to the Caribbean and to the Mediterranean between 1959-66. The Oslofjord carried a number of Polish and other Baltic immigrants to Canada until restrictions diminished this trade and she dropped the Halifax call entirely. Refitted for cruising during the winter of 1966-67 at Amsterdam she returned to service to a declining North Atlantic trade within the industry. The Oslofjord made only the occasional crossing for her annual overhaul or for positioning thereafter. She made her last transatlantic voyage for the Line on October 20, 1967, New York-Bergen-Stavanger-Kristiansannd-Copenhagen-Oslo. Chartered out to the Greek Line for a series of cruises out of Southampton in December 1967. Rechartered for a three-year period thereafter to the Italian Costa Lines in October 1968 and renamed Fulvia. The ship, now manned by Norwegian officers and Italian staff, was operating on a series of Mediterranean cruises. On July 19, 1968, while on a cruise with 721 passengers, an explosion occurred in the engine room 100 miles off Tenerife. The disabled ship's passengers, were disembarked into lifeboats and assisted by the French ship Acnerville. The flames grew so intense that her funnel melted as though it were a mass of plastic and the fire spread from stem to stern. The ship's last moments were recorded as listing heavily to port just before she took the plunge to the depths at 11:45 a.m. on the morning of the 20th. An interesting anecdote concerning the disaster was later related to me by one of the Norwegian officers who told me of two elderly English dowagers, who, when informed to evacuate the ship, were taking their tea. They had asked the officers "if they might finish up their tea before leaving the ship."

SAGAFJORD

Builder: Societe des Forges et Chantiers de la Mediterranee, Le Seyne, France

Completed: May 1965

Gross Tonnage: 24,002

Dimensions: 617′ x 79′ Depth: 53′ Draft: 27′

Engines: Two 9-cylinder, 2-stroke, single-acting Sulzer diesels, plus a bow thruster athwartship forward

Screws: Twin

Decks: Six

Normal speed: 20 knots (attained a speed of over 22.50 knots during her trials)

Passenger accommodations: 75 first and 719 tourist class (accommodations limited to 462 when cruising)

Officers and crew: 320

Registry: Norway

Maiden voyage: Oslo-Copenhagen-Kristiansand-New York on October 2, 1965

Built expressly for the Norwegian-America Line, the *Sagafjord* superstructure is constructed of aluminum. Equipped with moti stabilizers and fully air-conditioned. The *Sagafjord* is one of the first shi to also be fitted with six Bergen diesel locomotive-type auxiliary engines the first to ever be used on a ship. She is the Norwegian-America Lin flagship. Employed mostly as a cruise ship year-round, she did ma positioning voyages or trips to Norway for annual overhauling, in whi case she crossed on the Oslo-Copenhagen-Kristiansand-New York rou She would call at Stavangfjord instead of Kristiansand during the summ months. On January 5, 1971 she made a 93-day world cruise from N York, calling at 29 ports in the world. While on an annual world cru she would begin at New York and call at Port Everglades before headi out. In 1981 she underwent a major refit at a cost of $13 million. T result was an additional 15 deluxe cabins on the sun deck with priv terrace and panoramic windows. The work was done by Blohm & Vo Hamburg Germany between September and January 1981. In May 19 she began a series of 14-day cruises out of San Francisco to Alaska a British Columbia thus paving the way for the future and the cruise s era with new ports and new horizons. Due to the slackened trade on t North Atlantic and a not so sure future for liners in general, Norwegi: America Line decided to sell the *Sagafjord,* along with her running ma the *Vistafjord,* to Cunard Line for $83 million along with the goodwill NAL. Presently in their service under her original name.

STAVANGERFJORD

Builder: Cammell, Laird & Co., Ltd., Birkenhead, England
Completed: February 1918
Gross Tonnage: 14,015
Dimensions: 553' x 64' Depth: 33' Draft: 26'
Engines: Two 4-cylinder, quadruple expansion engines and two low-
  pressure turbines, double-reduction geared
Screws: Twin
Watertight bulkheads: Ten
Decks: Four
Normal speed: 15.50 knots
Passenger accommodations: 95 first, 238 cabin and 478 tourist class*
Registry: Norway
Maiden voyage: Kristiania**-Bergen-New York on April 29, 1918

*Originally carried: 117 first, 437 second and 983 third class.

**Now Oslo

Built expressly for the Norwegian-America Line at a cost of 4.8 million Norwegian kroner. Employed on the Kristiania-Bergen-New York run, the *Stavangerfjord* burned 120 metric tons of coal per day to fuel her engines. Laid up at New York from May until September 1918. In 1923 she added a call at Kristiansand and Stavanger and a call at Halifax westbound in 1924. Refitted for oil fuel in the first quarter of 1924 and converted to a cabin and third class ship in 1925-26. In 1931-32 she was taken to the Deutsche Schiff-und-Maschinenbau at Bremen and fitted with two Bauer-Wach low-pressure turbines. In April 1940 she was commandeered by the Germans and used as a hotel ship to accommodate troops at Trondheim, Germany. Returned back to the Line after the war, she made the first post-war commercial voyage in August 1945, from Oslo-Copenhagen-Kristiansand-Stavanger-Bergen-New York repatriating troops and maintained this route thereafter with an occasional call at Halifax westbound. This call was eliminated in mid-1961. Reconditioned in mid-1949 she was now a three-class ship carrying first, cabin and tourist classes. On December 9, 1953 the *Stavangerfjord* lost her rudder in a gale 500 miles east of Newfoundland and the ship hove for two days until the NAL's freighter *Lyngenfjord* took the ship in tow. While in tow the lines broke but she was able to make it back to Oslo on her own by the 19th but not without exacting communication between the Bridge and Engine room and over thousands of messages to steer the ship home. Reconditioned once again between October 1956-January 1957, she was the oldest passenger liner still in service when she made her last voyage for the Line on December 3, 1963, from New York-Stavanger-Kristiansand-Copenhagen-Oslo. She had served the company for 45 years and came to be known fondly amongst travellers on both sides of the Atlantic. Sold for scrap in Hong Kong to Patt Manfield Company, Ltd. and arrived on February 4, 1964 for breaking up.

Note: During her construction the British shipyard had refused Norwegian capital because of the war and the Government had ordered her to be finished as a freighter in March 1917; however, this was rejected later and she was finished as a passenger liner.

VISTAFJORD

Builder: Swan Hunter Shipbuilders, Ltd., Wallsend-on-Tyne, England
Completed: 1973
Gross Tonnage: 24,292
Dimensions: 627' x 82' Depth: 53' Draft: 27'
Engines: Two Sulzer 2-stroke, single-acting, nine-cylinder diesels plus an athwartship controllable pitch propeller forward
Screws: Twin
Watertight bulkheads: Eleven
Decks: Seven
Normal speed: 20 knots (attained a speed of 22.26 knots on her trials)
Passenger accommodations: 600 in a single first class
Officers and crew: 360
Registry: Norway
Maiden voyage: Oslo-Copenhagen-New York on May 22, 1973

The *Vistafjord* is one of the last transatlantic liners built as a dual purpose ship for world cruising. Engaged in the Oslo-Copenhagen-New York service and from New York to the Caribbean and Bermuda. After her first Caribbean cruise on June 12, 1973, New York-Ponce-Barbados-Martinique-St. Maarten-St. Croix, she made her first North Cape cruise from New York on June 26, with a 45-day itinerary (Iceland, Norway, Denmark, Finland, Sweden, Holland, the U.S.S.R., Germany, Scotland and Ireland). Employed primarily as a world cruise ship, the *Vistafjord* made an annual transatlantic voyage for drydocking and repositioning either in New York or Fort Lauderdale, or both. She has two swimming pools and her 10,000 square foot dining room, situated on the upper deck, seats 620 passengers. Her lido deck area affords over 10,000 square feet of leisure space. Eighty percent of her cabins are situated outside. *Vistafjord* is the line's flagship, built at a cost of some $32,000,000. Equipped with motion stabilizers and fully air-conditioned, she features an innovative garbage disposal that incinerates the refuse on board. Her aluminum superstructure and funnel, which weigh 520 tons, lower the ship's center of gravity, making her less topheavy and thereby a faster and a smoother sailing vessel. There are several suites with two offering private deck space as well. Full casino facilities, and the usual sauna, gymnasium, hairdresser, massage room, etc. Her stabilizers are the modern fold in and out type instead of the older retracting type. Sold to Cunard Line in mid-1983, along with her running mate, the *Sagafjord*, for $83,000,000, including the name and goodwill of the Norwegian-America Line. Presently in their service, the *Vistafjord* has retained her original name. The name "Cunard Vista" was originally contemplated.

Note: She made an unofficial maiden voyage with King Haakon and a number of Norwegian government officials around the Norwegian coast to Kristiansand, Stavanger and Bergen prior to her Atlantic crossing.

Polish Ocean Lines

BATORY

Builder: Cantieri Riuniti dell' Adriatico, Monfalcone, Italy
Completed: April 1936
Gross tonnage: 14,287
Dimensions: 526' x 71' Depth: 38' Draft: 25'
Engines: Two Burmeister & Wain 9-cylinder, 2-stroke, single-acting
  diesels
Screws: Twin
Watertight Bulkheads: Nine
Decks: Five
Normal speed: 18 knots
Passenger accommodations: 78 first and 786 tourist class (800 in a single
  class when cruising)
Registry: Poland
Maiden voyage: Gdynia-Copenhagen-New York on May 18, 1936, arriving
  on the 27th

Built expressly for the Polish Ocean Lines in arrangement with the Italian Government by bartering Polish coal for repayment. Employed in the Gdynia-Copenhagen-Southampton-New York-Halifax route westbound and cruising mostly to the Mediterranean. She made her last pre-war crossing with arrival at Hoboken, New Jersey on September 5, 1939. Fitted-out at Halifax in December 1939 as an army transport under the British Admiralty and left there on the 23rd for service on the North Atlantic. She participated in the evacuation at Dunkirk and did not return to peacetime service until April 5, 1947. In June-July of 1940 she had been used to transport £40 million pounds in gold bullion from Greenock, Scotland to Canada. Following an extensive refit at Antwerp she returned to commercial service as a tourist class ship in April 1947 and made only three voyages in 1951, her last on April 3rd from New York to Southampton-Cuxhaven-Copenhagen-Gdynia. In January of 1951 she had been denied docking facilities at New York because she had come from behind the Iron Curtain and had harbored a convicted spy with the knowledge of the captain. Refitted for a new service from Gdynia to Karachi and Bombay via Southampton and the Suez Canal in August 1951. She remained on this route until 1956 when she was again overhauled at Bremerhaven and placed once more on the transatlantic run from Gdynia to Copenhagen-Cuxhaven-Southampton*-Quebec-Montreal on August 26, 1957. Cuxhaven was later dropped in 1958 and she also made a number of direct trips to Boston in the mid-sixties. An occasional call at Leningrad, Le Havre, Helsinki or Bremerhaven was sometimes added to her itinerary in 1961 and she maintained her cruising schedule during the months of January through March out of London. In fact, in the course of her career the *Batory* made 22 cruises. Arrived Gdynia from London May 29, 1969 and withdrawn from service on June 1. Sold to the Gdansk District Board for use as a floating hotel at Gdynia, Poland. Sold for scrap to the Yau Wing Co., Ltd., Hong Kong, she left Gdynia on March 30, 1971 and arrived Hong Kong on May 11th. Demolition began June 1, 1971.

Sister ship: *Pilsudski.*

*Sometimes out of London.

Note: Ship actually owned by Polish Government.

CHROBRY

Builder: Nakskov, Skibsvaerft, Nakskov, Denmark
Completed: July 1939
Gross tonnage: 11,442
Dimensions: 478′ x 67′ Depth: 33′ Draft: 25′
Engines: Two 8-cylinder, 2-stroke, double-acting diesels
Screws: Twin
Watertight bulkheads: Eight
Decks: Four
Normal speed: 17 knots
Passenger accommodations: 60 first, 303 third and 804 steerage
Officers and crew: 260
Registry: Poland
Maiden voyage: Gdynia-South America on July 27, 1939

Launched on February 25, 1939, the *Chrobry* was destined for a short life. The outbreak of World War II prompted her withdrawal from service and placement under the auspices of the British Marine Transport. Fitted-out as an army transport in October 1939 at Halifax, Nova Scotia. She departed Halifax on December 23, 1939 for troop work in Europe. On May 14, 1940, the ship was attacked by German aircraft off Bodö, while in transit to Norway. She caught fire and her burnt-out hull sank in 67 latitude 40′ north longitude 13° 50′ east. Twelve crew members were killed and a number of troops during the attack and ultimate sinking.

Sister ship: *Sobieski.*

PILSUDSKI

Builder: Cantieri Riuniti dell' Adriatico Monfalcone, Italy

Completed: August 1935

Gross tonnage: 14,294

Dimensions: 526' x 71' Depth: 38'

Engines: Two 9-cylinder, 2-stroke, single-acting oil

Screws: Twin

Watertight bulkheads: Nine

Decks: Five

Normal speed: 18 knots

Passenger accommodations: 355 tourist and 404 third class

Registry: Poland

Maiden voyage: Gdynia-New York in September 1935

Engaged in the Gdynia-Copenhagen-Southampton-New York service. Made her last voyage for the Line on August 23, 1939, New York-Copenhagen-Gdynia. She called at Copenhagen for the first time on August 12, 1939, enroute to Gdynia. She was fitted-out as an armed merchant cruiser in World War II and sunk by a German submarine off the Humber River, England, on November 26, 1939, with the loss of eight crew members.

Sister ship: *Batory*.

Note: The *Pilsudski* and *Batory* were constructed for the Polish Ocean Lines by payments of Polish coal to the builders and the help of 12 countries who contributed to their construction.

SOBIESKI

Builder: Swan, Hunter & Wigham Richardson, Ltd., Newcastle-on-Tyne, England
Completed: May 1939
Gross tonnage: 11,030
Dimensions: 511′ x 67′ Depth: 36′ Draft: 25′
Engines: Two 8-cylinder, 2-stroke, double-acting diesel
Screws: Twin
Watertight bulkheads: Eight
Decks: Four
Normal speed: 17 knots
Passenger accommodations: 44 first and 860 tourist class
Registry: Poland
Maiden voyage: Gdynia-Buenos Aires in June 1939

She had been originally built for the South American trade. Commissioned by the allies during World War II as a transport and was fortunate in comparison with her sister *Chrobry* who also had been recently constructed when war broke out. Refitted in 1946, she sailed on Naples-Genoa-Cannes-Lisbon-New York. One of her noted passengers on one of these voyages was Ernest Hemingway. Sold to Russia in March 1950, and renamed *Gruziya*. She was scrapped at La Spezia, Italy in April 1975.

Sister ship: *Chrobry*.

STEFAN BATORY

Builder: Dok-en Werf Mij. Wilton-Fijenoord N.V. Schiedam, Netherlands
Completed: July 1952
Gross tonnage: 15,044
Dimensions: 502' x 69' Depth: 40' Draft: 29'
Engines: Two steam turbines double-reduction geared
Screws: Single
Watertight bulkheads: Eight
Decks: Five
Normal speed: 16.50 knots
Passenger accommodations: 39 first and 742 tourist class
Officers and crew: 321
Registry: Poland
Maiden voyage: Gdynia-Copenhagen-Rotterdam-London-Montreal on
  April 11, 1969

Built for the Holland-America Line and christened *Maasdam*. Sold to Polish Ocean Lines in December 1968 and renamed *Stefan Batory*. The ship was originally laid down as a cargo vessel but plans were altered while she was still on the stocks. Built as a passenger liner. The reason for her single screw was because of the original hull design. Employed in the Gdynia-Copenhagen-Rotterdam-London-Montreal service year-round. The call at Copenhagen was dropped in 1973 and she made an occasional call at Rotterdam, Cuxhaven, or Hamburg. She made her first voyage to New York on December 19, 1970 and in the years to come, though infrequently. She was the line's flagship. The *Stefan Batory* is somewhat of a special ship since she became one of the last ships to be engaged in

liner service with the exception of the last contender, the *QE2*. Ironically the Cunarder is a symbol of capitalism and the *Stefan Batory* was a communist example of sorts. However, when I travelled aboard in the fall of 1974, round-trip to London, I discovered some of the old traditions that could not be found any longer aboard the ships of today, i.e. unlimited baggage. Seeing passengers with steamer trunks reminded one of a bygone era. At dinner the band played music in the dining room reminiscent of Vienna in springtime. I presented one of my books to the captain and was invited to tea with all his officers in circle and presented with a paperweight commemorating fifty years of the company's service. It was all very Edwardian and lo and behold I found Salvador Dali's name on the passenger list. Sixty percent of the ship's cabins are inside and only 15% have private facilities. There was a main lounge and a number of public rooms. Two dining rooms, a swimming pool indoors, sauna and truly duty-free shops. She even had a few slot machines. Automobiles were carried as well. The *Stefan Batory* made her last voyage for the line on October 7, 1987, from Montreal to Gdynia completing her 140th voyage. She had carried 67,000 passengers eastbound and 57,000 westbound in the course of her service. I was on a cruise in October 1987 and was fortunate to see her in Montreal. I was able to get on board to look around. Her decks were buckling in the forecastle area but she looked pretty good otherwise. I thought it would be the last time I would see the ship since a deck steward told me she was soon going to the scrap yards. While on a later cruise I came out of my cabin at the port of Recife, Brazil to see the *Stefan Batory* docked alongside us. It reminded me of the *Patna* in Joseph Conrad's Lord Jim. Apparently, she had been making a number of cruises out of London since November 7, 1987, to South America and out of Hamburg to the West Indies. Sold to the City Shipping International Co., Inc. in 1989 (Swedish) and renamed *Stefan*.

Portuguese Line

IMPERIO

Builder: John Brown & Co., Ltd., Clydebank, Glasgow, Scotland
Completed: June 1948
Gross tonnage: 13,186
Dimensions: 531' x 68' Depth: 44' Draft; 28'
Engines: Four steam turbines, double-reduction geared
Screws: Twin
Collision bulkheads: One
Watertight bulkheads: Eight
Decks: Four
Normal speed: 17 knots
Passenger accommodations: 114 first, 156 cabin, and 118 tourist class
Officers and crew: 193
Registry: Portugal

Built expressly for the Portuguese Line and christened *Imperio*. Engaged in the Lisbon-Luanda-Beira trade with calls at Funchal, Las Palmas, Sao Tome, Luanda, Lobito, Maçsamedes, Cape Town, Lourenco, Marques, Beira, Mozambique, Nacala and Porto Amelia. Las Palmas and Nacala were occasional ports of call. The ship was fully air-conditioned and her moderate complement of passengers were afforded more room. She was requisitioned for troop service by the Portuguese Government in the spring of 1970 following nationalist uprisings in Portuguese-held Angola. I boarded the ship in May 1973 at Lisbon where she was laid up with a skeleton crew. The *Imperio* was sold for scrap to the Sun Hwa Steel & Iron Company in Kaohsiung, Taiwan. She arrived there on March 24, 1974. Demolition began on August 2, 1974 and was completed by September.

Sister ship: *Patria*.

INFANTE DOM HENRIQUE

Builder: Societe Anonyme, Cockerill-Ougree, Hoboken, Belgium
Completed: September 1961
Gross tonnage: 23,306
Dimensions: 42' x 84' Depth: 47' Draft: 27'
Engines: Four steam turbines double-reduction geared
Screws: Twin
Watertight bulkheads: Nine
Decks: Five
Normal speed: 20 knots
Passenger accommodations: 156 first, 862 tourist class
Officers and crew: 328
Registry: Portugal

Built expressly for the Portuguese Line and christened *Infante Dom Henrique*. Engaged in the Lisbon-East African ports-Beira trade. She had a cargo capacity for 724,553 cubic feet of grain, bales and refrigerated cargo space. Equipped with motion stabilizers and fully air-conditioned. The *Infante Dom Henrique* was the Line's flagship. She made calls also at Funchal on occasion with regular calls at Luanda-Lobito-Capetown-Lourenço-Marques-Beira. She was listed under the ownership of the Companhia Portuguesa de Transportes Maritimes in 1974 and dropped from Lloyd's Register in 1977 when her class was withdrawn because of reported defects. She was laid up on January 3, 1976. Converted to an accommodation hotel under the Panamanian flag in 1978. Reconditioned following her sale to Trans World Cruises in 1988 and re-entered service under the name *Vasco Da Gama*. Presently in their service. A nice looking liner, it's good to see she escaped the breaker's yard. Chartered to Seawind Cruise Line in 1991 and renamed *Seawind Crown*.

PATRIA

Builder: John Brown & Co., Ltd., Clydebank, Glasgow, Scotland
Completed: December 1947
Gross tonnage: 13,196
Dimensions: 531' x 68' Depth: 44' Draft: 28'
Engines: Four steam turbines double-reduction geared
Screws: Twin
Collision bulkheads: One
Watertight Bulkheads: Eight
Decks: Four
Normal speed: 17 knots
Passenger accommodations: 114 first, 160 cabin, and 118 tourist class
Officers and crew: 193
Registry: Portugal

Built expressly for the Portuguese Line and christened *Patria*. Engaged in the Lisbon-Sao Tome-Luanda-Lobito-Maçsamedes-Cape Town-Lourenço-Marques-Beira-Mozambique-Nacala-Porto Amelia trade with occasional calls at Funchal and Nacala. Fully air-conditioned, revenues fell drastically when the Portuguese Colonies in East Africa began seeking independence in the early seventies. The sovereignty given to the once held Cape Verde Islands also hastened her retirement. Made her last voyage for the Line on March 7, 1973, and was withdrawn on May 20 of that year. Sold to shipbreakers in Taipei in July 1973 and broken up.

Sister ship: *Imperio*.

SANTA MARIA

Builder: Societe Anonyme, John Cockerill, Hoboken, Belgium
Completed: September 1953
Gross tonnage: 20,906
Dimensions: 609' x 76' Depth: 43' Draft: 28'
Engines: Six steam turbines, double-reduction geared
Screws: Twin
Watertight Bulkheads: Nine
Decks: Five
Normal speed: 20 knots
Passenger accommodations: 156 first, 200 cabin, and 680 tourist class
Officers and crew: 369
Registry: Portugal
Maiden voyage: To the United States Lisbon-Port Everglades in January 1957, arriving on the 14th

Built expressly for the Portuguese Line, she was engaged in the transatlantic service from Lisbon-Funchal-Vigo-Tenerife-La Guaira-Curacao-Fort Lauderdale service in the winter season with the elimination of the calls at La Guaira and Curacao in the summer months. The *Santa Maria* set sail from Lisbon on January 9, 1961, on what was to become an international news event. On the morning of January 22 the *Santa Maria* was seized by twenty-four Portuguese and Spanish rebels under the leadership of Henrique Galvão, a Portuguese revolutionary. The rebels struck at 1:30 a.m. on the bridge. In the ensuing struggle that took place with the ship's personnel, the third mate was killed and two others wounded. The ship hoved off the Brazilian coast while being hunted by air and sea until spotted. Meanwhile, the rebels had set a course towards Martinique and the Windward Islands with 620 passengers aboard and 360 crew members. There were forty-one American passengers of the total complement. The ship was soon forced to land at Recife, Brazil on February 2 and the ship was officially handed over to Captain Maia on the 4th by the Brazilian authorities. The *Santa Maria* sailed from Recife on February 7 and arrived back in Lisbon on the 16th. She resumed her scheduled sailings on March 23rd. Equipped with motion stabilizers, she was fully air-conditioned. The ship also made calls at Havana but these were discontinued following the revolution in Cuba. She commenced her last voyage for the Line on March 15, 1973, from Lisbon. Sold for scrap to the Li Chong Steel & Iron Works Co., Ltd., for $87.00 per light ton displacement at Kaohsiung where she arrived on July 19, 1973. Scrapped in September of that year.

Sister ship: *Vera Cruz.*

UIGE

Builder: Societe Anonyme, John Cockerill, Hoboken, Belgium
Completed: July 1954
Gross tonnage: 10,001
Dimensions: 477′ x 63′ Depth: 37′ Draft: 26′
Engines: One 8-cylinder, two-stroke, single-acting Burmeister and Wain diesel
Screws: Single
Watertight bulkheads: Seven
Decks: Four
Normal speed: 16 knots
Passenger accommodations: 78 first and 493 tourist class
Officers and crew: 159
Registry: Portugal

Engaged in the Leixos-Lisbon-Las Palmas-Cabinda-Lobito-Moçamedes outbound and Moçamedes-Lobito-Luanda-Sao Tome Las Palmas-Funchal-Lisbon route homeward. The calls at Lobito and Las Palmas were occasional calls. Fully air-conditioned. The *Uige* was acquired when the Cia Portuguesa de Transportes, Carregadores Acoreanos, and Empresa Omsiama were merged into the Portuguese Line. Laid up on January 27, 1976 at Lisbon, she was sold for scrap four years later to the Baptista & Iramos Co., Ltd., at Lisbon with work commencing on February 7 and broken up by July 2, 1980.

VERA CRUZ

Builder: John Cockerill, S.A., Hoboken, Belgium
Completed: February 1952
Gross tonnage: 21,765
Dimensions: 610' x 76' Depth: 43' Draft: 28'
Engines: Six steam turbines double-reduction geared
Screws: Twin
Watertight Bulkheads: Nine
Decks: Five
Normal speed: 20 knots
Passenger accommodations: 148 first, 250 cabin, and 760 tourist class
Officers and crew: 361
Registry: Portugal
Maiden voyage: To the United States arrived Port Everglades on July 11, 1957

Built for the Portuguese Line and employed in the Lisbon-Vigo-Funchal-Tenerife-La Guaira-Curacao-Fort Lauderdale service westbound and Tenerife-Funchal-Vigo-Lisbon homeward. For a time she made calls at Havana. The trip to the United States was usually on a monthly basis and only westbound. A number of voyages were also made from Lisbon to Rio de Janeiro and East African ports as well. Equipped with motion stabilizers and fully air-conditioned. On February 2, 1961 she was diverted from Rio de Janeiro to Recife to pick up 108 distressed passengers from the *Santa Maria,* her sister ship, which had been taken over by political pirates while at sea. The *Vera Cruz* left Recife on February 5, 1961, for Tenerife-Funchal-Vigo-Lisbon with the passengers on board. For a time she did some troop work to Angola. Made her last voyage for the Line on January 7, 1973, Lisbon-Angola. Sold to Galbraith-Wrightson for scrap by the Yuita Steel & Iron Works, Co., Ltd., Kaohsiung, Taiwan. She left Lisbon for the last time on March 4, 1973, and arrived in Taiwan on April 19.

Sister ship: *Santa Maria.*

Red Star Line

II BELGENLAND

Builder: Harland & Wolff, Northern Ireland
Completed: June 1917
Gross tonnage: 27,132
Dimensions: 670' x 78' Depth: 49' Draft: 36'
Engines: Two sets of 4-cylinder triple expansion engines plus one low-pressure turbine
Screws: Triple
Watertight bulkheads: Eleven
Decks: Six
Normal speed: 17.50 knots
Passenger accommodations: 500 first, 624 second and 1,500 third class
Registry: United Kingdom
Maiden voyage: Antwerp-Southampton-New York in April 1923, arriving on the 14th

Launched on December 31, 1914, work was suspended due to hostilities. Completed as a cargo ship for the White Star Line in June 1917, and was christened *Belgic*. Commandeered as a transport during the First World War, she was released and returned to her builders in March 1922. Constructed with two funnels and three masts, she was rebuilt as a passenger liner and emerged from the shipyard with two masts and three funnels. Her upper deck area was 371 feet long. She had originally been intended for passenger service when ordered for the Red Star Line and was also converted to oil-firing at the time and renamed *Belgenland*. The third funnel was a dummy to give the ship symmetry. Acclaimed as luxury liner of the year in 1923, she was the largest ship to do cruises at the time and the first experimental ship for ship-to-shore telephone by the International Marine Radio Company. Engaged in the Antwerp-Southampton-New York service and cruising. In 1924 she made four London-New York voyages and in 1925 included a call at Halifax on her westbound crossings. She made her first world cruise out of New York on January 19, 1924 and also made one the following year. She would make three more in the future, one in 1928, 1930 and 1931. She made a number of booze cruises during Prohibition and the Depression years with one-day cruises out of New York for as little as £2.00 sterling and carrying up to 1,700 passengers. She made her last voyage for the Line on May 18, 1933 at the height of the Depression from New York to Antwerp. Laid up towards the end of 1934, she was transferred to the International Mercantile Marine's Panama Pacific Lines and renamed *Columbia*. Sold for scrap at Boness, Lothian, Scotland in April 1935 and broken up.

Note: The *Belgenland* flew the British flag while under the auspices of the Red Star Line, a Belgian corporation owned along with the White Star and Panama Pacific Line by the IMM of American financier J. P. Morgan.

FINLAND

Builder: William Cramp & Sons, Philadelphia, Pennsylvania, USA
Completed: September 1902
Gross tonnage: 12,222
Dimensions: 560' x 60' Depth: 42' Draft: 31'
Engines: Two sets of 3-cylinder triple expansion engines
Screws: Twin
Decks: Five
Normal speed: 15 knots
Passenger accommodations: 276 first, 359 second and 1,493 third class
Registry: U.S.A.
Maiden voyage: Antwerp-New York in October 1902, arriving on the 28th

Built for the Red Star Line and christened *Finland,* she was an integral part of J.P. Morgan's International Mercantile Marine and her registry often switched from American to Belgian and vice versa. Engaged in the Antwerp-New York service, she was laid up at New York following a return trip to the Mediterranean on December 28, 1914. She had also made two direct New York-Liverpool voyages that year beginning on August 22. She made another trip to the Mediterranean on January 12, 1915, followed by

two more and was once again laid up upon her return to New York on April 11. Between October and December of that year she made two trips to London for the American Line and later worked on the New York-Southampton run in 1916 until February 28, 1917, when she was laid up once again. Acquired by the U.S. Government for use as a transport on April 26, 1918, until November of the following year. She was converted to oil firing and re-entered service for the Red Star Line on April 7, 1920. Made a first-time call at Boston on February 16, 1921. She inaugurated a call at Halifax on January 4, 1922, westbound, and the next year made four sailings to Hamburg out of New York for the American Line beginning May 31. Simultaneously she was transferred to the American Line for eight more voyages. In October 1923 she was transferred to the International Mercantile Marine's Panama Pacific Line. She made her last official voyage for the Red Star Line on April 3, 1923, Antwerp-New York. The *Finland's* promenade deck was 273' long.

Sister ships: *Kroonland, Vaderland* and *Zeeland.*

Note: No record of service appears for the *Finland* between January 20, 1909, and November 8, 1909, the former date being when she left New York for Antwerp.

KROONLAND

Builder: William Cramp & Sons, Philadelphia, Pennsylvania, USA
Completed: June 1902
Gross tonnage: 12,241
Dimensions: 560′ x 60′ Depth: 42′ Draft: 31′
Engines: Two sets of 3-cylinder triple expansion
Screws: Twin
Watertight bulkheads: Eleven
Decks: Five
Normal speed: 15 knots
Passenger accommodations: 266 first, 380 second, and 1,512 third class
Registry: U.S.A.
Maiden voyage: Antwerp-New York in July 1902, arriving on the 22nd

Built for the Red Star Line, an American-owned subsidiary of the International Mercantile Marine, and christened *Kroonland.* She was engaged in the transatlantic service from Antwerp to New York. On October 9, 1913 the *Kroonland,* while on a westbound voyage, picked up the S.O.S. and came to the assistance of the Uranium Line immigrant ship *Volturno* ablaze in the North Atlantic and rescued 90 persons. Laid up at

New York on December 6, 1914 after returning from a trip to the Mediterranean. Prior to this she had made two direct New York-Liverpool voyages beginning August 15. With the outbreak of World War I, she was placed on the New York-Liverpool run on may 17, 1916. She made her last trip on this route from New York on August 5, 1917. Withdrawn from service and commandeered by the United States Government on April 25, 1918 as a transport and fitted-out. In October 1919 she was returned to her owners and returned to the New York-Antwerp run on March 24, 1920, after being converted for oil firing. On September 18, 1921, she made an eastbound call at Boston and a westbound call at Halifax for the first time on January 14, 1922. She made her last voyage for the Line in January 1923, Antwerp-New York, arriving on the 27th. Her promenade deck was 273 feet in length and her bulkheads were made of asphalt and cement. Transferred to the American Line in June 1923 for six voyages to Hamburg and subsequently to the Panama-Pacific Line. Sold for scrap in January 1927.

Sister ships: *Finland, Vaderland* and *Zeeland.*

Note: The Red Star Line, American Line and Panama-Pacific Line were part of the IMM combine of J.P. Morgan.

LAPLAND

Builder: Harland & Wolff, Belfast, Northern Ireland
Completed: 1908
Gross tonnage: 18,866
Dimensions: 606′ x 76′ Depth: 41′ Draft: 33′
Engines: Two sets of 4-cylinder quadruple expansion engines
Screws: Twin
Watertight bulkheads: Nine
Decks: Five
Normal speed: 18 knots
Passenger accommodations: 472 first, 698 second and 1,742 third class
Officers and crew: 370
Registry: United Kingdom
Maiden voyage: Antwerp-Dover-New York in April 1909, arriving at New York on the 10th

Built for the Red Star Line and christened *Lapland*. Engaged in the Antwerp-New York run, she made an eastbound call at Boston on March 28, 1914 for the first time. Used for troop work beginning in June 1917, she returned to commercial service on September 16, 1917. Later she was transferred to White Star Line management and placed in their Liverpool-New York run but also made sailings out of Southampton in 1919. The *Lapland* arrived at Cawsand Bay, Plymouth, England on April 28, 1912, carrying with her 172 of the *Titanic's* surviving crew members from New York. Her watertight bulkheads were made of cement. She made her last voyage for the White Star Line in August 1914, from Liverpool to New York and was transferred back to the Red Star Line. Resuming commercial service for the Line on December 24, 1919, New York-Antwerp, she was the only Red Star liner to sail for the line that year. She inaugurated calls at Halifax on January 28, 1922, westbound. Two years later on January 16, 1924, she made a voyage from New York to the Mediterranean and made a similar voyage that year. The *Lapland* was re-routed often during the Great Depression of the early twenties and on April 24, 1924, she was sailing from New York to Hamburg and the next month New York-London on May 24. In 1925 she made two more trips to the Mediterranean beginning on January 17, and a call at Halifax was incorporated into her itinerary both east and westbound. In 1926 there were three scheduled voyages to the Mediterranean beginning on January 16. Employed mostly as a cruise ship during The Depression until the close of 1933. In that year she steamed 30,000 miles cruising. She had made her final New York-Antwerp voyage across the North Atlantic on June 13, 1932. Sold for scrap to Japanese shipbreakers on October 26, 1933, for £30,000 sterling after having been laid up for some time at Antwerp.

PENNLAND

Builder: Harland & Wolff, Ltd., Northern Ireland
Completed: May 1922
Gross tonnage: 16,082
Dimensions: 574' x 67' Depth: 41'
Engines: Two sets of 4-cylinder triple-expansion engines plus one low-pressure turbine
Screws: Triple
Decks: Four
Normal speed: 16 knots
Passenger accommodations: 561 cabin and 250 third class
Officers and crew: 280
Registry: United Kingdom
Maiden voyage: Antwerp-Halifax-New York, arriving on April 13, 1926

Built for the White Star Line and christened *Pittsburgh*. She had originally been ordered for the American Line in 1913 but was transferred to the White Star Line while still on the stocks. Work on her had been held up during the First World War and she was not completed until May 1922. Transferred to the Red Star Line for management in January 1925, she passed into their service the following month. Notation should be made that the White Star Line and the Red Star Line were owned by the American conglomerate known as the International Mercantile Marine the brainchild of the famous financier J.P. Morgan, who sought to amalgamate all of the North Atlantic trade under his control. In pursuit of this, ships of the conglomerate were often shifted from one registry to another, i.e., British, American and Belgian. The *Pennland* made a call at Halifax westbound and was renamed officially in February 1926. She made her last voyage for the Line in 1935 and was later sold to Arnold Berstein. Resold to the Holland-America Line in June 1939, she became a British troop ship in May 1940. Sunk by German Flugzeugen aircraft on April 25 1941, off Crete while enroute from Alexandria, Egypt to the Gulf of Athens to evacuate British troops. She was hit by seven bombs, one of which penetrated her engine room killing four people.

Sister ship: *Westernland*.

VADERLAND

Builder: John Brown & Co. Ltd., Clydebank, Glasgow, Scotland
Completed: November 1900
Gross tonnage: 11,899
Dimensions: 561' x 60' **Depth:** 42' **Draft:** 31'
Engines: Two sets of 4-cylinder quadruple expansion engines
Screws: Twins
Watertight bulkheads: Ten
Decks: Four
Normal speed: 15 knots
Passenger accommodations: 323 first, 336 second and 1,646 third class
Registry: Belgium
Maiden voyage: Antwerp-New York in December 1900, arriving on the 20th

Built expressly for the Red Star Line and christened *Vaderland*. She was engaged on the North Atlantic run between Antwerp and New York. In 1914 she made a trip from New York to Liverpool direct, her last on October 8, 1914. She then made a series of five trips from Liverpool to Halifax and Portland, Maine beginning on December 2, 1914 while under White Star Line management, and in February of 1915 was renamed *Southland* when transferred. On the 16th of February she was fitted-out as a war transport at Halifax. Torpedoed by a German submarine on September 2, 1915 while trooping in the Aegean Sea, she was beached and repaired. Re-entering service her final demise was to come about on June 4, 1917 when she was again torpedoed by a German U-boat 140 miles off Tory Island Ireland, with the loss of four lives.

Sister ships: *Finland, Kroonland* and *Zeeland.*

Note: The Red Star Line, White Star Line and American Line were contingent lines under the International Mercantile Marine owned by American financier J.P. Morgan and ships were often transferred from one line to another as well as registries, i.e. Belgian, British and American depending on the political or economic situations prevalent at the time.

II WESTERNLAND

Builder: Harland & Wolff, Govan, Northern Ireland
Completed: December 1918
Gross tonnage: 16,231
Dimensions: 574' x 68' Depth: 41'
Engines: Two sets of 4-cylinder triple-expansion engines plus one low-
   pressure turbine
Screws: Triple
Decks: Five
Normal speed: 16 knots
Passenger accommodations: 572 cabin and 1,113 third class
Officers and crew: 280
Registry: Germany
Maiden voyage: Antwerp-New York in January 1930, arriving at New York
   on the 22nd

Built for the British Dominion Line and christened *Regina*. Transferred to
the White Star Line in December 1925. Resold to the Red Star Line at the
end of 1929 and renamed *Westernland* in 1930. The transferral of
ownership and registrations was a part of the operation of the
International Mercantile Marine, the powerful though unsuccessful
shipping conglomerate of J.P. Morgan, who owned the Dominion Line,
Red Star Line, White Star Line, Atlantic Transport Line, Leyland Line, the
National Line, and American Line and Baltimore Line to mention a few.
She made her last voyage for the Line on December 12, 1934, New York-
Antwerp. Sold to Arnold Berstein in 1935, she was resold to the Holland
America Line in June 1939. It may be worth noting that the IMM at one
time held a large percentage of HAL common stock. She became General
De Gaulle's flagship and served as headquarters for two months under the
Prince of the Netherlands at Falmouth, England in the beginning of the
War. In July 1940 she was taken to Liverpool and fitted-out as a transport
by the British Admiralty and in November of 1942 was converted to a
repair ship. She survived the war and was sold for scrap on July 15, 1947
to the British Iron & Steel Corporation at Blyth, Scotland. Demolition
began on August 1.

Sister ship: *Pennland*.

Note: During the First World War she was used temporarily by the
Admiralty in an uncompleted state and was released in 1918 when she
reverted back to the builder's yard. Built with only one smokestack, a
second was added when she had been sold to the White Star Line.

ZEELAND

Builder: John Brown & Co., Clydebank, Glasgow, Scotland
Completed: April 1901
Gross tonnage: 11,167
Dimensions: 562' x 60' Depth: 42' Draft: 31'
Engines: Two sets of 4-cylinder, single-stroke, quadruple expansion engines
Screws: Twin
Watertight bulkheads: Ten
Decks: Five
Normal speed: 15 knots
Passenger accommodations: 365 first, 324 second and 1,512 third class
Registry: Belgium
Maiden voyage: Antwerp-New York, arriving on April 23, 1901

The *Zeeland*, though under Belgian registry, was built for the Red Star Line, owned by J.P. Morgan's International Mercantile Marine, which also owned the British White Star Line in 1902. The ships of the combine often changed registries. The *Zeeland* was one of the first transatlantic liners to be fitted with wireless telegraphy. On April 19, 1910 she abandoned her regular run from Antwerp to New York and was transferred to the White Star Line's Liverpool-Queenstown-Boston service. She made her first trip to Montreal on November 3, 1914. Reverted back to Red Star Line service in October 1911 and resumed her former Antwerp-New York run. Transferred back to the White Star Line's Liverpool-Halifax-Portland, Maine service on November 13, 1914 and made three trips. She continued to work this route until summoned for troop work by the British Admiralty at the outbreak of World War I. In February 1915 she was officially sold to the White Star Line and renamed *Northland*. Returned to commercial service in August 1920 and was once again renamed *Zeeland*. Resumed her Antwerp-New York service after being converted to oil-firing. On February 24, 1921 she made a westbound call at Boston and on January 31, 1922 a call at Halifax heading eastbound enroute to Southampton. Converted to a cabin class ship in 1923, carrying cabin and third class passengers only. In 1924 she added Halifax to her westbound route. The *Zeeland* arrived at New York for the last time on October 18, 1926 and commenced her last voyage, New York-Antwerp, under the Red Star Line banner on October 23, 1926. Transferred to the International Mercantile Marine's Atlantic Transport Line in April 1927 and renamed *Minnesota*. Sold for scrap in October 1929 to Thomas W. Ward, Ltd., Inverkeithing, Scotland.

Sister ships: *Vaderland, Finland* and *Kroonland*.

Russian State Lines

ADMIRAL NAKHIMOV

Builder: Bremer Vulkan, Vegesack, Germany
Completed: 1925
Gross tonnage: 17,053
Dimensions: 572' x 69' Depth: 39' Draft: 30'
Engines: Two twin 4-cylinder triple expansion engines
Screws: Twin
Decks: Four
Normal speed: 16 knots
Passenger accommodations: 870 in a single class plus a number of saloon
  type passengers with deck chairs
Officers and crew: 346
Registry: Russia
Maiden voyage: May 1957

Built for the North German Lloyd and christened *Berlin*. Sunk by a mine off Swinemunde Bay, Poland on February 1, 1945. Raised by the Russians in 1949 and rebuilt at the Warnow Werft shipyards in East Germany. Her long slender funnels were replaced by the two shorter squat type and her samson posts fore and aft removed. Engaged in the Odessa-Eupatoria-Yalta-Novorossik-Sochi-Sukhumi-Batum service in the Black Sea.

Managed by the Black Sea Steamship Company, a subsidiary of the state-owned Morflot. On September 3, 1986 while on a cruise with 1,234 passengers and crew aboard she was rammed and torn open by a freighter. The liner began to sink rapidly making it nearly impossible to launch any of her lifeboats. The collision had occurred late at night near the port of Novorossik. The freighter, the *Pyotr Vasev*, an 18,604-ton bulk carrier, was also a Russian ship. Around 398 people lost their lives in one of the worst disasters at sea since the Second World War. It seems the sixty-one year old ship had not been built with watertight bulkheads which may have prevented some of the casualties. There was no fog at the time of the collision and nearly 50 vessels in the area had come to rescue the remaining passengers and crew. The total number of passengers given at the time were 888, all of whom were Soviet tourists. There were no casualties amongst the officers or crew. According to eyewitness accounts the blow to the stricken liner came between the engine room and the boiler room and virtually ripped the ship open to the sea sinking her within 15 minutes time. The total survivors, numbered 836, were plucked from the sea most of them clinging to rafts that floated free when the liner plunged to the bottom at around midnight that dark sunday evening. Seventy-nine bodies had been recovered and 319 people were still missing two days after the tragedy. During her career, the *Admiral Nakhimov* was mostly used as a liner and began cruising around the Crimean coast and the Caucasus in 1960 and also made calls at Sevastopol.

ANIVA

Builder: Deutsche Werft Reiherstiegwerft A.G., Hamburg, Germany

Completed: July 1938

Gross tonnage: 17,870

Dimensions: 598′ x 74′ Depth: 41′ Draft: 26′

Engines: Five single-acting, two-stroke M.A.N. 8-cylinder and one six-cylinder, single-acting two stroke diesel engine

Screws: Twin

Decks: Five

Normal speed: 17 knots

Passenger accommodations: 185 first, 164 tourist (German figures)

Registry: Russia

Built for the German-owned Hamburg-America Line and christened *Patria*. Allotted to Britain as a World War II reparation in May 1945 and renamed *Empire Welland* in July. Transferred to The Union of Soviet Socialist Republics in the spring of 1946 and renamed *Rossiya*; *Aniva* in 1985. She had entered service to the United States in 1947 and made about seven round trip voyages from Leningrad to New York and a few out of Odessa with a call at Piraeus westbound. Her last trip was made in February 1948 after which she was confined to European waters. Transferred to the Russian state-owned Black Sea Steamship Company which was an integral part of the government's Morflot and worked out of Odessa to Batum with calls at other Black Sea ports. Sold for scrap at Etajima-Hiroshima, Japan in February 1986.

Note: Photo as *Rossiya*

ALEKSANDR PUSHKIN

Builder: VEB Mathias-Thesen-Werft, Wismar, East Germany
Completed: June 1965
Gross tonnage: 20,502
Dimensions: 581' x 78' Depth: 43' Draft: 27'
Engines: Two Sulzer single-acting two stroke 7-cylinder diesels and a bow
  thruster forward
Screws: Twin
Decks: Five
Normal speed: 20.50 knots
Passenger accommodations: 763 in a single class*
Officers and crew: 365
Registry: Russia
Maiden voyage: Leningrad**-Bremerhaven-London-Le Havre-Quebec-
  Montreal in April 1966 arriving on the 13th

*Originally carried 130 first and 621 tourist class
**Now St. Petersburg.

Launched on March 26, 1964 she was built exclusively for the Russian state-owned Baltic Shipping Lines. Engaged in the North Atlantic trade from Leningrad-Channel ports-Montreal run with calls at Quebec westbound. Ports of call varied from time to time and Copenhagen was supplanted by Bremerhaven in 1969 and Le Havre added on after he initial call on March 29, 1970. She also made an occasional call at Rig. Sent cruising up the St. Lawrence and Saguenay Rivers during th summer months since July 1968 from Montreal to Quebec-St. Pierre Miquelon-Bagotville and on to Bermuda. She made five such cruises i 1970 and was later laid up when the St. Lawrence River would freeze u She returned to North Atlantic service on August 28, 1973 and later mad a cruise from Montreal to Havana on July 12, 1975. Constructed with 28 cabins most of these with the basic amenities. Refurbished in 1976 an 1981, she is one of five sisterships to be built on traditional lines with nice looking hull and superstructure. Staterooms have individual climat control and a three-channel radio for music and some cabins do not ha private facilities. There is an outdoor and indoor swimming pool an ample deck space. There are several lounges, two nightclubs, five bars ar the customary library, gymnasium, beauty parlour, barber shop. There a gambling facilities and slot machines. The *Aleksandr Pushkin* has bee engaged in many services over the past two decades and was last chartere out to an English firm who have employed the ship in worldwide cruisin On September 4, 1987 she made a 9-day cruise from Ulyanovsk to Zhigu Devushkin Island-Volgograd-Cossack Island-down the Don River Rostov. Ports which sound as mysterious to Westerners as once did a ri on the Siberian Railway. Presently in service.

Sister ships: *Ivan Franko, Mikhail Lermontov, Shota Rustaveli, Tar Shevchenko.*

AZERBAYDZHAN

Builder: Oy Wartsila Ab, Turku/Abo, Finland
Completed: December 1975
Gross tonnage: 16,361
Dimensions: 512′ x 72′ Depth: 53′ Draft: 19′
Engines: Two Vee 4-stroke Pielstick design, single acting 18-cylinder diesels, plus a bow thruster forward
Screws: Twin with controllable pitch
Decks: Five
Normal speed: 21.50 knots
Passenger accommodations: 650 in a single class
Officers and crew: 200
Registry: Russia
Maiden voyage: Odessa-Black Sea ports in January 1976

Built expressly for the Russian state-owned Black Sea Shipping Company. Engaged in a cruise service out of her home port of Odessa, the *Azerbaydzhan* and her four sister ships cruise mostly in the Black Sea and Mediterranean. Built with ice strengthened bow, stern and side doors, the *Azerbaydzhan* was constructed as a Passenger Ro/Ro Cargo/Ferry. The Ro/Ro abbreviation while well known to the shipping industry's own jargon means: "Roll on Roll off" just as "Obo" means a vessel which carries oil, bitumen and other cargoes such as grain, etc. The *Azerbaydzhan* also carries automobiles and has accommodations for 110 deck class passengers in reclining chairs. This has been little used over the past few years since the Black Sea Shipping Company has focussed on a more sophisticated European market as well as American to some extent. Fully air-conditioned and equipped with motion stabilizers the *Azerbaydzhan* is not luxurious by any means, but comfortable. The waitresses are very attractive and smile more so than in the past. The ship has the usual shops, beauty parlour, gymnasium, library/card room, bars, lounges, etc. Over the past few years the *Azerbaydzhan* has been sailing to various ports around the world from Scandinavia and the British Isles, Mediterranean, and offers Around the World Cruises. In the fall of 1987 she was making 14-day cruises out of Venice to Split-Piraeus-Izmir-Limassol-Alexandria-Heraklion-Santorini-Messina-Corfu-Dubrovnik with minimum fares beginning at $2,067. The ship's sales are marketed by CTC Lines in London and the U.S.A.

Sister ships: *Belorussiya, Gruziya, Kareliya, Kazakhstan.*

AZIYA

Builder: Bremer Vulkan, Vegesack, Germany
Completed: October 1924
Gross tonnage: 12,019
Dimensions: 510' x 62' Depth: 38'
Engines: Two sets of 3-cylinder triple expansion engines
Screws: Twin
Watertight bulkheads: Nine
Decks: Four
Normal speed: 13 knots
Passenger accommodations: 150 first, 270 second and 890 third class
  (North German Lloyd figures)
Officers and crew: 298
Registry: Russia
Maiden voyage: mid-1950

Built expressly for the North German Lloyd and christened *Sierra Morena*. Renamed *Der Deutsche* in June 1934. Ceded to the Russians as a World War II reparation in June 1946 and later renamed *Aziya*. Rebuilt at the East German shipyards of Warnow Werft in East Germany and re-entered service in mid-1950 under the banner of the Far East Steamship Company, a wholly owned subsidiary of the state-owned Morflot. Engaged in the Vladivostok-Petropavlovsk-Kamchatski trade in the Eastern regions of the Union of Soviet Socialist Republics. When she was rebuilt her sides were relined with corrugated steel. Removed from service in 1965 and later scrapped.

BELORUSSIYA

Builder: Oy Wartsila Av, Turku/Abo, Finland
Completed: 1975
Gross tonnage: 16,631 (Lloyd's Register listed as 13,631)
Dimensions: 512′ x 72′ Depth: 53′ Draft: 19′
Engines: Two Vee oil 4-stroke, single-acting, 18-cylinder diesels plus a
  bow thruster forward
Screws: Twin with controllable pitch
Decks: Five
Normal speed: 21.50 knots
Passenger accommodations: 350 in a single class
Officers and crew: 191
Registry: Russia
Maiden voyage: Odessa-European ports on January 15, 1975

Built expressly for the Russian state-owned Black Sea Shipping Company. Constructed as one of five sister ships the *Belorussiya* is a Passenger Ro/Ro Cargo/Ferry and has an ice strengthened bow. There are both a stern door and ramp to take on 256 cars and 23 lorries. Accommodations are for an actual complement of 504–390 in berths and 114 deck class. The former category has since been eliminated ever since she became a full cruise ship in the early eighties. Fully air-conditioned and equipped with motion stabilizers, the *Belorussiya* cruises mostly in Australian waters with sailings out of Southampton via Naples-Piraeus-Suez Canal-Aden-Colombo-Singapore-Freemantle-Melbourne-Sydney. In December she cruises in the South Pacific returning to England by the end of May. Refurbished in 1975 she has the customary public amenities of shops, beauty parlour, gymnasium, sauna, library/card room, a few bars, main lounge and main dining room. There is a swimming pool and discotheque, infirmary and photo gallery. Presently in service. Marketed by CTC Lines out of London and the U.S.A.

Sister ships: *Azerbaydzhan, Gruziya, Kareliya, Kazakhstan.*

FEDOR DOSTOYEVSKI

Builder: Howaldtswerke Deutsche Werft, Kiel, Germany
Completed: January 1987
Gross tonnage: 20,606
Dimensions: 578' x 72' Depth: 53' Draft: 20'
Engines: Four Sulzer single-reduction geared diesels with clutches and
 flexible couplings (two 4-stroke, 8-cylinder; two 4-stroke, 6-cylinder)
 plus a bow thruster forward
Screws: Twin (controllable pitch)
Decks: Five
Normal speed: 18 knots (attained a speed of 21 knots on her trials)
Passenger accommodations: 550 in a single class
Officers and crew: 280
Registry: Russia
Maiden voyage: Summer 1989, Black Sea area via Istanbul

Built for the South African-owned Safmarine and christened *Astor; Astor II* in late 1987. Chartered out to Morgan Leisure, Ltd., in the United Kingdom. Sold to the Russian state owned Morflot in January, 1988, for a reported 20 million German Marks and delivered in September at Lisbon. Renamed *Fedor Dostoyevski* she is currently being managed by the Black Sea Steamship Company and is engaged mostly in cruises in the Mediterranean and Black Sea areas. I had the privilege of travelling on the maiden voyage of this exquisite liner when she was owned by Safmarine back in February 1987, out of Southampton and must say she was in the top class of luxury ships at that time. Tradition was foremost for her former owners and even her decks were labelled: A, B, C, Main, Upper, Promenade. What a pleasantry compared to the confusing names of the cruise ships today, i.e., Emerald deck, or Princess deck. She lived up to her name calling of *Astor* and was in fact the second ship to have the name. Her predecessor built nearly identically the same in design and dimensions as well as outlay. The new ship only 39' longer in overall length. The *Fedor Dostoyevski's* cabins are fitted with two beds and most of the 295 cabins are situated outside. Cabins also have radio, telephone and climate control thermostat. The bathrooms have vacuum flushing and a wall hair-drier. There are two swimming pools, a gym, sauna boutique, several bars, main lounge lido deck area is very large. There are 32 suites and six are ultra suites. She is equipped with motion stabilizer and is fully air-conditioned. Presently in service under charter to the German tour operator Neckermann Seereisen.

FEDOR SHALYAPIN

Builder: John Brown & Company, Clydebank, Glasgow, Scotland
Completed: June 1955
Gross tonnage: 21,406
Dimensions: 607' x 79' Depth: 46' Draft: 28'
Engines: Four Pametrada steam turbines, double-reduction geared
Screws: Twin
Decks: Six
Normal speed: 20 knots
Passenger accommodations: 580 in a single class
Officers and crew: 400
Registry: Russia
Maiden voyage: Southampton-Sydney-Auckland on November 20, 1973

Built for the British Cunard Line and christened *Ivernia*. Renamed *Franconia* in 1962. Sold to the Russian state-owned Far Eastern Shipping Company through a Panamanian corporate shell set up for the purpose. The purchase price $1,000,000. Renamed *Fedor Shalyapin* she was engaged in cruising and liner service out of the Russian port of Vladivostok for a number of years. The decline in revenues forced the ship's inactivity between January 1972-1976. Later she was chartered out to the German tour operator Jahn Reisen but not before she had transported Cuban soldiers to the Middle East and East Africa via the Suez Canal in June of 1980. The chartering out of so many of the Russian state-owned ships provides their economy with an invaluable source of foreign exchange which is vital to its existence. The ship has changed little outwardly over the years and the liner still sports eight derricks and samson posts as well as her original smoke-stack. Today there is an outdoor pool on the aft deck. Since the charterers market the ship mostly to a European clientele little is known about shipboard amenities. She is, however, fully air-conditioned and equipped with motion stabilizers. There is a main dining room and main lounge. Also, a gift shop, beauty-barber salon, hospital. Entertainment: port lectures, bingo, etc. The ship is managed by CTC Lines in London and she is currently inactive.

Sister ship: *Leonid Sobinov.*

I GRUZIYA

Builder: Swan Hunter & Wigham Richardson, Newcastle-on-Tyne, England
Gross tonnage: 11,030
Dimensions: 511' x 67' Depth: 36' Draft: 25'
Engines: Two Kincaid double-acting eight-cylinder diesels
Screws: Twin
Decks: Four
Normal speed: 16 knots
Passenger accommodations: 60 first, 250 cabin and 450 tourist class
Registry: Russia

Built for the Polish Ocean Lines in May, 1939, and christened *Sobieski.* Sold to the state-owned Sovtorgflot of the Union of Soviet Socialist Republics and transfered to their subsidiary, Black Sea Steamship Company, and renamed *Gruziya*. Engaged in the Leningrad-Cuba-Indonesia service for a time as well as the Black Sea trade until withdrawn from service in April 1975. Sold for scrap in Italy and scrapped at La Spezia by the Cantieri Navale with work commencing on May 15, 1975 and completed by June of that year.

II GRUZIYA

Builder: Oy Wartsila Ab-Turku/Abo, Finland
Completed: June 1975
Gross tonnage: 16,631
Dimensions: 512' x 72' Depth: 53' Draft: 19'
Engines: Two Pielstick 4-stroke, single-acting, 18-cylinder diesels plus a bow thruster forward
Screws: Twin with controllable pitch
Decks: Five
Normal speed: 21 knots
Passenger accommodations: 480 in a single class
Officers and crew: 200
Registry: Russia
Maiden voyage: Odessa-Mediterranean ports on June 30, 1975

Built for the Russian state-owned Black Sea Shipping Company she is one of five sister ships. Unlike the quintet built for the North Atlantic trade in the mid sixties–early seventies in East German shipyards this group were contracted for in Finland. Built as Passenger Ro/Ro Cargo/Ferries the *Gruziya* and her sister ships have an actual capacity for 650 berthed passengers and 110 deck class. The complement has been reduced to the aforementioned figure since she and the other ships have been employed as cruise ships. The *Gruziya* has an ice-strengthened bow, and she has stern and side doors. The ship also has room for 256 cars and 23 lorries. Fully air-conditioned and equipped with motion stabilizers. Marketing for the ship is done through CTC Lines in London. Presently in service.

Sister ships: *Azerbaydzhan, Belorussiya, Kareliya, Kazakhstan.*

I ILYICH

Builder: Blohm & Voss, Hamburg, Germany
Completed: February 1933
Gross tonnage: 12,049
Dimensions: 524' x 66' Depth: 32' Draft: 25'
Engines: Two M.A.N. type 8-cylinder double-acting diesels
Screws: Twin
Decks: Four
Normal speed: 13 knots
Passenger accommodations: 900 in a single class
Officers and crew: 198
Registry: Russia

Built for the Hamburg-American Line and christened *Caribia*. Allotted to the United States on July 15, 1945, at the Potsdam Conference as a World War II reparation. She was subsequently transferred to the British in the autumn of 1945 and ultimately to the U.S.S.R. in 1946. Renamed *Ilyich* she was engaged in the Vladivostok-Petropavlovsk-Kamchatski service in eastern Russia under the subsidiary of the Far East Steamship Company an integral part of the state-owned Morflot. The *Ilyich* was in 1984 classified as being 'no longer seagoing' by Lloyd's and was stricken from the Register and assumed scrapped. She was modernized in 1973.

Sister ship: *Russ.*

IVAN FRANKO

Builder: VEB Mathias-Thesen-Werft, Wismar, East Germany
Completed: November 1964
Gross tonnage: 20,064
Dimensions: 574' x 82' Depth: 43' Draft: 27'
Engines: Two Sulzer 2-stroke, single acting, 7-cylinder diesels
Screws: Twin
Decks: Six
Normal speed: 20 knots
Passenger accommodations: 550 in a single class
Officers and crew: 370
Registry: Russia
Maiden voyage: Odessa-Mediterranean on November 14, 1964

Built expressly for the Russian-owned Black Sea Shipping Company and engaged in a service out of Leningrad to London and extensive cruising. She is fully air-conditioned and equipped with motion stabilizers. Accommodations are comprised of 88 outside cabins, 99 inside and two suites. In late 1964 she made a cruise out of Riga calling at Copenhagen-Gothenburg-Oslo-London-Casablanca-Algiers-Naples-Piraeus. In the spring of 1965 she operated in the Caribbean and was the first Soviet ship calling at the ports of Martinique-Guadalupe-Antigua-Curacao-Trinidad and Grenada. On the 18th of May, 1967, she called at Barcelona followed by Cadiz-Palma and Mahon Bay and was the first Soviet ship to do so after a lapse of three decades. In December, 1968, she cruised extensively out of London to the Canary Islands. For some years now the ship has been chartered out to the German tour operator Jahn Reisen. Her passenger certificate is for 750 passengers and she has a cargo capacity for 1,500 tons. Built with an icebreaker bow and hull. Refurbished in 1972 she was painted white for cruising. The ship has a gymnasium, sauna, gift shop, beauty and barber shop, gift shops, lounges and several bars. While most cabins have private facilities some of the inside staterooms in the lower decks must share. Her main dining room seats 376 and she has an enclosed heated swimming pool situated aft. Presently in service.

Sister ships: *Aleksander Pushkin, Mikhail Lermontov, Shota Rustaveli, Taras Shevchenko.*

KARELIYA

Builder: Oy Wartsila A.B. Turku/Abo, Finland
Completed: 1976
Gross tonnage: 16,631
Dimensions: 512′ x 72′ Depth: 53′ Draft: 19′
Engines: Two Vee Pielstick 4-stroke single-acting 18-cylinder diesels plus a bow thruster forward
Screws: Twin with controllable pitch
Decks: Five
Normal speed: 21 knots
Passenger accommodations: 650 in a single class
Officers and crew: 191
Registry: Russia
Maiden voyage: Odessa-Black Sea-European ports in December 1976

Built for the Russian state-owned Black Sea Steamship Co. and christened *Kareliya*. Renamed *Leonid Brezhnev* in 1982 after refurbishing. Renamed *Kareliya* in 1989. One of five sister ships built for the U.S.S.R. merchant fleet it was a surprise that the quintet were built in a Finnish shipyard since all previous Russian tonnage has been built in East Germany. Constructed as a Passenger Ro/Ro Cargo/Ferry she has a stern door and is ice-strengthened. As with the majority of all ships constructed she has a bulbous bow to eliminate drag. The *Kareliya* originally carried an additional 50 deck passengers in reclining salon seats. Employed as a cruise ship for some years now she is currently sailing out of London to Rotterdam-Madeira-Tenerife-Lanzarote-Casablanca-Gilbraltar-Lisbon and return on 14-night cruises. Minimum fares begin at £653 sterling. She is also making 7-night cruises to the North Cape; 13 and 16-day cruises to Scandinavia ports as well as to the Mediterranean. The ship has six suites and six deluxe cabins; the former include TV, cocktail cabinet, refrigerator and dining area with sitting room, and full bath and bidet. Some cabins have only showers and share facilities with some of the inside staterooms. There is a casino, sauna, cinema, nightclub and swimming pool. Air conditioned and stabilized the *Kareliya* offers more than one would expect from a Russian ship. Given the intense competition in the industry, the Russians are leaning more and more about epicureanism to secure a piece of the growing cruise business. She was refitted at the British Tyne shipyards in South Shields where 80 new cabins were added in 1982. Her salon and restaurant were also extended and refurbished. A cinema, night club and disco were installed. She also makes longer cruises to the Caribbean and South American ports.

Sister ships: *Azerbaydzhan, Belorussiya, Gruziya, Kazakhstan.*

KAZAKHSTAN

Builder: Oy Wartsila A.B. Turku/Abo Finland
Completed: June 1976
Gross tonnage: 16,631
Dimensions: 512′ x 72′ Depth: 53′ Draft: 19′
Engines: Two 9-cylinder Vee Pielstick 4-stroke, single acting diesels plus
 a bow thruster forward
Screws: Twin (controllable pitch)
Decks: Five
Normal speed: 20 knots
Passenger accommodations: 350 in a single class
Officers and crew: 191
Registry: Russia
Maiden voyage: New Orleans-Montego Bay-Curacao-Cartagena-San
 Andros Island-Playa del Carmen-Cozumel on December 19, 1976

Built for the Russian state-owned Morflot and placed in their Black Sea
Shipping Company fleet. Classified as a Passenger Ro/Ro Cargo/Ferry. She
has a full complement for 650 berthed passengers and 110 deck class. The
Kazakhstan holds 268 cars and 23 lorries when fully loaded. Her side door
and stern door and bow are ice-strengthened. She began her career
cruising in European waters as early as July 1, 1976, until positioned to
work out of New Orleans for a number of cruises to the Caribbean. She
reverted to cruises out of New York to Bermuda beginning June 15, 1977.
She made a maiden trans-Atlantic crossing on May 15, 1977, from New
Orleans to Tampa-St. Thomas-Las Palmas-Casablanca-Barcelona-Majorca-
Cannes-Genoa. Between December 24, 1977, and May 27, 1978, she ran
from New Orleans to Montego Bay-Curacao-La Guaira-Cartagena-San
Andros-Playa del Carmen and Cozumel. Her seven and fourteen-day
cruises were not a success nor an attempt at cruises to nowhere.
Repositioned in European waters she was modernized in 1984 at the
Hapag-Lloyd shipyards in Bremerhaven, West Germany. Presently
cruising out of Odessa to the Black Sea area with a Russian and Bulgarian
clientele.

Sister ships: *Azerbaydzhan, Belorussiya, Gruziya, Kareliya.*

LEONID SOBINOV

Builder: John Brown & Co., Clydebank, Scotland
Completed: August 1954
Gross tonnage: 21,846
Dimensions: 607' x 79' Depth: 46' Draft: 28'
Engines: Four steam turbines, double reduction geared
Screws: Twin
Collision bulkhead: One
Watertight bulkheads: Nine
Decks: Five
Normal speed: 20 knots
Passenger accommodations: 929 in a single class
Registry: Russia
Maiden voyage: Southampton-Sydney on February 25, 1974

Built for the Cunard Line and christened *Saxonia*. Renamed *Carmania* in 1962. Sold to the Russian state-owned Morflot and placed under the Far East Shipping Company in August 1973 after being reconditioned by the Swan, Hunter and Wigham Richardson shipyards at South Shields, England. Employed in a service between Vladivostok and Nahodko she was later used for cruising. Chartered out to Shaw Savill Line for a six-month period until a particular voyage prompted the Australian Government to ban all Russian passenger ships from entering her ports in December, 1979, notifying those in port to leave by February, 1980. The incident surrounded the *Leonid Sobinov* while enroute between Auckland and Sydney when during the early morning hours her lights were extinguished. Cranking cranes awoke a number of passengers who noticed a red submarine alongside. According to the 200 passengers who witnessed the incident both goods and personnel were taken off to the submarine and other goods exchanged. The *Leonid Sobinov* was later used by the Cuban Government to transport troops from Havana to the Middle East and East Africa via the Suez Canal in the summer of 1980. Since then it's been chartered out to numerous British based charterers who have based the ship to work out of Odessa for cruises in the Mediterranean. Unfortunately, the Russians run a tight ship and getting to visit one of their vessels is nearly impossible. I saw the *Leonid Sobinov* in Piraeus in early June 1985, and understood from some of her passengers that service and entertainment were of the first order. I had seen the ship at the same port while she was still the *Carmania* on one of her last cruises in 1973 and was at that time able to go aboard. And if my memory is accurate she was then one of the last liners to be built as a conventional ship. The Russians have done little to modernize her outwardly and this is a plus since the ship has very nice lines. In fact, she still has her derricks and samson posts for loading cargo, a vestige many older ocean liners have lost since their sell-off to companies operating the cruise circuit in an effort to make the ships look more contemporary in appearance.

Sister ship: *Fedor Shalyapin.*

MAKSIM GORKI

Builder: Howaldtswerk-Deutsche Werft, Hamburg, Germany
Completed: 1969
Gross tonnage: 24,981
Dimensions: 639' x 86' Depth: 53' Draft: 27'
Engines: Four steam turbines, double reduction geared
Screws: Twin
Decks: Six
Normal speed: 22 knots
Passenger accommodations: 600 in a single class
Officers and crew: 185
Registry: Russia
Maiden voyage: May 24, 1974, arrived New York from U.S.S.R.

Built for the German-Atlantic Line and christened *Hamburg*. Renamed *Hanseatic* in 1973. Sold to the Russian state-owned Black Sea Steamship Company on January 25, 1974, and renamed *Maksim Gorki*. Built at a cost of £5,600,000 she soon came to be known as "The Space Ship" because of her radically-designed smokestack which today blends in with the rest of the world fleet of cruise ships just fine. Soon after her purchase by the Russians she was chartered out to a Hollywood producer for the movie "Juggernaut" and renamed *Britannic*. Built exclusively as a cruise ship the Russians sent her cruising out of New York on May 28, 1974, to Bermuda following her initial crossing. Thereafter she made a series of sixteen voyages to Bermuda-Nassau-San Juan-St. Thomas-Martinique-St. Maarten-Antigua-Curacao-Aruba-Barbados. Her ports of call often alternated and sometimes changed. She would make an annual trans-atlantic crossing from New York-Le Havre-London-Bremerhaven-Riga for her drydocking. Westbound she would call at Hamburg in place of Bremerhaven. Her itinerary varied from time to time and she made cruises out of London as well. In November 1975, she was damaged by a bomb explosion while at San Juan. She was relocated to European waters leaving New York on December 5. Thereafter she was engaged in Mediterranean and Black Sea cruises as well as world cruises. On the night of June 19, 1989, while on a cruise with 573 passengers the *Maksim Gorki* struck an icefloe at 10:30 p.m. and sprang a leak 180 miles west of Spitsbergen Island, Norway, in the Arctic Ocean in latitude 77° 37' north, longitude 04° 09' east while in a fog. The ship sustained two gashes on her starboard side measuring 75 centimeters by 2.5 meters and 1 centimeter by 6 meters. The passengers were evacuated into the lifeboats which were lowered alongside until assistance could come. There were no casualties and the ship was anchored off Coles Bay on the 22nd. She arrived at Bremerhaven on July 4 for repairs and sailed on August 18, 1989, returning back to service. Presently in service.

MIKHAIL LERMONTOV

Builder: Mathias-Thesen-Werf, Wismar, East Germany
Completed: February 1972
Gross tonnage: 19.872
Dimensions: 578' x 77' Depth: 53' Draft: 27'
Engines: Two Sulzer single-acting 7-cylinder diesels (two bow thrusters athwartship forward)
Screws: Twin
Decks: Six
Normal speed: 20.50 knots
Passenger accommodations: 700 in a single class
Officers and crew: 365
Registry: Russia
Maiden voyage: Leningrad-Bremerhaven-Canary Islands on April 19, 1972

Built expressly for the Russian state-owned Morflot and placed under management of their subsidiary Baltic Steamship Company. She made her first voyage across the North Atlantic on June 9, 1972, Leningrad-Bremerhaven-London-Le Havre-Montreal. She made her first voyage to New York on May 28, 1973, sailing from Leningrad-Helsinki-Bremerhaven-London-Le Havre. This historic voyage reopened trade between the Soviet Union and the United States after twenty-five years. Fully air-conditioned and equipped with motion stabilizers. The liner was furnished with five bars and two swimming pools (one indoor), a sauna, two night clubs, library as well as two large public rooms. She began to maintain regular transatlantic service following her first call of a Russian-flag passenger liner (the last was the Vladimir on June 17, 1919). Her ports of call were Leningrad-Bremerhaven-London-Le Havre-New York. This began on a more scheduled basis beginning on July 13, 1973. In 1974 she made some cruises out of New York, Boston and Baltimore in 1976. One hundred and nine cabins situated outside were the only ones fitted with private facilities. Her outdoor space was quite adequate and the swimming pool was covered by a sliding roof. She made one of her first long cruises in early 1977, a 37-day cruise to Australia, and also made cruises from New York to the West Indies, Bermuda, Nova Scotia, and Quebec during the off season from New York. She had space for carrying 30 automobiles and afforded passengers nearly unlimited baggage space. By 1981 trans-atlantic sailings ceased out of New York and she engaged solely in cruising. Modernized in 1984 as a full cruise ship. Ran aground and sunk off Cape Jackson, South Island, New Zealand in heavy weather on February 16, 1986 and subsequently sank in latitude 41° 03' 30" south longitude 174° 12' 30" east. Blame originally attributed to the master of the vessel was later directed to the pilot who was aboard at the time of the disaster. One crew member died in the lowering of life boats.

Sister ships: *Aleksandr Pushkin, Ivan Franko, Taras Shevchenko, Shota Rustaveli.*

ODESSA

Builder: Vickers, Ltd., Barrow Shipbuilding Works, Barrow, England
Completed: 1974
Gross tonnage: 13,253
Dimensions: 446′ x 69′ Depth: 69′ Draft: 19′
Engines: Two Pielstick Vee 4-stroke, single-acting 16-cylinder diesels
Screws: Twin with controllable pitch propellers
Decks: Four
Normal speed: 19 knots
Passenger accommodations: 470 in a single class
Officers and crew: 260
Registry: Russia

Built for the Danish K/S Nordine A.S. and christened *Copenhagen* but never sailed for the company which went bankrupt. Sold to the Russian state-owned Black Sea Shipping Company in May, 1975, and delivered on July 18th. Renamed *Odessa*. In 1978 she worked out of New York to Bermuda and other routes. Presently chartered out to and managed by the West German Transocean Tours. Built with a full berth capacity for 550 passengers the *Odessa* is one of the more conventional looking liners in the Russian fleet. There are 241 cabins all of which are located outside, spacious and fully carpeted. Each has private shower/bath facilities, individual temperature controls, two lower beds, two-channel radio, telephone and some are fitted with television for video programs. There are two seatings for dining, a theatre hall, duty-free boutique, gift shop, heated outdoor swimming pool, sauna, gymnasium, hospital and library. Plenty of open deck space for games or just lounging around. Built on the idea of a Ro/Ro passenger type she has more of the lines of a conventional cruise ship. Presently engaged in a series of cruises marketed mostly in Europe. Most cruises are 9 to 18 days on up to 101 days mostly in the South Pacific and Far East as well as India via the Suez Canal, Mediterranean, Black Sea, Scandinavia, North Cape, Azores and Canary Islands, Baltic and the Black Sea. Prices begin at $2,565 for a 28-day cruise, $4,710 for 53 days; $7,150 for 79 days, and $9,085 for a 101-day cruise. German and English are spoken aboard the *Odessa*. Equipped with motion stabilizers she is fully air-conditioned.

RUSS

Builder: Blohm & Voss, Hamburg, Germany
Completed: July 1933
Gross tonnage: 12,931
Dimensions: 524' x 66' Depth: 32' Draft: 24'
Engines: Two M.A.N. 8-cylinder double-acting diesel engines
Screws: Twin
Decks: Five
Normal speed: 13 knots
Passenger accommodations: 900 in a single class
Officers and crew: 195
Registry: Russia
Maiden voyage: March 1952

Built for the German Hamburg-American Line and christened *Cordillera*. Sunk by an air attack off Swinemunde, Germany on March 12, 1945, while being used by the Nazis as a depot ship. Refloated by the Soviets in 1949 and towed to Antwerp for temporary repairs, completed by the Warno Werf at Warnemunde, East Germany. Engaged in the Vladivostok-Petropavlovsk-Kamchatski trade in the former Eastern U.S.S.R. under the banner of the Far East Steamship Co., part of the Russian state-owned Morflot. Presently in service.

Sister Ship: *I Ilyich*.

SHOTA RUSTAVELI

Builder: VEB Mathias-Thesen-Werft, Wismar, East Germany
Completed: 1968
Gross tonnage: 20,499
Dimensions: 574' x 82' Depth: 43' Draft: 27'
Engines: Two Sulzer 2-stroke, single-acting, 7-cylinder diesels
Screws: Twin
Decks: Six
Normal speed: 20.50 knots
Passenger accommodations: 550 in a single class
Officers and crew: 300
Registry: Russia
Maiden voyage: Odessa-Batumi-Mediterranean on June 30, 1968

Built expressly for the Russian-owned Black Sea Shipping Company the *Shota Rustaveli* is one of five sister ships. In September, 1968, she was rerouted from the Black Sea-Mediterranean circuit to Southampton where she inaugurated a round-the-world cruise. It was the first such trip for a Soviet ship. Fully air-conditioned and stabilized she has operated both as a cruise ship and a liner over the past two decades. She has an ice-strengthened hull and her actual berth capacity is for 650 passengers. She is a passenger and general cargo ship with three holds and four 3-1/2 ton cranes. Refurbished in 1982 she has been chartered out to Grand Viaggi tour operators for a number of years. When she was refitted for cruising her black hull was painted white. The ship has an indoor swimming pool, gymnasium and a number of bars, a gift shop, and a beauty parlour. While most cabins have private facilities some of the inside staterooms in the lower decks must share. Presently in service.

Sister ships: *Aleksandr Pushkin, Ivan Franko, Taras Shevchenko.* A fifth sister ship — the *Mikhail Lermontov* — sunk in 1986.

SOYUZ

Builder: Blohm & Voss, Hamburg, Germany
Completed: 1923
Gross tonnage: 23,009
Dimensions: 673' x 72' Depth: 47' Draft: 28'
Engines: Two sets of 4-cylinder steam turbines, single-reduction geared
Screws: Twin
Decks: Five
Normal speed: 19.25 knots
Passenger accommodations: 1,400 in a single class
Registry: Russia
Maiden voyage: September 1955

Built for the German Hamburg-American Line and christened *Albert Ballin; Hansa* in 1935. Sunk by a mine off Warnemunde, Germany on March 6, 1945. Refloated in 1949 by the Russians and renamed *Sovietsky* *Soyuz*. Contracted to *Soyuz* in 1953. Towed to Antwerp when she was refloated in 1950 for temporary repairs but completed at the East Germany shipyards of Warnow Werft at Warnemunde, East Germany. Part of her reconstruction work gave her corrugated steel sides of galvanized sheet steel shaped into parallel regular and equally curved ridges and hollows. Engaged in the Vladivostok-Petropavlovsk-Kamchatski trade. Overhauled at Taikoa Dockyard & Engineering at Hong Kong in 1972 and fitted with two new diesel generators. Operated by the state-owned Morflot under the management of the Far Eastern Steamship Company, a wholly owned subsidiary. She was the line's flagship at the time she entered service.

Note: When built as the *Albert Ballin* she was designed with two contemporary funnels of the time and had four masts. Scrapped in the 1980's.

TARAS SHEVCHENKO

Builder: VEB Mathias-Thesen-Werf, Wismar, East Germany
Completed: 1966
Gross tonnage: 20,027
Dimensions: 574' x 82' Depth: 43' Draft: 27'
Engines: Two Werk Spoor Sulzer 7-cylinder, 2-stroke, single acting
  diesels
Screws: Twin
Decks: Five
Normal speed: 20.50 knots
Passenger accommodations: 726 in a single class
Officers and crew: 260
Registry: Russia
Maiden voyage: Odessa-Mediterranean ports on April 26, 1965

Built exclusively for the Russian state-owned Black Sea Shipping Company. Employed mostly as a cruise ship the *Taras Shevchenko* was refurbished in 1973 and later her hull was painted white. The debut of Russian flag liners came into the world-wide international trade mostly for the purpose of accumulating American dollars and stemmed primarily from economic factors closely related to foreign exchange rather than prestige. The Russians content for some years on older pre-war tonnage began a new building program in the mid-sixties. Though conventionally attractive as conventional looking liners they lacked the vision in design of the liners built by many of their competitors who foresaw the emerging cruise market of the future. Equipped with motion stabilizers and fully air-conditioned the *Taras Shevchenko* was later chartered to a British syndicate and is managed by the London-based CTC Lines with a measure of success. Public rooms include lounge, music salon, cinema, library, gymnasium, gift shop, sauna, beauty salon, and two pools for adults as well as two children's swimming pools. Interiors are designed in tone with Ukrainian modes which mirror the sunshine of that republic. Presently engaged in cruising out of the Black Sea to the Mediterranean.

Sister ships: *Aleksandr Pushkin, Ivan Franko, Shota Rustaveli* (the *Mikhail Lermontov* sank in early 1986).

Scandinavian–American Line

FREDERIK VIII

Builder: A. G. Vulkan, Stettin, Germany
Completed: December 1913
Gross tonnage: 11,850
Dimensions: 542′ x 62′ Depth: 28′ Draft: 28′
Engines: Two sets of 8-cylinder triple expansion engines
Screws: Twin
Decks: Five
Normal speed: 17 knots
Passenger accommodations: 223 first, 179 second and 807 third class*
Officers and crew: 308
Registry: Denmark
Maiden voyage: Copenhagen-Oslo-Christanssand-New York on
   February 5, 1914

*Originally carried: 356 first, 378 second, and 911 third class.

Built at a cost of 5,500,000 Danish Krone expressly for the Scandinavian-American Line, she was launched on May 27, 1913 and was the pride of Denmark for many years on the North Atlantic ferry. Converted to a cabin class ship in 1923 her accommodations were reduced. Engaged in the Copenhagen-Oslo-New York service. Carrying mostly Eastern European immigrants to the United States she left New York on Valentine's Day, February 14, 1917, and was laid up in Denmark until November 1918. Made five trips transporting 7,500 British prisoners of war from December 1918 to January 1919 between Warnemünde-Lubeck-Steffin-England. She returned to service arriving back in New York on March 31, 1919. In 1920 she was the first ship to be fitted with the Anschütz gyro-compass, automatic pilot and course recorder. The auto-pilot was connected to the steering wheel by means of a bicycle chain, which altered the steering wheel accordingly. On March 30, 1924, she inaugurated a call at Halifax on the westbound trip to New York and called there from then after westbound. On October 15, 1924 she made her first cruise: Copenhagen-

Lisbon-Barcelona-Monaco-Genoa-Naples-Palermo-Algiers-Gibraltar Copenhagen. She called at Boston for the first time on May 12, 1926 while headed eastbound calling there on occasion. The *Frederik VIII* had five holds which could hold 303,000 cubic feet of grain and 278,000 cubic feet in bales. She had fifteen derricks. Below there were ten boilers and a crew of 44 stokers and firemen until her boilers were fitted with Erith-Riley mechanical stokers in December of 1915. Unfortunately, she burned a lot of coal and was very expensive to operate and she hardly ever filled her cabin space. She had been the largest Scandinavian ship up until the Norwegian-America Line's *Stavengerfjord* made her debut in 1918. According to an old Danish sailor whom I met on more than one occasion aboard liners, on the Christmas eastbound voyage in 1925 Mr. Sven Stausholm related the story of two stowaways aboard the *Frederik VIII*. Following an argument up on the boat deck and a fist fight one of the men fell and landed on one of the ventilators and was killed. His body burned he was buried at sea. Mr. Stausholm was a young cook aboard the ship at the time. By 1935 the Great Depression hit hard worldwide and the company requested a new subsidy from the Danish Government. This was declined and her government subsidy ran out on January 1, 1936. The fierce competition from NAL helped to seal her fate. She left New York for the last time on December 7, 1935 and made her last trip for the Scandinavian-American Line on December 23, 1935, in the form of a Christmas Cruise from Copenhagen-Aarhus on the Jutland peninsula of Denmark with 3,000 passengers aboard. Sold for scrap to Hughes Bolkhow at Blyth, Scotland in November 1936 for £28,100. Resale market value of the scrap was £57,012. She left Copenhagen for the last time on November 12th and arrived at the breaker's yard on the 18th. She was dismantled by April 1937, after lying idle for some time. She was the largest Danish ship until the debut of the *Dana Regina* in 1924.

Note: The *Frederik VIII's* engines produced 11,000 horsepower and she was the 322nd ship built by the Vulkan shipyards. She was taken over by the Danish DFDS (United Shipping Lines) in 1925 when the major Danish shipping companies formed a union.

DANA ANGLIA

Builder: Aalborg Vaerft A/S, Aalborg, Denmark
Completed: 1978
Gross tonnage: 14,399
Dimensions: 502' x 80' Depth: 27' Draft: 19'
Engines: Two Pielstick Vee 9-cylinder 4-stroke single acting diesels plus
  two bow thrusters athwartship forward
Screws: Twin with controllable pitch
Decks: Four
Normal speed: 21.10 knots
Passenger accommodations: 43 Commodore first class, 760 tourist and
  440 dormitory class with couchette
Officers and crew: 80
Registry: Denmark
Maiden voyage: Aalborg-London-Harwich-Copenhagen-Esbjerg on
  May 1, 1978

Built for the Danish union of ship owners knows as DFDS Scandinavian Seaways, launched on June 24, 1977 and christened in the Poole by the Duchess of Gloucester on May 4, 1978. Classified as a passenger Ro/Ro Cargo/Ferry she has berths for 1,249 passengers and 107 deck passengers according to her registration certificate. She can carry 470 cars and 135 TEU's. She has a bow door with a stern door as well for rapid loading and unloading on her overnight voyages from Esbjerg to Harwich — a 393 mile trip. On board there is an a la carte restaurant as well as a cafeteria, two lounges, and two bars. Also, a sauna and duty free shopping area. The *Dana Anglia* first class quarters are quite spacious and furnished with a mini-bar, four-band radio and spacious windows. They also serve the best coffee and the smörgasbord buffet will satisfy the hungriest palate. She was built with extensions on her exhausts but these were removed to enable the ship to pass under Tower Bridge when she arrived in England for her christening. Her engines can produce 20,000 horsepower and she features a very long continuous sun deck for summer travelers. There is one main elevator located mid-ships. She has worked the Hook of Holland-Harwich service while under time charter to Sealink between January 1987 until November 23, 1988 when she worked the Copenhagen-Oslo route unitl Feburary 11, 1989. Since December 29, 1989 she has been working the Esbjerg service. Presently in service.

DANA REGINA

Builder: Aalborg Vaerft A/S, Aalborg, Denmark
Completed: 1974
Gross tonnage: 14,399
Dimensions: 506' x 80' Depth: 47' Draft: 20'
Engines: Four Burmeister & Wain 4-stroke, 8-cylinder diesels plus two bow thrusters with pitch propellers
Screws: Twin
Decks: Three
Normal speed: 21.50 knots
Passenger accommodations: 56 Commodore first class, 803 tourist, and 98 couchette class
Officers and crew: 127
Registry: Denmark
Maiden voyage: Copenhagen-London-Harwich-Esbjerg on July 1, 1974

Launched on August 31, 1973 she was constructed at a cost of 101,500,000 Danish Krone. Built expressly for the Danish DFDS Federated Union of Ship Owners and christened *Dana Regina*. The company carried on the legacy of the former Scandinavian-American Line and since 1989 has been operating under the name of Scandinavian Seaways. The *Dana Regina* is classified as a passenger Ro/Ro Cargo/Ferry with space for 330 automobiles and 43 trailers. She has both a bow door, stern and side door for loading and unloading. Constructed with an ice strengthened hull. Public rooms include a number of conference rooms, a disco and nightclub, cafeteria and grill as well as an a la carte restaurant. There is one deluxe cabin. There are 878 berths. Engaged in the Esbjerg-Harwich route on an overnight turn-around schedule. Since October 12, 1983, she was running on the Copenhagen-Oslo route overnight turn-around service until June 1, 1990. Sold to the Swedish EST Line in January, 1989, she was chartered back to Scandinavia Seaways for a year and delivered on June 2, 1990. Renamed *Nord Estonia*. Presently in service.

HAMBURG

Builder: Nobiskrug Werft GmbH, Rendsburg, Germany
Completed: 1976
Gross tonnage: 13,141
Dimensions: 515' x 79' Depth: 45' Draft: 20'
Engines: Two 10-cylinder Stork Werkspoor, 4-stroke, single acting diesels
Screws: Twin
Decks: Four
Normal speed: 22 knots
Passenger accommodations: 80 Commodore first class, 527 tourist, 152 economy, 274 couchettes, and 40 deck-chair class
Registry: Bahamas
Maiden voyage: Hamburg-Harwich on November 8, 1989

Built for the Norwegian Jahre Line and christened *Kronprins Harald*. Sold to the Danish DFDS on February 27, 1987, and renamed *Hamburg* after being rebuilt at the Blohm & Voss Shipyards in Hamburg. Classified as a passenger Ro/Ro Cargo/Ferry she has space for 135 TEU's, 65 12-metre trailers and 400 automobiles. There are three conference rooms aboard seating from 16 to 64 persons. Engaged in the overnight route from Hamburg to Harwich year-round. Round trip summer season fare with cabin is £119. Though classified as a ferry boat her outward appearance is pleasing to the eye. The ship offers duty free shopping, a disco and theatre, lounge and dining room as well as cafeteria. On the night of November 8, 1989, while steaming out of the Elbe River she collided with the Ro/Ro cargo ship *Nordic Stream* just nine miles south of Helgoland at 9:45 p.m. while battered by 70-mile an hour winds blowing off the North Sea. The *Nordic Stream* was heading into the Elbe channel when the accident occurred. Three people were killed including a crew member and twelve injured. The ship was holed in her starboard quarter, above and below the waterline. Her 277 passengers were taken back to Bremerhaven. The ship then proceeded to Hamburg for repairs returning to service on December 20th. I recall the incident quite well since I had come from Hamburg just a few days before. Scheduled to return on the ship on the November 9th voyage out of Harwich. When I arrived at Liverpool Street station to catch the boat-train the news was in the Daily Mirror. The *Hamburg* is presently in service.

HELLIG OLAV

Builder: Alexander Stephen & Sons, Ltd., Glasgow, Scotland
Completed: 1902
Gross tonnage: 10,136
Dimensions: 515′ x 58′ Depth: 41′ Draft: 27′
Engines: Two sets of 6-cylinder triple expansion engines
Screws: Twin
Decks: Four
Normal speed: 15.50 knots
Passenger accommodations: 123 first, 129 second, and 837 third class
Officers and crew: 211
Registry: Denmark
Maiden voyage: Copenhagen-Christiania*-Christianssand-New York on March 25, 1903, arriving at New York on the 9th

*Now Oslo

Launched on December 16, 1902, she was buit at a cost of £205,770 sterling. Built expressly for the Danish Scandinavian-American Line and christened *Hellig Olav*. Laid up at New York on January 29, 1917 until April 26th and again on June 4, 1918 unitl October 1918. The *Hellig Olav* began carrying only second and third class passengers from 1922 onward and became a cabin class ship in the following year. She inaugurated an eastbound call at Boston on March 11, 1923, and a westbound call at Halifax on June 8, 1924, incorporating this port into most of her crossings both directions. She occasionally called at Boston either way. Engaged in the Copenhagen-Oslo-Scandinavian ports-New York run her tonnage was later reduced to 9,939 tons. She made a Baltic cruise on August 1, 1925: Copenhagen-Stockholm-Helsinki-Stockholm-Copenhagen. She made her last voyage for the Line in September, from New York-Halifax-Oslo-Copenhagen and was laid up on October 7, 1931. Sold for scrap to Hughes Bolckow Ltd. at Blyth Scotland on March 5, 1984 for £14,750 sterling. She left Copenhagen under her own power on March 9th and arrived at the breakers yard on the 14th. The resale market value of her scrap was estimated at £21,550.

Sister ships: *Oscar II, United States.*

Note: She crossed the Atlantic 418 times.

KING OF SCANDINAVIA

Builder: Dubigeon Normandie S.A., Nantes, France
Completed: 1975
Gross tonnage: 20,581
Dimensions: 567' x 73' Depth: 26' Draft: 20'
Engines: Four Vee, 12-cylinder 4-stroke single-acting diesels
Screws: Twin
Watertight bulkheads: Thirteen
Decks: Six
Normal speed: 21.50 knots (Attained a speed of 22 knots on her trials)
Passenger accommodations: 104 Commodore first and 1,071 tourist class
Officers and crew: 135
Registry: Denmark
Maiden voyage: Copenhagen-Gothenburg-Newcastle-Esbjerg on May 25, 1981

Built for the Finnish Silja Line and christened *Wellamo*. Sold to the DFDS on April 23, 1981, and renamed *Dana Gloria*. Placed on the Line's Esbjerg-Newcastle run year round with a secondary route, Newcastle-Gothenburg in the May/June to August/September period. She ran from Copenhagen-Oslo beginning October 12, 1983 until December 19, 1983. Chartered back to the Silja Line on January 26, 1984, for sixteen months and renamed *Svea Corona*. Returned on May 18, 1985, she underwent an overhaul and her couchette sleeping space was removed and replaced by a wine shop. Offered up for sale for $4.2 million but no buyers materialized. The Line then decided to send the ship to the drydock shipyards of Joseph Meyer Werft at Papenburg, Germany on November 7, 1988. The *Dana Gloria* was then cut in two literally and a 22.20 metre mid-body inserted thus increasing her length from 504' overall to 567'. Redelivered on February 9, 1989, when she re-entered service on the Oslo route she now carried a complement of 1,175 passengers in cabins as opposed to her former capacity of 799. Classified as a passenger Ro/Ro Cargo Ferry she is like most ferries certified by Lloyd's Register for short international voyages. Aboard the gigantic vessel are several conference rooms with a total seating capacity for 312 persons. There is a sauna and swimming pool, children's playroom and several restaurants and buffets seating 550, cafes and night club lounges, a disco and bars. The *King of Scandinavia* also can carry 285 automobiles and forty twelve-metre trailers. Her passenger certificate allows for her to transport 1,300 people. Entertainment on all the Line's ships are featured as well as a cinema, boutique and the popular duty-free shopping arcade. First class accommodations offer a mini-bar and spacious cabins. Equipped with Sperry fin stabilizers and fully air-conditioned. Her engines produce 24,000 brake horse power. Originally on the Gothenburg-Newcastle-Esbjerg route she is now working on the Copenhagen-Oslo run. She has a bow door and stern door both with ramps and her hull is ice strengthened. Presently in service on the Copenhagen-Oslo run with a call at Helsingor outbound.

OSCAR II

Builder: Alexander Stephan & Sons, Ltd., Glasgow, Scotland
Completed: 1901
Gross tonnage: 10,012
Dimensions: 515′ x 58′ Depth: 41′ Draft: 27′
Engines: Two sets of 6-cylinder triple expansion engines
Screws: Twin
Decks: Four
Normal speed: 15.50 knots
Passenger accommodations: 160 first, 191 second and 931 third class
Registry: Denmark
Maiden voyage: Copenhagen-Christiania*-Christianssand-New York in February, 1901, arriving at New York on the 20th

*Now Oslo

Built at a cost of 4,800,000 Danish Krone. Launched on November 14, 1901. Engaged on the Copenhagen-Oslo-Scandinavian ports-New York run. On February 18, 1903, while enroute to New York, she encountered heavy seas and her starboard engine broke down. Following its repair the next day, she sprang a leak in the No. I and No. II holds and the compartments flooded. She changed course and arrived at Ponta Delgada in the Azores where she arrived on the 27th. Following temporary repairs she sailed back to Glasgow on March 16th. A year later she grounded at Christianssand and sprang another leak. She was beached in order to prevent her from sinking. Taken to Kiel, Germany and repaired. Detained at New York from August 28, 1917, because of hostilities until the 6th of October, 1918. Resumed regular services Copenhagen-New York on March 29, 1919 following refurbishing and calling at Christianssand homebound only. In 1921 she carried only second and third class passengers and became a cabin class ship in 1923 with accommodation for cabin and third classes. She had maintained regular scheduled sailings throughout most of the First World War until her detainment in New York. She made her first call westbound at Boston on May 21, 1923, and called occasionally thereafter. The following year she called at Halifax for the first time westbound on March 17 and incorporated this port into her regular itinerary. The *Oscar II* made her last voyage for the Line on January 6, 1931, New York-Oslo-Copenhagen, and was subsequently withdrawn. Laid up indefinitely she appears to have been a victim of the Great Depression and was later sold for scrap to Hughes Bolckow Ltd. for £14,250. Arrived at the breaker's yard on September 10, 1933.

Sister ships: *Hellig Olav, United States.*

Note: She crossed the Atlantic 398 times.

PRINCE OF SCANDINAVIA

Builder: Flender Werft A.G., Luebeck-Siems, Germany
Completed: May 1975
Gross tonnage: 14,905
Dimensions: 552' x 78' Depth: 53' Draft: 20'
Engines: Four Pielstick single-acting 12-cylinder diesels plus two bow thrusters forward with controllable pitch propellers
Screws: Twin
Watertight bulkheads: Fourteen
Decks: Five
Normal speed: 26 knots
Passenger accommodations: 23 Commodore first class, 870 tourist, and 512 dormitory class with couchette
Registry: Denmark
Maiden voyage: Gothenburg-Amsterdam-Felixtowe on March 29, 1982

Built for the Swedish Tor Line and christened *Tor Britannia*. Passed on to the Danish-owned DFDS (United Steamship Company)* on November 2, 1981, along with the purchase of the Tor Line. She retained her name until chartered for a time and was temporarily renamed *Scandinavian Star* in 1981. She acquired her original name the following year. Laid up mid-January to March 12, 1982. Engaged in the Gothenburg-Amsterdam/Felixtowe service with Harwich replacing Felixtowe from April 1, 1983. She dropped the call at Amsterdam on October 1, 1983 and her route became Esbjerg-Harwich. She also ran between Copenhagen-Gothenburg in 1988-1989 for a time and reopened the Gothenburg-Amsterdam route on October 2, 1989. Taken to the Blohm & Voss shipyards in Hamburg for refitting between November 8, 1990 and January 11, 1991, and renamed *Prince of Scandinavia*. Employed in the service between Gothenburg and Harwich. Classified as a passenger Ro/Ro Cargo/Ferry she has space for 420 automobiles and sixty 12-metre trailers as well as 116 TEU's. She has six conference rooms, a swimming pool, cinema, disco, sauna and a number of bars. There is also duty-free shopping, a bank for currency exchange, one club lounge, a cafeteria, restaurant and children's play area. There is also a main lounge and her catering services offered both a la carte and buffet style. Equipment with motion stabilizers and in-cabin temperature control. Her engines can generate an astounding 45,600 horse power. Presently engaged in the Harwich-Esbjerg service year-round with limited sailings in winter. Regular service offers overnight sailings with two to three sailings weekly. Presently in service.

Sister ship: *Princess of Scandinavia.*

Note: The company originally known as the Scandinavian-American Line has over the years changed its name from DFDS to DFDS Scandinavian Seaways.

*Bahamas subsidiary and transferred to DFDS (Danish) on March 26, 1982.

PRINCESS OF SCANDINAVIA

Builder: Flender Werft A.G., Luebeck-Siems, Germany
Completed: April 1976
Gross tonnage: 14,893
Dimensions: 552′ x 78′ Depth: 53′ Draft: 20′
Engines: Four Pielstick single-acting, 12-cylinder diesels plus two bow thrusters with controllable pitch propellers
Screws: Twin
Watertight bulkheads: Fourteen
Decks: Five
Normal speed: 26 knots
Passenger accommodations: 23 Commodore first class, 884 tourist class, and 512 dormitory class with couchette
Registry: Denmark
Maiden voyage: Felixtowe-Gothenburg on December 10, 1981

Built for the Swedish Tor Line and christened *Tor Scandinavia*. Resold to the Danish DFDS (United Steamship Company) on December 10, 1981. The transfer took place officially on January 1, 1982, and the ship retained her original name. A temporary change of name took place in 1982 when she was chartered out and converted to an exhibition ship at the World Expo in Vancouver, B.C. with renaming to *World Wide Expo*. Between October 25, 1982 and February 25, 1983 she made a South Pacific voyage as such on December 10, 1982, Copenhagen-Suez Canal-Singapore-Bangkok-Brunei-Manilla. Reverted to her original name in 1983 and resumed service on the Gothenburg Felixtowe/Amsterdam on March 3rd. Originally on the Felixtowe-Gothenburg-Amsterdam service with three to

four sailings weekly. She later was placed on the Gothenburg-Harwich overnight service and on September 24, 1983 the Amsterdam call wa dropped. In 1984 she also ran out of Esbjerg-Harwich. She has two ster doors and ramps for loading and unloading plus two side doors. Classifie as a Passenger Ro/Ro Cargo/Ferry. The *Tor Scandinavia* is equipped wit motion stabilizers and in-cabin temperature control. Shipboard amenitie include two bars, a cafeteria, restaurant, duty-free shopping, swimmin; pool, sauna, disco, cinema, one club lounge and restaurant. There are als six conference rooms with seating accommodations for from 15 to 6 people. For children there is a playroom area. The service spee maintained is 23 knots enabling her in conjunction with her sister ship t maintain two to three sailings per week from England and Denmark. Sh has a 45,600 horse power capacity. Reopened the Gothenburg-Amsterdam Route on February 2, 1989/Gothenburg Harwich September 25, 1989 wit an occasional trip to Newcastle as well as Gothenburg-Copenhagen. O September 25, 1989 a fire deliberately set in a laundry room killed tw passengers by smoke inhalation. The fire had been set by a derange employee. Renamed *Princess of Scandinavia* in early 1991 following refit at the Blohm & Voss shipyards in Hamburg, Germany betwee January 17, 1991 and March 11, 1991. Presently in service.

Sister ship: *Prince of Scandinavia.*

Note: The company originally the Scandinavian-American Line late became known as DFDS (United Steamship Company) and in recent year as Scandinavian Seaways.

QUEEN OF SCANDINAVIA

Builder: Oy Wartsila AB, Turku, Finland
Completed: March 1981
Gross tonnage: 25,940
Dimensions: 547' x 96' Depth: 30' Draft: 21'
Engines: Four Vee 4-stroke, single-acting 12-cylinder diesels
Screws: Twin
Watertight bulkheads: Thirteen
Decks: Six
Normal speed: 22 knots
Passenger accommodations: 82 Commodore first, 1,469 tourist class plus 150 couchette and 66 deck class passengers
Registry: Denmark
Maiden voyage: Copenhagen-Helsingborg-Oslo on June 1, 1990

Built for the Finnish Silja Line and christened *Finlandia*. Sold to the Danish-owned DFDS on May 11, 1990 and renamed *Queen of Scandinavia*. Classified as a passenger Ro/Ro cargo vessel she has space for 70 twelve-metre trucks and 450 cars. Her passenger certificate is for a total of 2,000 passengers. Aboard are duty-free shopping, a cinema, sauna, disco, several bars, restaurants and lounges. Engaged in the Copenhagen-Oslo service in an overnight service with a stop at Helsingborg outbound. Equipped with motion stabilizers and fully air-conditioned. The *Queen of Scandinavia* was built for cold waters and has an ice-breaker bow. She is presently in service.

SCANDINAVIA

Builder: Dubigeon-Normandie S.A. Prairie-au-Duc, Nantes, France
Completed: 1982
Gross tonnage: 26,747
Dimensions: 607' x 89' Depth: 30' Draft: 22'
Engines: Two B&W 9-cylinder, 2-stroke single-acting diesels plus two
   bow thrusters athwartship forward with controllable pitch propellers
Screws: Twin
Decks: Five
Normal speed: 18 knots
Passenger accommodations: 1,606 in two classes (First Commodore and
   tourist)
Officers and crew: 380
Registry: Bahamas
Maiden voyage: New York-Freeport on October 2, 1982*

*Made a presentation cruise prior. Miami-Port Canaveral-Philadelphia-
Boston-Port Jefferson-New York arriving on September 25, 1982.

Launched on May 19, 1982, she was built expressly for the Danish-owned
DFDS wholly-owned subsidiary of Scandinavian World Cruises. Engaged
in the New York-Freeport-Nassau trade route under a ten-year contractual
agreement with the Bahamian Government to carry passengers and cars
between Miami and mainland provided the ships were under Bahamian

registry. This odd looking ship was beset by troubles from the outset. Her
shallow draft gave her stability problems because of her height. She
remained at Boston for a time until cement could be poured into the
ship's hull to make her steady at sea. The New York-Grand Bahama route
turned out to be a failure and the ship was diverted to work out of Miami-
Port Canaveral to the Caribbean. She left Freeport for the last time on
November 23, 1983, when this route was abandoned entirely. Left New
York for the last time on November 29, 1983 for Copenhagen. Began
sailing on the Copenhagen-Oslo route on December 19th. Classified as a
passenger Ro/Ro Cargo Ferry she has a rear door for quick loading and
unloading. She can carry 350 cars, 175 on the main deck and 175 on a
raised platform deck. Equipped with motion stabilizers and fully air-
conditioned. The ship has duty-free shopping, a number of restaurants,
pool, gymnasium, sauna, beauty parlour, hair stylist, cafeteria, several
lounges and bars. Her staterooms were larger than most vessels of this
type. Approximately 480 are situated outside and feature lower twin beds.
Cabins also have closed-circuit television, radio, telephone and
temperature control dial, vacuum flushing and heated bathroom tile
floors. One lounge seats 700, the other 600 for shows and the main dining
room accommodates 650. She made her last voyage for this Line on
April 8, 1985, Oslo-Copenhagen. Sold on April 15, 1985, to Sundance
Cruises and renamed *Sundancer* in October. Passed on to Admiral Cruise
Lines ownership when Sundance was merged with Eastern and Western
Steamship Lines on October 1, 1986. The sale price for the ship was $10
million. Resold to the Norwegian-owned Royal Caribbean Line in 1990
and renamed *Viking Serenade*. Presently in their service.

SCANDINAVIAN SEA

Builder: Upper Clyde Shipbuilders, Ltd., Clydebank, Glasgow, Scotland
Completed: 1970
Gross tonnage: 10,736
Dimensions: 489′ x 66′ Depth: 27′ Draft: 22′
Engines: Two Pielstick 4-stroke, single-acting, 18-cylinder diesels, single-reduction geared, plus a bow thruster forward
Screws: Twin (controllable pitch)
Decks: Six
Normal speed: 22.50 knots
Passenger accommodations: 580 in a single class plus 527 deck class
Officers and crew: 270
Registry: Bahamas
Maiden voyage: Port Canaveral-Freeport on February 12, 1982

Built for the Norwegian-owned Bergen Line and christened *Blenheim*. Resold to the Danish DFDS-Scandinavian Seaways on November 24, 1981, and renamed *Scandinavian Sea* in 1982 after being refitted at Blohm and Voss shipyards, Hamburg, Germany. Between November 1, 1981 and January 18, 1982, making her positioning voyage from Hamburg-Port Canaveral the same day. Engaged in a cruise service from Port Canaveral, Florida, to Grand Bahama Island under Scandinavian Cruises, a wholly-owned subsidiary of DFDS. The ship was able to carry 120 cars and offered the usual amenities of sauna, bars, lounges, climate control staterooms, boutiques, gymnasium, duty-free shopping etc. The federation of shipping known as DFDS (United Steamship Company) fell on hard economic times in 1983 with its Scandinavian World Cruises losing $32,100,000 that year. The following year losses amounted to $20,000,000 thereby forcing the company to sell off a number of ships. The *Scandinavian Sea* was engaged in short day cruises between Port Canaveral and sometimes Jacksonville-Freeport. On March 9, 1984, while on an eleven-hour cruise with 946 passengers from Cape Canaveral she caught fire and returned to port. The fire raged for 46 hours and 19 people had to be treated for smoke inhalation. The inferno was finally extinguished on March 11. Her passengers and crew were evacuated safely but there was extensive damage to cabin accommodations and the electrical system. Several of her decks had heat-buckeled and 30% of the ship had been gutted. She listed heavily to starboard due to the heavy intake of water from extinguishers. Later taken in tow to Jacksonville, Florida. Declared a total loss on April 2nd and put up for sale. The company had been negotiating to sell off the ships sailing under the Scandinavian World Cruises subsidiary and the fatal incident of the *Scandinavian Sea* sealed the company's future. Sold to Greek shipping magnate Antonios Lelakison May 5, 1984. Resold to an American syndicate the Pan Ocean Navigation Company and renamed *Venus Venturer*. Resold to the Bajamar Shipping Company (Panama) in late 1986 and rebuilt as a cruise ship under the name *Discovery One* in 1987; *Discovery I* later on. Presently in their service.

Note: DFDS sold off the Scandinavian World Cruises subsidiary in July 1985 to American interests and retained only a 5% interest in the company thereafter.

SCANDINAVIAN STAR

Builder: Dubigeon-Normandie S.A., Prairie-au-Duc, Nantes, France
Completed: 1971
Gross tonnage: 10,513
Dimensions: 463' x 72' Depth: 23' Draft: 18'
Engines: Two Vee Pielstick 4-stroke single acting, 16-cylinder diesels plus
  two bow thrusters forward with controllable pitch propellers
Screws: Twin
Decks: Four
Normal speed: 20 knots
Passenger accommodations: 963 in a single class
Officers and crew: 246
Registry: Bahamas

Built for the French Nouvelle Compagnie de Paquebots and christened *Massalia*. Sold to the Swedish Stena Line in 1984 and renamed *Stena Baltica; Island Fiesta*. Resold to the Danish Scandinavian Seaways of DFDS in 1984 and renamed *Scandinavian Star*. Built as a passenger Ro/Ro cargo ship she was converted for cruising. She retained her stern door and her original passenger berth capacity was increased from 874 to the present figure. Refurbished in 1987 she was engaged in one-day cruises out of the port of Tampa year-round to the Gulf of Mexico. Sailings were daily leaving at 9 a.m. and returned in the evening at 10 p.m. Every 28 days the *Scandinavian Star* made a three-day cruise to Cozumel. Special features of the ship included complete air-conditioning throughout the ship and fin motion stabilizers. There was a swimming pool and extensive outdoor space. There was a casino with several slot machines, etc., disco, movie hall, electronic game room, bars, cabaret lounge and changing facilities with lockers and showers for those without cabins. A main dining room served all passengers. Shipboard amenities included get-acquainted parties, bingo, horse racing game. Broadway style revues and Calypso music at poolside. The duty-free shopping was a major feature and source of revenue for the ship. Meals for passengers were served buffet style three times a day. Minimum fares began at $79 and there were special discounts for senior citizens, children and groups. Cabin accommodations were an additional charge of from $30 to $60. Marketed in the United States under the Sea Escape logo. On March 16, 1988, fire broke out in her engine room while at sea with 700 passengers aboard. Two injured seamen were air-lifted by helicopter to shore and the ship was towed to Cancun where she was repaired. Later on in her career she began making longer cruises in Scandinavian waters and was again the victim of fire. On April 7, 1990, while on a cruise off the coast of Norway in the North Sea the ship was engulfed in flames. The fire which began suspiciously it was later learned had been set by a disgruntled Danish crew member who had prior convictions of setting fires. He died in the disaster but also caused the deaths of an additional 157 people. Taken in tow to the port of Lysekil the day after, she continued to smoulder and was declared a total loss. The S.O.S. sent out by the ship had first been picked up by a short-wave radio operator in Sweden named Ulf Wigh who relayed the ship's May Day signal to expedite assistance to the stricken ship. The ship was later resold to Danish owners and is currently being rebuilt under the name *Candi*.

UNITED STATES

Builder: Alexander Stephen & Sons, Ltd., Glasgow, Scotland
Completed: 1903
Gross tonnage: 10,146
Dimensions: 515' x 58' Depth: 41' Draft: 27'
Engines: Two sets of six-cylinder triple expansion engines
Screws: Twin
Decks: Four
Normal speed: 15.50 knots
Passenger accommodations: 145 first, 72 second and 1,382 third class
Registry: Denmark
Maiden voyage: Copenhagen-Christiania*-Christianssand-New York in June 1903, arriving at New York on the 16th

*Now Oslo

Ordered for the Danish Thingvala Line she was purchased while still on the stocks by the Scandinavian-American Line in May 1903 as one of a trio ordered for the immigrant trade to America. The name "U.S. President" was first contemplated. Built at a cost of £203,750 and launched on March 30, 1903. Engaged in the Copenhagen-Christiania-Christianssand-New York service. On April 16, 1908 while enroute to Copenhagen out of New York she collided with the American *SS Monterey* about one hour after leaving New York. She was beached after her engine room flooded. Refloated and repaired at New York on April 21st. Two years later she ran aground in the Oslo Fjord on March 12, 1910. Her passengers were evacuated and the ship taken back to be tightened at Burmeister & Wain,

Copenhagen. The *United States* seems to have been plagued with a number of mishaps during her career and was grounded during a fog not long thereafter. From November 1922 she began carrying only second and third class passengers with accommodations for 876 passengers and was in 1923 considered as a cabin class ship. Laid up at Copenhagen January 14, 1917–April 19, 1917. She had been detained at New York during the First World War from September 27, 1917, until November 22, 1918, when she left on the eastbound voyage for Scandinavia. Called at Boston first time on February 16, 1921. On April 13, 1924, a westbound call at Halifax was incorporated into her itinerary and she made a second call at Boston on June 6, later on that year. Her tonnage was later reduced to 9,993 tons in 1924. She made her last transatlantic voyage for the Line from New York-Halifax-Copenhagen on November 10, 1934. She was withdrawn from service on September 21, 1934. She crossed the Atlantic Ocean 462 times and steamed 1,796,926 nautical miles. Sold to the Cantieri Marzocco, Livorno Italy for scrapping on July 25, 1935 for £24,000. Set on fire in Copenhagen on September 3 by Danish Communists so as to prevent her future use as a troop ship by Italian Fascists in the war against Ethiopia. Left Copenhagen under tow on September 22, 1935 for the breaker's yard under tow by the Dutch tug *Zwartezee* for Italy.

Sister ships: *Hellig Olav, Oscar II.*

Note: Her engines produced 9,000 horsepower.

Spanish Line

ARGENTINA

Builder: Swan Hunter & Wigham Richardson Ltd., Wallsend-on-Tyne, England
Completed: February 1913
Gross Tonnage: 10,137
Dimensions: 480' x 61' Depth: 36' Draft: 25'
Engines: Two 4-cylinder, quadruple expansion engines and two low-pressure turbines
Screws: Twin
Watertight bulkheads: Nine
Decks: Four
Normal speed: 17 knots
Passenger accommodations: 250 first, 100 second, and 75 third class
Registry: Spain

Built expressly for the Spanish Line and christened *Reina Victoria Eugenia*. Renamed *Argentina* in 1931. Engaged in the Spain-Havana-Vera Cruz service. Reallocated to the Spain-South America Trade in 1931. Sunk by an air attack at Barcelona between January 16 and 23, 1939 during the Spanish Civil War. Refloated and sold for scrap in 1945.

Sister ship: *Uruguay*.

BEGOÑA

Builder: Bethlehem Steel Corp., Fairfield Yard, Baltimore, Maryland, USA
Completed: 1945
Gross Tonnage: 10,139
Dimensions: 455' x 62' Depth: 38' Draft: 29'
Engines: Two steam turbines double-reduction geared
Screws: Single
Watertight bulkheads: Seven
Decks: Four
Normal speed: 17.50
Passenger accommodations: 123 special tourist and 830 tourist class
Officers and crew: 200
Registry: Spain

Built for the United States Department of Commerce and christened *Vassar Victory*. Sold to the Italian Sitmar Line in 1947 and renamed *Castelbianco; Castel Bianco* in 1953. Sold to the Spanish Line in 1957 and renamed *Begoña*. Employed in the Genoa-Naples-La Coruna-Vigo-Canary Islands-Central America-Cuba trade until May 1958, when she was reallocated to the Southampton-Santander-La Coruna-Vigo-Tenerife-Port of Spain-La Guaira-Curacao-Kingston service calling at San Juan instead of Curacao homeward. Equipped with motion stabilizers and fully air-conditioned. She was the Line's flagship. She made her last voyage for the Line on September 27, 1974, Southampton-Vigo-Tenerife-Port of Spain-La Guaira-Kingston. On October 10th while enroute she had an electric and boiler room breakdown in mid-Atlantic with 771 passengers aboard. The German tug *Oceanic* happened to be sailing in ballast from Cabo Verde to Halifax and was about 160 miles from the disabled *Begoña*. The Spanish Line contracted with the German tug to tow the ship to Barbados, the nearest haven, in order to disembark her passengers. Arriving at the scene where the *Begoña* lie at anchor on the 12th, she was taken in tow and pulled into Barbados on October 17 at 6 a.m. The passengers were flown to their destinations paid by the Spanish Line for their inconvenience and towed back to Castellon, Spain where she arrived on November 8. Sold for scrap to Manuel Desguaces Varela, she arrived at the breaker's yard on November 28, 1974, in tow by the tug Ibaizabal Uno with a skeleton crew aboard. Subsequently broken up. the *Begoña* was the last passenger liner to sail for the 100-year old Spanish Line thus ending a long legacy of passenger service.

Sister ship: *Montserrat.*

II COVADONGA

Builder: Compania Euskalduna, Bilbao, Spain
Completed: August 1953
Gross Tonnage: 10,226
Dimensions: 487' x 62' Depth: 40' Draft: 26'
Engines: One 10-cylinder, 2-stroke single-acting Sulzer diesel
Screws: Single
Watertight bulkheads: Eight
Decks: Three
Normal speed: 16.50
Passenger accommodations: 105 first and 248 tourist class
Officers and crew: 135
Registry: Spain
Maiden voyage: Bilbao-Santander-Gijon-Vigo-Lisbon-New York-Havana-
Vera Cruz on August 27, 1953

Built expressly for the Spanish Line, she was launched as the *Monasterio de la Rabida* but her name changed before completion. Originally laid down as a cargo liner for the Spanish Empressa Nacional Elcano, she had been purchased by the Spanish Line while still on the stocks. She made a special cruise from La Coruna to London in May 1953 before sailing across the Atlantic. Engaged in the Bilbao-Santander-Gijon-Vigo-Lisbon-San Juan-Vera Cruz-New York service, she sometimes made a call at Norfolk, Virginia. The eastbound route began New York-La Coruna-Gijon-Santander-Bilbao. During her earlier years she made scheduled calls at Cadiz and Havana but eliminated these ports in 1962. The call at New York had been eliminated by mid-1962 westbound and was entirely eliminated by 1968 when she failed to meet U.S. Coast Guard Safety regulations for the transportation of American citizens. Commenced her last voyage for the Line on December 3, 1972, Bilbao-Vigo-Lisbon-San Juan-Vera Cruz-Tampico-Miami-Bilbao. Arriving at Bilbao on January 19, 1973, she was laid up and soon sold for scrap to Messers. Desguaces Varela Donalillo of Castellon, Spain. She left Bilbao for the last time on March 30, 1973 and arrived at the breaker's yard on April 4th.

Sister ship: *Guadalupe.*

II CRISTOBAL COLON

Builder: Sociedad Espanola de Construccion Naval, Ferrol, Spain
Completed: September 1923
Gross Tonnage: 10,833
Dimensions: 499′ x 61′ Depth: 36′ Draft: 26′
Engines: Four steam turbines, single-reduction geared
Screws: Twin
Watertight bulkheads: Ten
Decks: Three
Normal speed: 17 knots
Passenger accommodations: 1,100 in first, second and third class
Registry: Spain
Maiden voyage: To America, Cadiz-Barcelona-Vigo-New York, arriving on March 4, 1927

Built expressly for the Spanish Line and christened *Cristobal Colon*. Engaged in the transatlantic trade from Spain to Mexico and Central America. Employed mostly in a direct service from Cadiz-Barcelona-Vigo-New York trade, she began in 1929 to call at Havana and in January 1930, at Vera Cruz. At the outbreak of the Spanish Civil War the *Cristobal Colon* departed New York on July 25, 1936, eastbound, the last of four transatlantic trips she had made that year. The Spanish Government ordered the ship to return immediately but a number of insurrectionists among the crew took over the ship and forced her to land her passengers at Southampton. Following a call at Cardiff, Wales, she sailed for Vera Cruz. On October 24, 1936 she was wrecked on North Rock, Bermuda by her crew.

Sister ship: *Habana.*

GUADALUPE

Builder: Sociedad Espanola de Construccion Naval, Bilbao, Spain
Completed: March 1953
Gross Tonnage: 10,226
Dimensions: 487′ x 62′ Depth: 40′ Draft: 26′
Engines: One 10-cylinder, two-stroke, single-acting Sulzer diesel
Screws: Single
Watertight bulkheads: Eight
Decks: Three
Normal speed: 16.50 knots
Passenger accommodations: 106 first and 244 tourist class
Registry: Spain
Maiden voyage: Bilbao-Santander-Gijon-Vigo-Lisbon-New York-Havana-Vera Cruz on March 21, 1953

Launched as the *Monasterio de Guadalupe* for the Empresa Nacional Elcano, she was purchased by the Spanish Line before completion. Her name was contracted to *Guadalupe* before entering service. Engaged in the Bilbao-Santander-Gijon-Vigo-Lisbon-San Juan-Vera Cruz-New York route outward calling at La Coruna-Gijon-Santander-Bilbao homeward. She formerly made a call at Cadiz but this was eliminated in 1962 along with the call at Havana. From 1961 until mid-1962 she called at New York westbound but eliminated this port by 1968 due to her failure to pass U.S. Coast Guard safety regulations for embarking U.S. citizens. She made her last voyage on January 6, 1973, from Bilbao-Vigo-Lisbon-San Juan-Vera Cruz-Miami-Port Arthur, Texas-Aviles, arriving Bilbao on March 2nd. Laid up at Bilbao until sold for scrap to Manuel Desguaces Varela at Castellon. She left Bilbao for the breaker's yard on April 10, 1973, arriving two days later. Broken up in May 1973.

Sister ship: *Covadonga.*

II HABANA

Builder: Sociedad Espanola de Construccion Naval, Bilbao, Spain
Completed: August 1923
Gross Tonnage: 10,551
Dimensions: 500' x 61' Depth: 36' Draft: 30'
Engines: Four steam turbines, single-reduction geared
Screws: Twin
Watertight bulkheads: Ten
Decks: Three
Normal speed: 16 knots
Passenger accommodations: 101 in a single class*
Officers and crew:
Registry: Spain
Maiden voyage: To America, Cadiz-Barcelona-Vigo-New York, arriving on February 13, 1927

*Originally carred: 1,100 in three classes.

Built expressly for the Spanish Line and christened *Alfonso XIII*. Renamed *Habana* in 1931. Engaged in the transatlantic trade from Spain to Mexico and Central America. Engaged in the direct service from Cadiz-Barcelona-Vigo-New York with occasional calls at Havana begun in February 1929; Vera Cruz in February 1930. Laid up at Bordeaux, France during the Spanish Civil War in July 1936, she was used to immigrate Jews fleeing from Germany in 1938. Gutted by fire at Bilbao, Spain in 1943, she was rebuilt as a cargo-passenger liner with a limited accommodation for 12 persons in a single class. Rebuilt at the Todd Brooklyn Shipyard, New York and given the present complement of passengers. Returned to scheduled service in April 1947. In 1952 she made only one voyage, her last, on July 1st from New York-La Coruna-Gijon-Santander-Bilbao-Cadiz-Barcelona. Sold to the Pescanova S.A. on May 12, 1962 and renamed *Galicia* following her conversion to a fish factory. Broken up by Hierros Ardes at Vigo, Spain in April 1978.

Sister ship: *Cristobal Colon*.

URUGUAY

Builder: William Denny & Bros., Ltd., Dumbarton, Scotland
Completed: March 1913
Gross Tonnage: 10,348
Dimensions: 482′ x 61′ Depth: 36′ Draft: 25′
Engines: Two 3-cylinder, triple expansion
Screws: Triple
Watertight bulkheads: Eight
Decks: Four
Normal speed: 17 knots (attained a speed of 18.64 knots on her trial runs)
Passenger accommodations: 250 first, 100 second and 75 third class
Registry: Spain

She was christened *Infanfa Isable de Borbon*. Renamed *Uruguay* in 1931. Engaged in the Spain-Havana-Vera Cruz service and reallocated to the Spain-South American trade in 1931. Sunk by an air attack at Valencia, Spain, between January 16 and 23, 1939, during the Spanish Civil War. Refloated on July 27, 1942 and sold for scrap.

Sister ship: *Argentina.*

Swedish–American Line

DROTTNINGHOLM

Builder: Alexander Stephan & Sons Ltd., Glasgow, Scotland
Completed: April 1905
Gross tonnage: 11,055
Dimensions: 538' x 60' Depth: 41'
Engines: Steam turbines single-reduction geared
Screws: Triple
Watertight bulkheads: Seven
Decks: Four
Normal speed: 17.50 knots
Passenger accommodations: 183 first, 486 second and 922 third class*
Officers and crew: 219
Registry: Sweden
Maiden voyage: Gothenburg-New York arriving on June 9, 1920

*Originally carried: 426 first and 280 second.

Built for the British Allan Line and christened *Virginian*. Passed on to the Canadian Pacific Line in 1916 when the Allan Line was absorbed. Resold to the Swedish-American Line in early 1920 and renamed *Drottningholm*.

Engaged in the Gothenburg-New York service and later added a call at Copenhagen. On May 2, 1924 she inaugurated a westbound call at Halifax and incorporated the port in her itinerary, sometimes calling there both east and westbound. She called at Boston for the first time eastbound on May 9, 1926. The *Drottningholm* had been converted to oil-firing from a coal burner and her original Parson steam turbines replaced between December 1921 and May 1922 by the presently stated type of propulsion. Converted to a cabin and third class ship in February 1925, she earned notoriety by having brought the famous Swedish actress Greta Garbo to the United States. In April 1924 she was chartered by the Allies to bring diplomats across the North Atlantic and was later used for repatriation work under the office of the International Red Cross. Resumed scheduled sailings in March of 1946 from Gothenburg to New York and was the first liner to commence peacetime voyages since the war. Famous in her own right she was the first ship to be driven by the then revolutionary Parson steam turbines with their direct acting force upon the shaft exerting great force back in 1905. She made only two voyages in 1948, then made her 440th and last voyage for the Line on February 13, 1948, New York-Gothenburg, and was subsequently sold to the Home Lines in the same month and renamed *Brasil; Homeland* in 1951. Sold for scrap to Sidarma S.A. at Trieste, Italy and arrived there on March 29, 1955 for breaking up after a long service of 50 years under three flags.

I GRIPSHOLM

Builder: W. G. Armstrong, Whitworth & Co., Ltd., Newcastle-on-Tyne, England
Completed: November 1925
Gross tonnage: 19,105
Dimensions: 590' x 74' Depth: 43' Draft: 29'
Engines: Two 6-cylinder, four-stroke, double-acting Burmeister & Wain diesels
Screws: Twin
Watertight bulkheads: Ten
Decks: Five
Normal speed: 16 knots
Passenger accommodations: 210 first, 710 tourist class*
Registry: Sweden
Maiden voyage: Gothenburg-New York on November 21, 1925

*Originally carried: 170 first, 481 second, and 1,010 third class.

Built expressly for the Swedish-American Line, she was engaged in the Gothenburg-Copenhagen-New York service and cruising. She called at Boston eastbound for the first time on April 30, 1926. In February 1927 she made her first extensive cruise to the Mediterranean. Thereafter, she made an annual cruise to South America. *Gripsholm* was the first motorship involved in the North Atlantic run at the time of her debut. In March 1942 she was chartered by the United States Government at a cost of $17,000 per day until March 1946, for use as a diplomatic exchange ship. Following the war she ferried Japanese, Germans and Italians to their fatherland and repatriated allied soldiers on her return trips under the office of the International Red Cross. During this extensive duty of repatriation she carried over 27,000 war personnel and covered 120,000 miles. She soon became the most well-known mercy ship of the war. Reconditioned for peace time service, she returned in March 1946 from New York to Gothenburg. The *Gripsholm's* interior modes were so elaborate that she was often referred to as "The Castle Afloat." She had been built at a cost of 14 million Swedish Krona. On July 18, 1952 she rescued 45 people from the burning Norwegian freighter *Black Hawk,* 75 miles outside of New York. The *Gripsholm* was the first ship to gain popularity as a cruise ship. In 1949 she was refitted at Kiel, Germany and given a new stem with an increase in overall length from 574 feet to 590 feet. Her funnels were also replaced with larger stacks. She made her last commercial voyage for the Line on December 29, 1953, from Gothenburg to New York and was sold under a joint ownership scheme with the North German Lloyd in January 1954, and sailed under the Bremen-Amerika Line banner. The Swedish-American Line retained a 50 percent interest in the ship until the Germans purchased her outright in January 1955. Renamed *Berlin,* she was sold for scrap in Italy in October 1966.

II GRIPSHOLM

Builder: Ansaldo SpA Cantieri Navale, Sestri-Genoa, Italy
Completed: April 1957
Gross tonnage: 22,725
Dimensions: 631′ x 82′ Depth: 50′ Draft: 27′
Engines: Two 9-cylinder, two-stroke single-acting diesels.
Screws: Twin
Watertight bulkheads: Eleven
Decks: Five
Normal speed: 18 knots
Passenger accommodations: 175 first and 682 tourist class (450 in a single first-class when cruising)
Officers and crew: 364
Registry: Sweden
Maiden voyage: Gothenburg-Copenhagen-Halifax-New York on May 14, 1957

Built expressly for the Swedish-American Line, she soon came to be known as the "Golden Yacht" with her sleek clipper bow. Christened by Her Royal Highness Princess Margaretha of Sweden on the day of launching, April 8, 1956. Engaged in the Gothenburg-Copenhagen-Bremerhaven-New York run with an occasional call at Halifax westbound as well as cruising. Most of her long cruises were to the Mediterranean, South America, West Africa, the Pacific and the North Cape. Though built as a dual purpose ship she cruised for most of the year making only the annual transatlantic voyage for her drydocking. The *Gripsholm's* fore funnel was a dummy but concealed a staircase leading to a passenger observation platform at the top. Fully air-conditioned and equipped with motion stabilizers, she became a symbol of luxury coupled by her expensive tariffs which a discriminating clientele were most eager to pay out. The *Gripsholm* had a cargo capacity for 82,500 cubic feet and was equipped with a water evaporating system capable of turning 175 tons of sea water into fresh water each day. In 1959 the call at Halifax was dropped and the Bremerhaven call eliminated by 1964. By 1967 she was cruising extensively year-round for the most part. She made her last transatlantic voyage on August 26, 1975, from New York to Copenhagen-Gothenburg and was laid up at the Balestrand Fjord in Norway on September 17 pending disposition. Sold to the Greek-owned Karageorgis Line and delivered to them at Sande Fjord, Norway on November 26, 1975. Renamed *Navarino*. A proposed resale was to take place on November 26, 1981 to the Finish-owned Commodore Cruise Line but on the same day that the transfer of ownership was to take place, the ship partially capsized and sank at Skaramanga, Greece. Damage to her machinery and accommodations was severe and she was declared a total loss. Righted in March 1982, she was given some preliminary repairs and sold to a company named Multiship Italia. Renamed *Samantha,* she was to be used as a floating condominium-style timesharing cruise ship. However, when the owner of the company allegedly absconded with some $3 million in funds she was later sold to Greek interests. Nothing seemed to materialize for the ship and she was sold for scrap for $3.9 million and towed to Italy by the salvage tug *Tinos*.

II KUNGSHOLM

Builder: Blohm & Voss, Hamburg, Germany
Completed: November 1928
Gross tonnage: 20,067
Dimensions: 609' x 78' Depth: 43' Draft: 29'
Engines: Two 8-cylinder, four-stroke, double-acting Burmeister & Wain diesels
Screws: Twin
Watertight bulkheads: Ten
Decks: Five
Normal speed: 17.50 knots
Passenger accommodations: 115 first, 489 second, and 940 third class
Officers and crew: 344
Registry: Sweden
Maiden voyage: Gothenburg-New York on November 24, 1928

Built exclusively for the Swedish-American Line at a cost of 18.2 million Swedish Krona, she was launched on March 17, 1928 and completed by October 13th. The following day three men were killed by an explosion in the engine room while she was on her sea trials. Despite this terrible beginning, her career was a successful one for the most part. Engaged in the Gothenburg-Copenhagen-New York service and pleasure cruising. In 1939 she was set to cruise out of New York to the West Indies. Following the completion of one of these cruises, she was laid up due to hostilities on October 14, 1939. Seized by the United States Government on January 2, 1941 and converted to a transport and renamed *John Ericsson*. She was later officially sold to the U.S. Government on January 2, 1942. During her services as an American transport the *Kungsholm* carried over 170,000 troops across the North Atlantic during the course of the war. Following the war she was used as a warbride ship with altered accommodations for 279 mothers and 177 babies. She also made a few voyages under the management of United States Lines during peacetime. On March 7, 1947, while lying at pier 90 in New York, fire broke out around 2:24 p.m. caused by a short circuit. The fire was extinguished at 5:45 p.m. but caused $1,500,000 in damage to the ship. Sold back to the Swedish-American Line in July of that year she was sent to the Ansaldo shipyards in Genoa in December to be repaired. Sold to the Greek-owned Home Lines on April 8, 1948 for a consideration equal to the cost of repairing the ship and renamed *Italia*. Resold to an American syndicate in 1964 and converted to a casino and 500-room hotel at Freeport, Bahamas. Renamed 'The Imperial Bahama Hotel'. The company soon went bankrupt and she was offered up for sale in June 1965. When no offers materialized she was sold for scrap to Spanish shipbreakers and arrived at Bilbao, Spain on September 8, 1965.

III KUNGSHOLM

Builder: De Schelde N.V., Flushing, Netherlands
Completed: October 1953
Gross tonnage: 21,164
Dimensions: 60' x 77' Depth 49' Draft 26'
Engines: Two Burmeister & Wain 8-cylinder, two-stroke, single acting diesels
Screws: Twin
Collision bulkheads: One
Watertight bulkheads: Eight
Decks: Five
Normal speed: 19 knots
Passenger accommodations: 176 first, and 723 tourist class (accommodations limited to 400 when cruising)
Officers and crew: 355
Registry: Sweden
Maiden voyage: Gothenburg-Copenhagen-New York on November 24, 1953

Built for the Swedish-American Line exclusively, she was christened *Kungsholm* by Her Royal Highness Princess Sybilla of Sweden on the 18th of April 1952, the day of her launching. Despite her non-existent outside promenade deck, all of her cabins were situated outside. She was also the first to have a private bathroom for every stateroom on the ship. Engaged in the North Atlantic trade from Gothenburg-Copenhagen-New York she also made calls to Bremerhaven eastbound and Halifax on occasion westbound. Three months out of the year she was sent cruising and made her first round-the-world cruise in January 1955, lasting 97 days and calling at 21 ports. Fitted with motion stabilizers in 1961, she was fully air-conditioned. Her fore funnel was a dummy and her masts were telescopic so they could be retracted allowing passage under low bridges. The *Kungsholm* made a World Cruise also in 1956, 1960-62. She abandoned the call at Halifax by mid-1960 and Bremerhaven as well by 1964. She made her last voyage for the Line in the form of a cruise leaving New York for the last time on September 1, 1965, headed for the Mediterranean and later Scandinavia. Sold to the North German Lloyd in October 1965 and renamed *Europa*. Resold to the Italian Costa Line in October 1981 and renamed *Columbus C.; Costa Columbus* in 1984. She rammed the breakwater wall at Cadiz, Spain on September 29, 1984. Taken in tow she later sank. Refloated she was sold for scrap in Barcelona in June 1985.

Note: She arrived at New York for the first time on December 3, 1953.

IV KUNGSHOLM

Builder: John Brown & Co., Ltd., Clydebank, Glasgow, Scotland
Completed: March 1966
Gross tonnage: 26,678
Dimensions: 660' x 87' Depth: 51' Draft: 28'
Engines: Two 9-cylinder, two-stroke, single-acting diesels
Screws: Twin
Collision bulkheads: One
Watertight bulkheads: Nine
Decks: Five
Normal speed: 21 knots
Passenger accommodations: 110 first, and 656 tourist class
  (accommodations limited to 500 when cruising)
Officers and crew: 450
Registry: Sweden
Maiden voyage: Gothenburg-Copenhagen-New York on April 22, 1966

Built for the Swedish-American Line at a cost of some 100 million Swedish Krona. She was one of the last passenger liners to be built by the famous shipyards of John Brown, builder of the three Queens, and one of the last to be conservatively decorated in old world fashion with plenty of wood panelling. The *Kungsholm* made her debut at a time when the transatlantic ferry had nearly reached its nadir and the new age of cruising was just emerging. Though she made annual transatlantic voyages, they were for the most part positioning voyages or crossings for her annual overhaul. When she made the voyage it was on the New York-Copenhagen-Gothenburg run. Employed mostly as a cruise ship she travelled worldwide. Her forward funnel was a dummy and was used as a storage area. She was plagued by air-conditioning problems from time to time but the exquisite outlay of her public rooms and charming staterooms earned her the position of the best of the best luxury liners for her time. On January 15, 1971, she made a 94-day world cruise and called at 23 ports. She was the Swedish-American Line's flagship. Equipped with motion stabilizers and fully air-conditioned. Her on-board amenities included several lounges, bars, library, sauna, gymnasium, barber and beauty shop, boutique, etc. The oil crisis of the mid-seventies had sealed the fate of the Greek Line, Italian Line and now knocked on the door of the Swedish-American Line, who decided to end its services with the sale of the *Kungsholm*. She made her last voyage for the Line on August 28, 1975, New York-Hamilton (Bermuda)-Prince Edward Island-Quebec-Halifax. Returning to New York on September 10th, she sailed the following day for Newcastle, England to be delivered to her new owners, the Norwegian-owned Flagship Cruises, who took over the ship on the 19th. She retained her original name. Resold to the British-owned P & O Lines in September 1978 and underwent a major refit. She emerged with her fore-funnel having been removed and was renamed *Sea Princess* in January 1979. Transferred to their subsidiary Princess Cruises in November 1986. Transferred back to P&O in May 1991. Presently in service.

I STOCKHOLM

Builder: Blohm & Voss, Hamburg, Germany
Completed: May 1900
Gross tonnage: 12,835
Dimensions: 571' x 62' Depth: 38' Draft: 32'
Engines: Two 3-cylinder, triple expansion engines
Screws: Twin
Watertight bulkheads: Ten
Decks: Four
Normal speed: 15 knots
Passenger accommodations: 154 first, 355 second, and 867 third class
Officers and crew: 200
Registry: Sweden
Maiden voyage: Gothenburg-New York on December 11, 1915

Built for the Holland-America Line and christened *Potsdam.* Sold to the Swedish-American Line in September 1915 for 4.9 million Swedish Krona and renamed *Stockholm.* The *Stockholm* had a promenade deck 195 feet long. Employed in the Gothenburg-New York run, she made only six trips to New York in 1916 because of the war. On July 15, 1917 she rescued 868 passengers from the Norwegian-America Liner *Kristianiafjord* when the ship was wrecked seven miles off Cape Race, Newfoundland and brought them to Norway. Converted to a cabin and third class ship in early 1923, she began to call at Halifax in either direction, the first westbound on January 15, 1924. On May 21, 1926 she called at Boston for the first time. She made her last voyage for the Line on October 13, 1928, New York-Gothenburg, and was subsequently sold to the Norwegian firm of Odd Co. A/S and converted to a whale factory ship with renaming to *Solgimt.* Captured by the German raider Pinquin in the Antarctic Ocean on January 14, 1941 and taken to Bordeaux where she was used as a tanker. Scuttled by the Germans at Cherbourg as a blockship to the harbour entrance in June 1944. When it became impossible to refloat her after the war, she was blown-up on August 30, 1946.

Note: The *Stockholm* carried 55 first, 23 second and 53 third class passengers on her maiden voyage to New York, where she arrived on December 26, 1915. On her last voyage for the Line on October 13, 1928, she had arrived at the port three days earlier prior to her departure on the 9th. Many liners had long stay-overs before the turn-around voyage as compared with today's sometimes ten-hour turn-around and less.

III STOCKHOLM

Builder: Cantieri Riuniti del'Adriatico, Monfalcone, Italy
Completed: 1938
Gross tonnage: 30,090
Dimensions: 642′ x 83′
Engines: Three low speed C.R.D.A.-Sulzer 10-cylinder, two-stroke diesels
  (Shaft output = 14,155 kilowatts)
Screws: Triple
Decks: Six
Normal speed: 20 knots
Passenger accommodations: 1,350 in first, tourist-cabin & third class
  (620 when cruising)
Registry: Sweden

Built expressly for the Swedish-American Line, she was the brainchild of designer Eric Christiansson. Born in 1901, he had gone to sea at the tender age of 14 on the barquentine *Jonstorp*. As technical designer for Swedish American Line's parent company, the Brostroms Group, Christiansson laid down the plans for what was to be the paragon of luxury liners during the apex of ocean liner opulence and technology. The dream ship, however, was not to be. She had been built on the same ship wrights where a previous hull designated to be *Stockholm* had been destroyed while fitting-out. The second attempt was more fortunate and was launched in May 1938 and fitted-out during 1941 at Monfalcone. All her cabins were situated outside in the first and tourist-cabin classes. Featuring a view of the outside world each was furnished with a full-size twin bed, spacious wardrobe area and, in many, a separate sitting area. The majority afforded passengers with en-suite bathrooms with bathtub. The decor was in the hotel style. Externally, the *Stockholm* was a product of the then transitional motorship profile with a strong streamlined superstructure, two moderate funnels, a raked stem and cruiser stern: A stark contrast to the two-stacked turbine driven steamers of the previous decade. She also was fitted with anti-rolling tanks. Her cabins arranged on either side of a single wide central hallway extended the full length of the deck, as opposed to the more conventional layout with twin parallel alleyways. The complicated spacious layout was achieved by the use of divided funnel uptakes. Public rooms consisted of a smoking room, two veranda cafes, writing room, card room and library, the main lounge and the Showboat Restaurant. Taken over by the Italian Government during the war and renamed *Sabaudia* for military service. On September 9, 1943, she was boarded by a platoon of German marines while tied up at Trieste. The same day, Italy had capitulated to the Allies. The Italians aboard were ordered ashore, while the Nazis held the ship for a number of days until railway wagons could be commandeered and brought alongside to carry off her interiors. Later moved out into the harbour, she was struck and set on fire by allied bombers on July 6, 1944. She lay burned-out, half sunken and keeled over on her starboard side with a swell lapping in and out of her swimming pool and upper deck windows. Her three engines were later salvaged when the hull was refloated. Scrapped in 1949-1950.

IV STOCKHOLM

Builder: A. B. Gotaverken, Gothenburg, Sweden
Completed: February 1948
Gross tonnage: 12,396
Dimensions: 525' x 69' Depth: 39' Draft: 25'
Engines: Two 8-cylinder, two-stroke, single-acting Gotaverken diesels
Screws: Twin
Decks: Four
Normal speed: 19 knots
Passenger accommodations: 28 first and 557 tourist class (350 in a single class when cruising)*
Officers and crew: 219
Registry: Sweden
Maiden voyage: Gothenburg-New York on February 21, 1948

*Originally carried 113 first, 282 tourist class

Built expressly for the Swedish-American Line, launched on September 9, 1946, she was the first ship to be built on Swedish soil for the company. Classified as a cargo-passenger liner, she was engaged in the Gothenburg-Copenhagen-Bremerhaven-New York service with a call at Halifax in either direction; during the winter months westbound only. The call at Bremerhaven was occasional. Refitted in November 1953, she was fitted with Denny-Brown stabilizers in 1956. The *Stockholm* also did cruising after her passenger accommodations had been enlarged in 1953. On the night of July 25, 1956 the *Stockholm,* while on an eastbound voyage out of New York, rammed and sunk the Italian liner *Andrea Doria* in a calm fog at 11:22 p.m. off the Nantucket Shoals. The reinforced ice-breaker bow of the *Stockholm* pierced the *Doria's* starboard side causing the liner of only three years service to list heavily. Five crew members aboard the *Stockholm* were killed when their quarters located forward were crushed by the great impact. The *Stockholm's* lifeboats were sent to pick up survivors from the sinking *Andrea Doria,* which went down eleven hours later. The *Stockholm,* still afloat, made her way back to New York and disembarked her passengers. Repaired at the Bethlehem Steel Company shipyards in Brooklyn, where she remained until November 5th. Her mangled bow replaced by a new one, she returned to service in December. A formal inquiry found both ships at fault with relation to the proper readings of the navigational equipment and the altering of ship's course when approaching another ship that appears on the radar screen. Something both ships failed to do on that fatal night. Resuming service from New York to Copenhagen-Gothenburg on December 8, 1956, the *Stockholm* remained in service for another three years and made her last voyage for the Line on December 4, 1959, New York-Halifax-Bremerhaven-Copenhagen-Gothenburg. Sold to the East German Freier Deutsche Gewerkschafts-Bund on January 3, 1969, and renamed *Volkerfreundschaft; Volker* in 1985. Resold to Swedish owners in 1988, operating under the name Neptunus Rex Enterprises and renamed *Fridtjob Nansen.* She is presently registered at the port of Vila, Vanuatu, in the Efate Islands (formerly the New Hebrides).

United States Lines

I AMERICA

Builder: Harland & Wolff Ltd., Belfast, Northern Ireland
Completed: September 1905
Gross tonnage: 21,329
Dimensions: 687' x 74' Depth: 52'
Engines: Two 4-cylinder quadruple expansion engines
Screws: Twin
Watertight bulkheads: Twelve
Decks: Five
Normal speed: 17.75 knots
Passenger accommodations: 674 cabin and 1,256 third class*
Registry: United States of America
Maiden voyage: New York-Bremen-Danzig on August 27, 1921

*Originally carried 55 first, 87 second and 582 third class.

Built for the German Hamburg-American Line and christened *Amerika*. Laid up on July 24, 1914 and seized by the United States at Boston, Massachusetts on August 6, 1917 following U.S. entry into the First World War. Converted to a transport on October 15, 1918 and had her name anglicised to *America*. On the night before she was to enter service as a trooper, the *America* sank at her pier at New York when some of her ballast intake valves were left open accidentally. Refloated on December 12, 1918 and fitted-out at the New York Naval Shipyard, she was used mostly for repatriation work rather than as a troop ship. Released in September 1919, she was transferred to the U.S. Mail Line in July 1921 and subsequently to the United States Lines on August 31, 1921 upon dissolution of the former. Engaged in the New York-Plymouth Cherbourg-Bremen service. She added a call at Cobh in January 1924. The *America* was converted to a cabin and third class ship in March 1923 and her passenger complement reduced greatly as a result. During the peak years of immigration to the United States she was recorded as having ferried 387 first, 379 second and 1,332 third class on one particular voyage according to the records of the Trans-Atlantic Passenger Movement annual reports. Rebuilt in 1926 after being nearly destroyed by fire at Newport News, Virginia on March 10, 1926 during an overhauling. Rebuilt, she returned to service in April 1928 sailing to Cherbourg-Southampton-Bremen. She made her last commercial voyage from Hamburg-Cherbourg-Plymouth-Cobh arriving at New York on September 4, 1931 and was subsequently returned to her registered owners, the U.S. Department of Commerce, and laid up in the reserve fleet along the James River. Recommissioned as a troop ship in January 1941 under the name *Edmund B. Alexander*. Refitted for oil firing in May 1942 and her two tall funnels replaced by a single squat type. Laid up once again, this time on the Hudson River on May 26, 1949 after extensive repatriation work. Sold for scrap on January 27, 1957 at Baltimore, Maryland to the Bethlehem Steel Corporation and broken up. The *America* was the first ocean liner to have an a la carte restaurant. She ranked very high in her day as a luxury liner.

II AMERICA

Builder: Newport News Shipbuilding & Drydock Co., Newport News, Virginia, USA
Completed: July 1940
Gross tonnage: 33,961
Dimensions: 723' x 94' Depth: 56' Draft: 33'
Engines: Six steam turbines, high pressure, double-reduction geared; intermediate pressure and low pressure, single reduction geared
Screws: Twin
Watertight bulkheads: Fourteen
Decks: Six
Normal speed: 22.50 knots
Passenger accommodations: 516 first and 786 tourist class*
Officers and crew: 675
Registry: United States of America
Maiden voyage: New York-St. Thomas-San Juan-Port au Prince-Havana on August 10, 1940

*Originally carried: 475 first, 467 second and 343 tourist.

Built expressly for the United States Lines and floated out of drydock. Her forward funnel was a dummy and her aft funnel was later raised fifteen feet due to poor smoke exhaust ventilation. This gave the ship better symmetry since the forward funnel was a bit higher to begin with. Internally she was a very luxurious liner with public rooms appointments from art deco to contemporary. Requisitioned for troop work in June 1941 following a series of cruises to the Caribbean and renamed *West Point*. She was used as a transport until after hostilities and during the course of the war carried over 400,000 troops and steamed over 500,000 miles. The

America's engines generated 37,400 ship horse power. Released in February 1946 she underwent a $6 million dollar refit and recovered her original name. She resumed transatlantic crossings on November 14, 1946 from New York-Cobh-Southampton-Le Havre. This was her intended route and the maiden crossing which she had to forego because of the war. On her first voyage outward, she made a fast crossing from Ambrose Lighthouse to Daunt's Lightship in 4 days, 22 hours and 22 minutes at a speed of 24.54 knots. She inaugurated a call at Bremerhaven in October 1951 and incorporated the port into her regular itinerary. In November 1960 she was converted to a first and tourist class ship. She began to do more cruising in the sixties when transatlantic travel began to slacken, but she lacked the ability to compete with the ships built for this trade since she did not have an outdoor pool or large lido area. In September 1963 she was the victim of a labor dispute between American and Hispanic crew members and her voyage had to be cancelled, her passengers sent home. The ensuing results caused the ship to be laid up at the Todd Shipyards in Hoboken, New Jersey. She remained there until the following February when she resumed service. She made her last voyage for U.S. Lines Bremerhaven-Southampton-Le Havre-Cobh arriving at New York on October 27, 1964. In August she was sold to the Greek-owned Chandris Lines for $4,250,000 who increased her passenger capacity from the original 1,046 berths to 2,294 for the immigrant trade to Australia. Delivered in November and renamed *Australis*. Resold to Venture Cruises in July 1978 for $2.5 million dollars and renamed *America*. Resold to Chandris Lines and $1 million dollars and renamed *Italis*. Laid up in Piraeus since September 1979. Renamed *Noga* in 1980. Resold in 1984 to Silver Moon Ferries Ltd., of Piraeus, Greece (Panama flag) and renamed *Alferdoss*. Presently laid up Perama, Greece.

Note: Her fore-funnel was removed in 1979.

GEORGE WASHINGTON

Builder: A.G. Vulkan, Stettin, Germany
Completed: November 1908
Gross tonnage: 23,788
Dimensions: 722' x 78' Depth: 50'
Engines: Two 4-cylinder, quadruple expansion engines
Screws: Twin
Watertight bulkheads: Twelve
Decks: Six
Normal speed: 18.50 knots
Passenger accommodations: 500 first, 524 second and 901 third class
Registry: United States of America
Maiden voyage: New York-Bremen-Danzig on September 3, 1921

Built for the North German Lloyd and christened *George Washington*. Laid up at New York on August 4, 1914 with the outbreak of World War I and seized by the United States in April 1917. Commissioned as a troopship and converted on September 6, 1917. She retained her original name ironically and came to be nicknamed 'Big George' by the troops. Returned to the United States Shipping Board in November 1919 and managed for them by the U.S. Mail Line from August 1920 until its collapse on August 31, 1921 when she was handed over to the newly formed United States Lines. Engaged in the New York-Channel ports-Bremen service year-round. She made a Mediterranean cruise on February 14, 1922 from New York. Her regular service that year was New York-Plymouth-Cherbourg-Bremen-Danzig. In 1925 she added the call at Cobh and dropped Danzig, and her accommodations changed to first, second tourist cabin and third class in January. By 1927 she was running from New York to Bremen via Cherbourg and Southampton. She made her last commercial voyage from Hamburg-Cherbourg-Plymouth-Cobh arriving at New York for the last time on October 16, 1931. Returned to the U.S. Shipping Board and laid up in the Patuxant River, Maryland as a reserve troopship. Taken over by the British in 1940 and brought to Halifax, Nova Scotia for refitting as a transport and renamed *Catlin* in January 1941. The British decided not to use her and she was returned to the United States in April 1942 and recovered her original name. Completed by the United States for war service with conversion to oil-firing; the elimination of a funnel and new accommodations for 6,500 armed men. The refit took place at the Todd shipyards in Brooklyn, New York in June 1942 and she entered service in April of 1943 with a new squat-like funnel. Decommissioned in March 1947 and put up for sale. When no buyers appeared she was laid up at Baltimore where was destroyed by fire off Hawkins Point on January 16, 1951. The remaining hulk sold for scrap to the Boston Metal Company at Baltimore, Maryland where breaking up commenced on February 14th. During her career as a liner and her combined war services, the *George Washington* steamed over 185,000 miles and carried more than 160,000 persons. She also transported President Wilson across the Atlantic for the signing of the Treaty of Versailles and had three separate promenade decks for passengers.

LEVIATHAN

Builder: Blohm & Voss, Hamburg, Germany
Completed: May 1914
Gross tonnage: 48,943
Dimensions: 950' x 100' Depth: 64'
Engines: Four sets of steam turbines
Screws: Quadruple
Watertight bulkheads: Thirteen
Decks: Seven
Normal speed: 24 knots (attained a speed of 27.07 knots on her trial runs)
Passenger accommodations: 835 first, 652 second and 2,117 third class
Officers and crew: 1,150
Registry: United States of America
Maiden voyage: New York-Cherbourg-Southampton on July 4, 1923

Built for the German Hamburg-American Line and christened *Vaterland*. Laid up at New York on July 30, 1914 upon completion of her second voyage and seized by the United States on April 4, 1917 upon U.S. entry into the First World War. Commissioned as an army transport on July 25, 1917 and renamed *Leviathan*. Transferred to the United States Lines by the U.S. Shipping Board in 1923. Reconditioned by naval architect Francis Gibbs, who would later design the superliner *United States,* and converted to oil-firing in September 1919. Reconditioned once again in 1923 for U.S. Lines, her gross tonnage was increased to 59,957 according to American rule measurement and thereby making her the largest ship in the world. This proved to be costly when the Line had to pay over $2 million dollars in dry-dock and harbour dues based on her net tonnage. Gross tonnage was reduced to the present figure in 1931. She had been converted to carry first, second tourist-cabin and third class in January 1925. Engaged in the New York-Cherbourg-Southampton service year-round. During her career as transport she carried as many as ten thousand troops on each voyage and was fondly known by American troops as the 'Levi Nathan.' Prohibition and the Great Depression caused the *Leviathan* to be withdrawn from service in December 1933. In June 1934 she made five round trips, her last from Southampton on September 8th via Le Havre-Plymouth. She arrived at New York on the 14th and was put up for sale. Sold for scrap in January 1938 she left New York for the last time on January 25th steaming for the breaker's yard at Rosyth, Scotland. As majestic a liner as the *Leviathan* was, she earned the reputation as being the 'Great White Elephant' since she never earned a profit. She was broken up by June 1938.

Note: On her maiden voyage she carried: 807 first class, 487 second class and only 493 third class passengers.

MANHATTAN

Builder: New York Shipbuilding Corp., Camden, New Jersey, USA
Completed: 1932
Gross tonnage: 24,289
Dimensions: 705′ x 86′ Depth: 47′
Engines: Six steam turbines single-reduction geared
Screws: Twin
Watertight bulkheads: Eleven
Decks: Six
Normal speed: 20 knots
Passenger accommodations: 567 cabin, 461 tourist and 196 third class
Officers and crew: 481
Registry: United States of America
Maiden voyage: New York-Cobh-Plymouth-Le Havre-Hamburg on August 10, 1932

Built expressly for the United States Lines, she and her sister ship were the first orders placed by the Line, having operated older and appropriated tonnage prior to. Her smokestacks were later raised fifteen feet due to poor exhaust, which left the deck areas with black soot. Though not as large or as fast as originally contracted for between the then owners of the company and the United States Shipping Board who had made a large subsidy to build the ships, they were very attractive and moderate in all their characteristics. Engaged in the New York-Channel ports-Hamburg service, the *Manhattan* opened travel from New York to Genoa-Naples on December 30, 1939 until June 10, 1940 when Italy entered the war. On January 12, 1941 the *Manhattan* ran aground five miles north of Lake Worth, Florida while on a cruise from New York to San Francisco via the Panama Canal. She remained fixed for 22 days. Her passengers were removed by the Coast Guard cutter *Vigilante,* which took them to Palm Beach where they could make other arrangements for their respective destinations. The ship was finally freed on February 4th and managed to make her way back to New York for repairs, which when completed, amounted to almost 2 million dollars. Requisitioned for troop work in June 1941 and renamed *Wakefield.* Misfortune was to reappear when she caught fire on September 3, 1942 while on a westbound convoy. She remained ablaze for seven days and had to be abandoned. Taken back to Boston for repairs, her entire promenade deck had to be removed and completely rebuilt. Resuming troop work in April 1944, she was destined never to sail again as a commercial liner. Performing various duties during and after the war, such as repatriating, she was active until the early fifties. Laid up in the Hudson River as a reserve ship by the U.S. Department of Commerce where she slowly rusted away until finally sold for scrap to the Union Mineral & Alloy Corporation for a meagre $263,000 and broken up at the Lipsett yards in Kearny, New Jersey in July 1964 arriving in tow.

Sister ship: *Washington.*

PRESIDENT ADAMS

Builder: New York Shipbuilding Corp., Camden, New Jersey, USA
Completed: April 1921
Gross tonnage: 10,558
Dimensions: 522' x 62' Depth: 42'
Engines: Two 4-cylinder triple expansion engines
Screws: Twin
Watertight bulkheads: Thirteen
Decks: Three
Normal speed: 14 knots
Passenger accommodations: 140 cabin and 428 third class
Officers and crew: 117
Registry: United States of America
Maiden voyage: New York-Boulogne-London on September 6, 1921 as *Centennial State*

Built for the United States Government and christened *Centennial State*. Managed by the U.S. Mail Line until taken over by the United States Lines on August 31, 1921. Renamed *President Adams* in April 1922. Engaged in the New York-Queenstown-Plymouth-Cherbourg-London route in January 1922. On June 15, 1922 she called at Boston while on an eastbound voyage and called there on occasion thereafter on her outbound voyages. Passage on the President Adams and her four sister ships stood at $120.00 one-way in cabin class. She made her last voyage on December 26, 1923 following her sale to the Dollar Line two months prior. Upon completion of her voyage, she was handed over at New York on January 23, 1924. Passed on to American President Lines ownership in 1938 following a reorganization plan between the Dollar Line and the U.S. Maritime Commission-retainer of the U.S. Shipping Board. Renamed *President Grant* in 1939. She struck a submerged reef in the South Pacific while transporting troops during the Second World War. Fixed on the reef, her crew laboured for almost one hundred days to free the ship. When nearly completed, a great wave struck and split her hull in two on February 26, 1944.

Sister ships: *President Garfield, President Monroe, President Polk* and *President Van Buren.*

PRESIDENT ARTHUR

Builder: A.G. Vulkan, Stettin, Germany
Completed: September 1900
Gross tonnage: 10,421
Dimensions: 523' x 60' Depth: 38'
Engines: Two 4-cylinder quadruple expansion engines
Screws: Twin
Watertight bulkheads: Thirteen
Decks: Four
Normal speed: 15 knots
Passenger accommodations: 304 second and 355 third class
Registry: United States of America
Maiden voyage: New York-Bremen-Danzig on September 15, 1921

Built for the German Hamburg-American Line and christened *Kiautschou*. Sold to the North German Lloyd in 1903 and renamed *Prinzess Alice*. Seized by the United States Government at Manila,

Philippines in early 1917 and commissioned as a transport on April 27th and renamed *Princess Matoika*. Released in September 1919 and laid up. Transferred to the United States Mail Line in August 1920 and subsequently to United States Lines on August 31, 1921 after only four voyages. Renamed *President Arthur* in April 1922. Engaged in the New York-Plymouth-Cherbourg-Bremen-Danzig run eastbound and called at Southampton-Cherbourg-Cobh westbound. The call at Danzig was dropped in 1923 and she was converted to a cabin and third class ship. Commenced her last voyage for the Line on October 2, 1923 from Bremen and was laid up upon arrival at New York on November 1st. Withdrawn from service she was later chartered to the American-Palestine Line in 1925 with service from New York to Naples-Haifa beginning March 12th. Sold to the Palace Line in 1926 and renamed *White Palace*. In 1926 she was resold once again to the Los Angeles Steamship Company and renamed *City of Honolulu*. Damaged by fire on May 25, 1930 at Honolulu, she was able to make the voyage back to Los Angeles. Laid up pending her disposal after having sailed under many houseflags she was sold for scrap in Japan in 1933.

PRESIDENT GARFIELD

Builder: New York Shipbuilding Corp., Camden, New Jersey, USA
Completed: June 1921
Gross tonnage: 10,558
Dimensions: 522' x 62' Depth: 42' Draft:
Engines: Two 4-cylinder triple expansion engines
Screws: Twin
Watertight bulkheads: Thirteen
Decks: Three
Normal speed: 14 knots
Passenger accommodations: 140 in cabin class
Registry: United States of America
Maiden voyage: New York-Queenstown-Plymouth-Cherbourg-London on
  May 31, 1922

Built expressly for the United States Government as one of a series of cargo-passenger liners sometimes known as 522's by their overall length. Christened *Blue Hen State*, she was managed by the U.S. Mail Line until taken over by the United States Lines on August 31, 1922, one year after the former's bankruptcy. Renamed *President Garfield* in 1922, she was employed in the New York-Queenstown-Plymouth*-Cherbourg-London trade. Sold to the Dollar Line on the West Coast in September 1923 with delivery scheduled for early 1924. She commenced her last voyage for U.S. Lines on January 9, 1924 eastbound and was handed over to the Dollar Line on February 6, 1924. Consolidated into the American President Lines in 1938 following reorganization of the Dollar Line and renamed *President Madison* the following year. Requisitioned as a transport in April 1942 and renamed *Kenmore*. Two years later she was converted to a hospital ship in February 1944 under the name of *Refuge*. Sold for scrap in 1948.

Sister ships: *President Adams, President Monroe, President Polk* and *President Van Buren.*

*The port of Plymouth was dropped in 1924.

PRESIDENT HARDING

Builder: New York Shipbuilding Corp., Camden, New Jersey, USA
Completed: December 1921
Gross tonnage: 13,869
Dimensions: 535′ x 72′ **Depth:** 41′
Engines: Four steam turbines, single-reduction geared
Screws: Twin
Decks: Three
Normal speed: 18 knots
Passenger accommodations: 320 cabin and 364 third class
Registry: United States of America
Maiden voyage: New York-Plymouth-Cherbourg-Bremen on March 25, 1922 as Lone Star State

Built for the United States Government and christened *Lone Star State*. Transferred to the United States Lines in 1922 and renamed *President Taft* in April; *President Harding* in June 1922. The *President Harding* originally carried first and third class passengers but was converted to a cabin and third class ship during the first quarter of 1926. Engaged in the New York-Plymouth-Cherbourg-Bremen route and added a call at Southampton-Cobh in 1925 westbound. Rerouted to a new service out of New York to Algiers-Genoa-Naples in February 1928, she reverted back to her original service two months later. Classified as a cargo-passenger line, the *President Harding* and a number of other ships with the same measurements were known as 535's because of their overall length and the large number which had been built. Transferred to the Antwerp Navigation Company, an American subsidiary under the Belgian flag, at the outbreak of World War II and in observance of America's Neutrality Act in February 1940 and renamed *Ville de Burges*. She ceased to carry passengers at this time since many of her voyages brought her within the war zone of the English Channel. Sunk by Nazi bombers in the River Scheldt, Holland on May 14, 1940.

Sister ship: *President Roosevelt*.

PRESIDENT MONROE

Builder: New York Shipbuilding Corp., Camden, New Jersey, USA
Completed: August 1920
Gross tonnage: 10,513
Dimensions: 522' x 62' Depth: 42'
Engines: Two 4-cylinder triple expansion engines
Screws: Twin
Watertight bulkheads: Thirteen
Decks: Three
Normal speed: 14 knots
Passenger accommodations: 140 in cabin class
Registry: United States of America
Maiden voyage: New York-Boulogne-London on October 25, 1921 as
  Panhandle State

Built for the United States Government and christened *Panhandle State*.
Managed by the U.S. Mail Line until their bankruptcy and subsequently
taken over by the newly created United States Lines on August 31, 1921.
Renamed *President Monroe* in April 1922. Employed in the New York-
Queenstown-Plymouth-Cherbourg-London service. In the following year
she was sold to the Dollar Line on the West Coast in September of 1923
and delivered to them in early 1924—the same year the port of Plymouth
was dropped. She made her last voyage for the Line on February 6, 1924
from London and was handed over to the Dollar Line upon her arrival on
March 12th at New York. Passed on to American President Lines in 1938
following reorganization of the Dollar Line. Renamed *President
Buchanan* in 1940. Converted to a hospital ship during the Second World
War and renamed *Emily H. Weder*. Sold for scrap in 1948.

Sister ships: *President Adams, President Garfield, President Polk* and
President Van Buren.

PRESIDENT POLK

Builder: New York Shipbuilding Corp., Camden, New Jersey, USA
Completed: March 1921
Gross tonnage: 10,513
Dimensions: 522′ x 62′ Depth: 42′ Draft:
Engines: Two 4-cylinder triple expansion engines
Screws: Twin
Watertight bulkheads: Thirteen
Decks: Three
Normal speed: 14 knots
Passenger accommodations: 236 cabin and 408 third class
Officers and crew: 117
Registry: United States of America
Maiden voyage: New York-Plymouth-Cherbourg-Bremen-Danzig on
April 8, 1922 as *Granite State*

Built for the United States Government and christened *Granite State*. Managed by the U.S. Mail Line until taken over by the United States Lines in August 1921. Renamed *President Polk* in June 1922. She is classified along with her four sister ships as cargo-passenger liners. Engaged in the New York-Queenstown-Plymouth-Cherbourg-London trade. The call at Plymouth was dropped in 1924. Sold to the Dollar Line of Robert Dollar in September 1923 with delivery for the coming year. Converted from a second and third class ship to a cabin and third class in 1923. She made her last voyage for United States Lines on January 23, 1924 from London and was handed over to the Dollar Line upon her arrival at New York on February 20th. Consolidated into the new American President Lines in 1938 and renamed *President Taylor* in 1940. Stranded off Canton Island in the Pacific Ocean on February 13, 1943 while working as a transport and abandoned.

Sister ships: *President Adams, President Garfield, President Monroe* and *President Van Buren.*

PRESIDENT ROOSEVELT

Builder: New York Shipbuilding Corp., Camden, New Jersey, USA
Completed: January 1922
Gross tonnage: 13,869
Dimensions: 535' x 72' Depth: 41'
Engines: Four steam turbines, single-reduction geared
Screws: Twin
Decks: Three
Normal speed: 18 knots
Passenger accommodations: 320 cabin and 338 third class
Registry: United States of America
Maiden voyage: New York-Plymouth-Cherbourg-Bremen on February 18, 1922 as *Peninsula State*

Built for the United States Government and christened *Peninsula State*. Transferred to the United States Lines in 1922 and renamed *President Pierce* in May; *President Roosevelt* in June. Engaged in the New York-Plymouth-Cherbourg-Bremen route until re-routed to a new service to Algiers Genoa-Naples in January 1928. She reverted back to her original itinerary in April. The *President Roosevelt* also called at Southampton on certain voyages and by 1932 was working New York-Plymouth-Le Havre-Hamburg with a call at Le Havre-Southampton-Cobh* homeward. During her career she came to the rescue of the sinking British steamer *Antigone* by listening to her direction finders as soon as she picked up the S.O.S. on January 24, 1926 at the early hour of 3:00 a.m. Converted to a cabin class ship in early 1926, she originally carried first and third. The *President Roosevelt* was classified as a cargo passenger liner. Requisitioned for troop work in June 1941 she was converted to an attack transport in 1943 and renamed *Joseph T. Dickman*. Sold for scrap in 1948.

Sister ship: *President Harding.*

*The port of Cobh was added in 1925.

PRESIDENT VAN BUREN

Builder: New York Shipbuilding Corp., Camden, New Jersey, USA
Completed: October 1920
Gross tonnage: 10,533
Dimensions: 522' x 62' Depth: 42'
Engines: Two 4-cylinder, triple expansion engines
Screws: Twin
Watertight bulkheads: Thirteen
Decks: Three
Normal speed: 14 knots
Passenger accommodations: 140 cabin class
Registry: United States of America
Maiden voyage: New York-Boulogne-London on September 20, 1921 as
  Old North State

Built for the United States Government and christened *Old North State*. Managed by the United States Mail Line until their failure and taken over by the United States Lines, newly created by the United States Shipping Board. Officially handed over on August 31, 1921 and renamed *President Van Buren* in April 1922. She made her maiden voyage as *President Van Buren* in August 1922. Employed in the New York-Queenstown-Plymouth-Cherbourg-London service until sold to the Dollar Line in September 1923 with delivery slated for early 1924. She commenced her last voyage for U.S. Lines on February 20, 1924 and was handed over upon her arrival at New York on March 19th. Consolidated into the American President Lines after reorganization of the Dollar Line in 1938 and renamed *President Fillmore* in 1940. Converted to a hospital ship in 1942 and renamed *Marigold*. Sold for scrap in 1948.

Sister ships: *President Adams, President Garfield, President Monroe* and *President Polk.*

Note: The port of Plymouth was dropped in 1924. Photo ship in Dollar Line colours.

REPUBLIC

Builder: Harland & Wolff Ltd., Belfast, Ireland
Completed: September 1907
Gross tonnage: 17,910
Dimensions: 600′ x 68′ Depth: 52′
Engines: Two 4-cylinder quadruple expansion engines
Screws: Twin
Watertight bulkheads: Eleven
Decks: Five
Normal speed: 14 knots
Passenger accommodations: 587 cabin, 903 tourist third and 527 third
  class
Registry: United States of America
Maiden voyage: New York-Plymouth-Cherbourg-Bremen on
  April 29, 1924

Built for the British firm of Furness, Withy & Co., and christened *Servian*. Sold to the Hamburg-American Line upon completion and renamed *President Grant*. Laid up at New York on July 23, 1914 in anticipation of war. Interned there, she was seized by the United States Government on April 4, 1917 and converted to a troopship on July 30, 1917, when she was commissioned as such. Released in October 1919 and laid up once again. Transferred to the newly established United States Lines in 1924 and positioned on the North Atlantic run from New York-Plymouth-Cherbourg-Bremen. On her maiden voyage she carried a small complement made up of 238 cabin class and 48 third class passengers. She ran under the name of *President Buchanan* for a time until renamed *Republic* in 1924. Converted to oil-firing in 1927 and converted to a cabin class ship. Her original complement consisted of first, second and tourist class, but she began a new intermediate class known as tourist-third in May 1925, which was to become known as tourist class in later years within the industry. Built with six masts, her third and fourth were removed at the time of her conversion from coal to oil fuel. The *Republic* made her last commercial voyage from Hamburg to New York via Cherbourg-Plymouth-Cobh and arrived at New York on July 28, 1931. Transferred title of ownership was then passed to the United States War Department. She was subsequently laid up until requisitioned for troop work in July 1941 and was later utilized as a hospital ship in February 1945. Decommissioned in February 1946 and laid up. Sold for scrap at Baltimore, Maryland in 1952.

UNITED STATES

Builder: Newport News Shipbuilding & Drydock Co., Newport News,
  Virginia, USA
Completed: 1952
Gross tonnage: 38,216
Dimensions: 988' x 99' Depth: 72' Draft: 32'
Engines: Four steam turbines, double-reduction geared
Screws: Quadruple
Decks: Eight
Normal speed: 33 knots
Passenger accommodations: 871 first, 508 cabin and 551 tourist class
  (709 when cruising)
Officers and crew: 1,068
Registry: United States of America
Maiden voyage: New York-Le Havre-Southampton on July 3, 1952

Built expressly for the United States Lines and employed on the North
Atlantic run from New York to Southampton via Le Havre with a call
Cobh in the summer and on to Bremerhaven in winter. The *United States*
also made cruises with a limited complement of passengers in a single
class category. She won the coveted Blue Riband on her maiden crossing
from Cunard's *Queen Mary* by making the run from Ambrose Lighthouse
to Bishop Rock in 3 days, 10 hours and 40 minutes at a mean speed of
35.59 knots. The *United States* is the largest ship ever to be constructed in
America at a cost of over $73 million. The flagship of the Line, she had
recaptured the prestige of winning the Blue Riband lost for over a century
to foreign competitors. Equipped with motion stabilizers and fully air-
conditioned, she is the fastest merchant ship in the world with a potential
speed of over 36 knots. Designed with wartime specifications, she has a
troop capacity for 14,000 fully equipped personnel. Her superstructure is
made of aluminum and she is considered to be virtually fireproof with all
interior furniture made of lightweight metals and non-flammable
materials. The only wood aboard the ship was reputed to be the grand
piano and the butcher's block (the latter no doubt removed since the
Health Department outlawed them). Her first class cinema seats 350
people. The main deck's enclosed promenade deck flooring is composed of
a blue-coloured non-flammable composition. The termination of a Federal
operating differential subsidy hastened the superliner into an early
retirement when the contract ended in 1969. Towards the end of her
career she made a first call eastbound at Boston on May 1, 1969 and her
last commercial voyage on November 1, 1969 from Bremerhaven-
Southampton-Le Havre-New York. Losses on the continued operation of
the liner after the end of the subsidy had cost the Line between $4 and $5
million. On February 6, 1973, the Federal Government took title of the
ship by repurchasing the superliner for $4,600,000. (Her then book value
estimated at $12 million dollars.) Sold to real estate developer, Richard
Hadley of Seattle, Washington for $5 million dollars (her estimated scrap
value at the time). Hadley formed United States Cruises and greatly
reduced the ship's gross tonnage measurement from its original 50,924 to
the present figure. U.S. Cruises original intentions were to attract the
yuppie market with plenty of deck space for jogging, tennis, golf,
swimming, etc. Though the ship had withstood the elements quite well
over the years, the cost of refitting was grossly underestimated and the
superliner remained in a state of limbo. Still laid up in Norfolk, Virginia
where she had been retired, she sits, her shadow against the murky water
casting an almost eerie figure of a ghost ship with a cloudy future.

Note: The *United States'* four gigantic propellers weigh 13 tons each and
are 20 feet in diameter.

WASHINGTON

Builder: New York Shipbuilding Corp., Camden, New Jersey, USA
Completed: 1933
Gross tonnage: 23,626
Dimensions: 705' x 86' Depth: 47'
Engines: Six steam turbines, single-reduction geared
Screws: Twin
Watertight bulkheads: Eleven
Decks: Six
Normal speed: 22.50 knots
Passenger accommodations: 580 cabin, 400 tourist and 106 third class
Registry: United States of America
Maiden voyage: New York-Cobh-Plymouth-Le Havre-Hamburg on May 10, 1933

Built expressly for the United States Lines and engaged in the New York-Channel ports-Hamburg trade and cruising. Avoiding the English Channel for German submarines that might break America's Neutrality Act, the *Washington* was sent to Genoa and Naples on January 13, 1939 to assist in the evacuation of thousands of civilians. In October the U.S. State Department chartered the ship on the 19th, when she left Brooklyn Army Base to evacuate 3,500 American citizens from Shangai, with Japanese aggression imminent, until July 1940 when hostilities began to worsen in Europe. She was then re-routed to cruising in American waters until United States entry into the war whereof she was requisitioned for troop work on June 16, 1941 and renamed *Mount Vernon*. She was the second transport to bear this name, the first having been an ex-German liner of the First World War. Decommissioned on January 19, 1946, she was chartered from the U.S. Maritime Commission and began carrying her complement of passengers in a single class category. She operated on the New York-Cobh-Southampton-Le Havre-Hamburg-route calling at Halifax homebound from February 1948 until October 12, 1951. she made her last voyage from Hamburg-Bremerhaven-Southampton-Le Havre-Cobh-New York arriving on the 19th of October 1951. Turned over to the United States Department of Commerce, she was utilized to transport troops and their families between New York and Bremerhaven. Laid up in the Hudson River after her repatriation work, she was sold for scrap to the Union Mineral & Alloys Corporation for $238,126 at the Lipsett shipbreakers located in Port Newark, New Jersey. She arrived in tow all rusted due to the years in reserve.

Sister ship: *Manhattan.*

Zim Lines

ALIYA

Builder: Cammell, Laird & Co., Ltd., Birkenhead, England
Completed: September 1913
Gross Tonnage: 11,015
Dimensions: 530' x 61' Depth: 33' Draft: 26'
Engines: Two sets of 8-cylinder, quadruple expansion engines plus two low-pressure turbines double-reduction geared with hydraulic couplings
Screws: Twin
Watertight bulkheads: Eight
Decks: Three
Normal speed: 15 knots
Passenger accommodations: 35 first, 741 tourist class
Registry: Israel
Maiden voyage: Haifa-New York on April 29, 1953

Built for the Norwegian-America Line and christened *Bergensfjord*. Sold to the Home Lines in November 1946 and renamed *Argentina*. Resold to the Zim-Israel Lines in 1952 and renamed *Jerusalem*; subsequently renamed *Aliya* in 1957. Engaged in the Haifa-Piraeus-Naples-Marseilles service as well as the transatlantic run to New York though she mostly worked the Mediterranean route after 1955. She made her last voyage from New York on August 31, 1955 to Naples-Piraeus-Haifa. On some of her eastbound crossings she called occasionally at Halifax. Laid up in May 1958 and finally sold to the Terreste Marittima for scrapping at Spezia, Italy in October 1959, after having served under three house flags.

Note: She was the first ship to sail for the newly formed Zim Lines. Photo as *Jerusalem*.

SHALOM

Builder: Chantiers de L'Atlantique, de St. Nazaire, Penhoet-Loire, France
Completed: March 1964
Gross Tonnage: 25,320
Dimensions: 628' x 82' Depth: 49' Draft: 27'
Engines: Four C.E.M. Parsons-Atlantique steam turbines double-reduction geared
Screws: Twin
Collision bulkheads: One
Watertight bulkheads: Eleven
Decks: Six
Normal speed: 20 knots (attained a speed of 24 knots on her trials)
Passenger accommodations: 72 first, 130 intermediate class, and 887 tourist class (700 in a single class when cruising)
Officers and crew: 460
Registry: Israel
Maiden voyage: Haifa-Naples-Marseilles-Malaga-New York on April 17, 1964

Built expressly for the Zim-Israel Lines she was the first ship order to be placed for the Line. Flagship of the fleet, she was built at a cost of £7.5 million. The names "King Solomon" and "King David" were first contemplated as names for the vessel. Engaged in the Haifa-Piraeus-Naples-Marseilles-Barcelona-Ponta Delgada-New York service. Although built for Mediterranean service she had very little open deck space and the food service was not on a parity with other liners. She worked the transatlantic run between April and October and cruised in the Caribbean or the Mediterranean the remainder of the year. Fully air-conditioned and equipped with Denny Brown stabilizers and private facilities in all cabins. She had two outdoor pools and one indoor; a gym and sauna room,

library, several lounges and bars. She also made occasional calls at Cannes, Lisbon and Palma d'Marjorca and at least two Mediterranean cruises each year to coincide with Hebrew holidays. In the early hours of the morning of November 26, 1964, just 28 miles southeast of Ambrose Lighthouse, the *Shalom* collided with the Norwegian tanker *Stolt Nagali* while headed for her first Caribbean cruise with 700 passengers aboard. The *Shalom* had entered into a thick fog bank and hit the tanker full speed. The tanker had been on a coastwise trip from Philadelphia to New York. Fortunately the tanker was in ballast and remained afloat after the *Shalom* tore off the stern section of the ship, killing nineteen crew members of the Norwegian ship. The *Shalom* sustained no casualties. The *Shalom* steamed into New York harbour with a mangled bow the same afternoon and was later taken to Newport News, Virginia and repaired. She re-entered service on the transatlantic circuit April 1, 1965. As was the case with the *Andrea Doria* and *Stockholm* collision in the same area both ships had each other visible on the radar screen at least an hour before the collision. The Zim-Israel Lines were not very good ship operators when it came to passenger liners and the operating cost for the ship ran over $25,000 per day. The low volume of trade on the Atlantic also helped to seal her fate. She made her last voyage fore the Line in May 1967 and arrived at New York on the 18th. Sold to the German-Atlantic Line in May 1967 for $5 million and renamed *Hanseatic* following delivery in October. Resold to Home Lines in July 1973 and renamed *Doric*. Resold to the Greek-owned Royal Cruise Line in January 1981 and renamed *Royal Odyssey* in early 1982. Resold to the Greek-owned Regency Cruises in 1987 and delivered in November 1988, with renaming to *Regent Sun*. Presently in their service.

Note: The *Shalom* made a pre-maiden publicity voyage from Haifa-Turkey-Greece-Italy-Yugoslavia on March 27, 1964.

Index